Fiction by T. Allen Winn

Dark Thirty

The Perfect Spook House

The Detective Trudy Wagner Series

Road Rage

North of the Border

Memoir

The Caregiver's Son,
Outside the Window Looking In

**Historical fictional short story featured in
Beach Author Network's book 'Shorts'**

For Your Amusement

'True nostalgia is an ephemeral composition of disjointed memories.'

- Florence King

T. Allen Winn's

Cornbread and Buttermilk

Good Ole Fashion
Home Cooked Nostalgic Nonsense

Cornbread and Butttermilk
Copyright © 2015
T. Allen Winn

All rights reserved. This publication may not be reproduced, stored in a retrieval system, or transmitted in any form: recording, mechanical, electronic, or photocopy, without written permission of the publisher. The only exception is brief quotations used in book reviews

Comments:
Contact T. Allen Winn
TALLENWINN@mail.com, and
T. Allen Winn's Face Book

Coenbread and Buttermilk is a fictional novel. Any reference to real people or historical events or places is coincidental. All places are used fictitiously and the author's imagination has shaped them to fit the story.

ISBN: 978-1-941069-27-1

Published by ProsePress
75 Red Maple Drive,
Pawleys Island, South Carolina 29585

www.Prosepress.biz
proseNcons@live.com

Acknowledgements

This is dedicated to those still above dirt and also for those who have passed on, contributing to making life's memories memorable. Putting it to print is my way of keeping the tales alive once I have joined those who passed before me. And kudos to Foster Parents, walking a mile or two in your shoes certainly taught me valuable lessons, one of the toughest and inspirational times in my life.

From a modest good ole southern upbringing and beginning in Abbeville, S.C, all is good looking back and remembering. It brought a smile to my face putting my ole spin on these tales and proudly blaming those people and situations that helped shape who I am.

Hopefully this will inspire you to do the same. When those who tell and share them are gone, often are the tales they told, buried forever along with them. Word to the wise; listen when we ole folks have something to say, no matter how silly or boring it might seem. The Lord gave you two ears and one mouth for a reason, I'm just saying. Write this stuff down. Keep it. Share it. Enjoy it.

This is an excerpt from
CORNBREAD AND BUTTERMILK
recorded by
Grand Ole Opry Legend and Entertainer Little
Jimmy Dickens in 1956, bless his heart.

"When you was just a little boy
remember how your ma
Just before suppertime,
how she laid down the law
You young'ns wash behind your ears,
your dirty hands and then
Eat cornbread and buttermilk to
grow you into men

Keep a eatin' that cornbread and buttermilk,
a country boy's delight
I eat it ev'ry mornin', I eat it noon & night
Some people like fried chicken,
while others like their ham
But cornbread and buttermilk
made me what I am"

Part I

1   Remembering Back When

4   Black Skillet Cornbread

9   Toby

14   A Grade Full of Firsts

23   Burning a Hole in My Pocket

28   The Red Camel Club

33   I'm Rooming with Papa so it must be Christmas

38   Little Mountain

45   Let's Make a Deal, Monty Hall

52   My Black Mama

56   A Dollar a Day is All You Pay

64   BFFF

71   Counting Cows (Road Warriors Post Apocalypse)

78   Fall is for Fairs

84   Talking out the Fire

89   Speaking in Tongues

95   The Backyard Grocery

101   Walk-In's and Drive-In's

110   Win, Lose or Draw

117   But You Doesn't Hasta Call Me Tommy

125   Everyone probably has an Uncle Floyd (Puth-up, The Expanded Version)

- 131 Cowboys and Indians
- 137 Me and Teco
- 143 Breaking an Arm Ain't That Hard To Do
- 149 Myths and Madness
- 153 Don't Peek out the Window, Something Might be Peeking Back
- 162 Smokey Mountain High
- 167 A Pig's Tale
- 173 The Constant Gardener
- 181 The Pusher
- 188 Nothing but Cornbread Crumbs, Fire up another Skillet
- 189 Regrets, I've had a Few

Part II

194 Fostering Four and Much More
197 Like Yesterdays' Garbage
202 Possession is Nine Tenths
211 Confounding Fathers
216 Tour of Duty
223 Let's Take This Show on the Road
228 Help me, My Clothes are Shrinking
233 An Amazon among Men
238 Tail of the Why Monkey
246 Boys will be Boys Because They Are
253 The Legend of Lizard Man
257 Four Equals Three
261 Accessorizing with Spaghetti
265 Fostering Hatred
270 Screams from Very Dark Places
275 Terrible Two's for a Reason
280 Three Too Many
284 Training Day Blues
290 The Little Red Headed Stranger
296 Helicopter Tommy
303 Crying Uncle

Part I

The Beginning of Remembering Back When

Remembering Back When

In the time before political corrective-ness destroyed the world as I once knew it, there existed a land of uniqueness; that place where kids could be kids no matter what age they really were. Foolishness was accepted or at least tolerated. You were actually allowed to make bad decisions and say the wrong things without being persecuted to the end of time. It was okay for us to play cowboys and Indians, be army soldiers, and possess pretend guns. In each game of any kind there was usually a winner and the rest were losers. That was all right. We knew there would be an eventual winner and we accepted our fate regardless of the outcome. The world accepted it too.

We could actually own weapons and play with cap guns, dart guns, water pistols or even point sticks, broom handles or even fingers at one another and then say bang-bang, you're dead. Fake blood stained the ground and we died deaths worthy of Oscar winning performances. Yes, we actually played with guns but we didn't kill anyone; well we did, but we took turns dying. It was fun. I liked that time much better than the warped one I live in now.

Those very same broom handles served as our trusty steeds, our horses, usually named Trigger or Silver, Flicka or even Buttermilk. Both good guys and bad guys were a part of our everyday backyard fun. You took turns being each. Using one's imagination was a way of life on those long summer afternoons. Being an Indian or a no good varmint was a good bad thing. We got to be both sooner or later.

There was no FFF, 'forced family fun.' Families actually

did things together. The arrival of summer and school out meant we'd be going on vacation somewhere and we, the kids, couldn't wait. Those long hot summers were too short to suit most of us. Bored, hardly; we stayed outside from sunup to sundown, long after dark thirty most days. No one stayed inside and having to do so was met with much resistance and procrastination. Excuses, oh yeah, we had a slew of them; anything to prolong our alliance with nature's outdoor wonderland.

School, in my eyes, was a necessary evil, but somewhere you had to go and usually we liked most of it once we got back in the swing of things.

Teachers were to be feared, fear meaning you respected them, or feared not doing what they told us. If a teacher said you had done something wrong, then your parents took this as the gospel, no argument and no disagreements. Neither parents nor kids hired lawyers to plea their case. We were always guilty as charged. And yeah, we were whipped, paddled and spanked, by the teachers, our parents, grandparents, or anyone else who wanted to take their turn. Most of the time we deserved those dreaded beatings, as we called them, for something we had done or were about to do. Adults ruled and sided with one another. There was no law to protect us. The law was pretty simple, break the rules and pay the consequences. Sometimes you even got to pick your switch off the tree.

Grandparents were not just old people. We enjoyed going to their house, being spoiled by them, and yes, we even listened to their crazy little stories of long ago times. Home cooking, wonderful desserts and churning ice cream were just part of my fond memories. Nowadays grandparents require these quirky little catchy names, Memaw, Mimi, Grams, Pe-paw and on and on. For me it was simple; Granny and Papa. To keep my grannies separate and straight when talking about them, they were referred to as Granny Bowie and Granny Winn. I had only one papa so his was simply Papa. Back in my day, they actually loved being called Granny, Papa, Grandmother, and Grandfather and were not offended by it making them sound old. They were old. They got it, we got it and they loved every minute of it.

Most anything can trigger a nostalgic memory; a movie, a snow storm, something someone has said, or an old photograph. For good or bad we can venture down a trail as warm as yesterday or one from a zillion years in our past. For that reason, mine will follow no particular path. These snippets in my life are organized in no chronological order. Flashes, excerpts, moments in time, lucky just to remember them, they're woven and shaped, often having been buried and forgotten until like magic they appear. Capturing them before they become lost again is the key.

If I haven't chased you away by now, then grab you a glass of sweet tea or a cup of coffee, or maybe even a bottle of coke with salted goobers poured inside, sit back and enjoy my good ole southern home cooked nostalgic nonsense, and if it puts a smile on your face, then my job is done.

Black Skillet Cornbread

Fact: Cornbread is not supposed to taste like cupcakes.
Fact: Cornbread should never resemble muffins.
Fact: Real cornbread does not come inside a box marked ready mix or cornbread mix.
Fact: You can only cook homemade southern cornbread in a cast iron skillet.
Fact: Only with this recipe can you add diced onions and have one of the ingredients for making perfect southern dressing.

Don't get snookered by that waitress in a restaurant asking, '*Would you like biscuits or cornbread with your meal or a mixture of both?*' Pass on the cornbread. It tastes like dessert. Go for the biscuits if you have a choice. To really throw her off her game ask her if she has any *cathead* biscuits. Real southerners know what I'm talking about; those oversized mutations that only granny could whip up.

In case you're wondering, I'm southern born and raised, born in L.A. That's Lower Abbeville, a community of 5000 or so nestled about midway between South Carolina's state capitol, Columbia and the upstate city of Greenville, pert near in the middle of nowhere. About and pert near are actual location indicators in the south, just like over, up or down yonder. For my Granny Bowie, every place was referenced as over yonder. Over yonder can be across the room, on the next street, in another town, state or even country or continent. It's all inclusive. I'm rambling a tad off point but we southerners are excellent ramblers. It's in our genes and jeans, whichever fits your fancy.

CORNBREAD AND BUTTERMILK

Cornbread in my humble opinion is a delicacy, served up with most meals, especially those which include butter beans, pink eye purple hulled peas, any sort of greens, turnip salad, collards or even spinach. If you gave me the choice between having cornbread and buttermilk or a tenderloin steak for supper, I'd grant the cow a stay of execution, milk it instead. At the end of every utter is southern gold, just needing to be churned and bottled by the gallon or half gallon. I grew up with kinfolk or friends milking their own and churning buttermilk.

It's tough to beat a cold glass of farm churned buttermilk unless the glass of milk contains precisely crumbled homemade cornbread. Garnish it with either a slice of onion or preferably spring onions, those green ones with bulbs on the ends, plucked directly from the dirt. Eat the onions on the side or better still, cut them up in the buttermilk and cornbread. Add a little salt and pepper and then stay out of my way until I'm done. Turning up that bowl to your mouth to get that last little bit is a tradition in my family. It goes along with smacking your lips and patting your full belly. Sometimes unbuttoning your pants and loosening your belt is not a bad idea, especially if you have just had that second bowl or topped off the first.

If you're not of the southern persuasion you may be wondering what this churning thing is. Picture a barrel with a lid with a hole in it and a plunger mounted through the hole. You work that batch of freshly retrieved milk with the churn, plunging it to perfection. Buttermilk is what you have left after you've finished making butter. Foregoing further explanation, just Google it and discover for yourself, the lost art of churning. We used to go to my great grandmother's house to fetch fresh churned buttermilk.

Granny Holmes, my granny's mama, always had some fresh churned on hand. We'd take that ride out in the country where she lived. Rides in the country are as southern as it gets. Granny Holmes was a short little woman, hair in a bun and few teeth, but she was the real deal, and not many kids can say they had two grannies, one papa and a great grandma all at once. I was an only child but had grandparents galore. My mama's side of the family appreciated fresh buttermilk and a skillet of homemade cornbread. It was a staple at their tables. I can't imagine a week without cornbread. Heck, I usually have buttermilk and cornbread several times a week. The first thing I want after returning from vacation is you guessed it, B&C.

What do you need to make cornbread?
Read and learn.

A large Cast Iron Skillet
Canola Oil or any oil will do
(Crisco from a can was used in my day)
Self Rising Corn Meal (not corn meal mix or ready mix)
Fat Free Buttermilk or
Freshly Churned Buttermilk is even better
One Large Egg (or Egg Substitute or Egg White,
thinking a tad bit healthier)
Salt & Pepper
Pre-heat the oven on Bake @ 495°
Coat the skillet with oil and sprinkle in a light dusting

of corn meal (best to use a seasoned cast iron skillet)
and place it in the oven while it's coming to temperature.
Allow the corn meal to brown –
should only take a couple of minutes
While the corn meal is browning in that skillet,
in a mixing bowl
Add two cups of corn meal
Lightly sprinkle salt and pepper and
mix with a spoon
Add approx. one and half cups of buttermilk and mix
until meal becomes a paste
Add an egg and stir in thoroughly
(do remove the egg from the shell)
Add a tablespoon of oil and mix it in
Remove the skillet with the browned corn meal
Add the premixed cornbread mixture into
the skillet

*I have my own technique for this that gives it character by
spooning and swirling it*

Allow approximately twenty five minutes or until bread has browned and hardened. (If the smoke alarm goes off, you've waited just a tad too long.)
Remove from skillet by flipping the corn bread onto a plate

If you did it right, it should look like this on the plate.

Ways to enjoy:
Serve with your home cooked veggies-meal (speckled butter beans, pinto beans, turnip salad, collard greens, etc.)
Slice and butter a wedge
My favorite (the ultimate southern meal, buttermilk and cornbread) – crumbled in a bowl of buttermilk, lightly salted and peppered with a slice of onion added
My dad used sweet milk and no onion; yuck, I'm just saying…

Toby

A horse is a horse, of course. Now try to get that tune out of your head, Mister Ed. Can you say Wilbur? A talking horse, what a concept and it was one of my all time favorite weekly programs on CBS from October 1, 1961, to February 6, 1966. Mister Ed was a striking Palomino but not the only well known breed of my childhood. Let's not forget Trigger, Roy Roger's faithful steed. Trigger was more reserved and never spoke unless spoken to and only then following commands by Roy.

The story line of each Mister Ed episode was pretty much the same, stemming from the fact that Mister Ed was a notorious troublemaker and would only speak to Wilbur, his owner. Other running jokes capitalized on poor Wilbur being accident prone, inadvertently causing harm to himself and others. There were the nosey neighbors to contend with as in most sitcoms of that era. Who could forget the eye candy, Carol, Wilbur's wife. Slapstick and funny, most times predictable, but we didn't change that dial just the same. There was no remote control. Channel surfing was too difficult and hadn't been invented.

BME, before Mister Ed, there was Francis the talking mule, originating in 1946 in a novel by David Stern, with seven movies featuring the antics in the 1950s. Francis was an Army mule, like Ed, spoke to only one person, and in this case it was to a young soldier played by Donald O'Connor. Famous horses, talking and the non-talking kind have graced the movie and television screens. As mentioned, Trigger, Roy Roger the cowboy's horse was one of the most popular, but not as popular was another singing westerner's mount, Champion. So who did he belong to? That would be good ole Gene Autry. Don't sweat it. Google caught me up to speed. I did remember Dale Evans' horse's name. Go figure. Buttermilk was not a tough one for me. Bullet was their trusty dog. I might have named him cornbread though. Innovation introduced us to a jeep in the cowboy saga. It too had to be named; Nellie Belle was a good'un. Sticking to the happy trails theme, The Lone Ranger rode Silver while Tonto rode who? That would be a little pinto named Scout.

One could not exclude a couple of my favorites, Fury that aired on NBC from 1955 to 1960, featuring, a soon to be Mister Mission Impossible, Peter Graves as a ranch owner operating the Broken Wheel Ranch. Graves played Jim and had an adopted son Joey, who befriends the black stallion named Fury. If you're old as dirt, you couldn't forget the show's opening: the beloved stallion running inside the corral and approaching the camera as the announcer reads: "FURY!..The story of a horse...and a boy who loves him."

Then there was *My Friend Flicka* with a similar plot, a ten year old boy living on Goose Bar Ranch, just outside of Cheyenne, Wyoming, with his practical father, Rob; his mother, Nell, and his older brother. It was originally before my television viewing time, airing on CBS in 1956-1957, but then later on NBC, with reruns on ABC and on CBS between 1959 and 1966. Even the Disney Channel ran the reruns in the 1980s.

So, all this horsing around I'm doing is just a lead-in to my very first introduction to the four hoofed wonder that would forever impact my little imaginative life. Playing broom horses and naming our mounts were part of our make-believe playing. Securing the best picked name was crucial. You wanted to be riding Trigger or Silver into the sunset, not Francis or Mister Ed, or even a girl's horse, Buttermilk; not that having an imaginary talking broomstick horse named Buttermilk would have necessarily been a bad thing to me. My first memory of the creature called a horse is not so much a memory as it was my grandparents and parents sharing the all but forgotten experience with me. There is a valuable lesson to be learned about what I am *fix'in* to share with you. I'm southern; I can say *fix'in*, even in print. Pay very close attention when your elders tell stories of your childhood; especially those lap-slappers that you might have been too young to recall and probably too embarrassed to hear when in the company of your peers. When the elders are gone, so are the tales.

Taking those Sunday afternoon rides into the country was common practice back in my time. We'd load as many as we could cram in one vehicle and drive to the outer regions of civilization. One of those tiny circus clown cars had nothing on us and we had no seatbelts to restrict the confines. Double stacking was not out of the ordinary. One of our favorite destinations was Uncle Ben and Aunt Dot's house. Uncle Ben was one of my granny's brothers, part of the Holmes clan. Going to the country was an adventure. Of course, an ulterior motive often existed for the adults; freshly made buttermilk and seasonal garden vegetables could be there for the taking if offered, and they usually were. I had cousins to play with and they had all sorts of animal critters I didn't see that often, except in the country.

One such critter was a horse named Toby. So the story goes as recapped by those long in tooth and gone now, little

Tommy couldn't wait to get to Uncle Ben's and Aunt Dot's so that he could go see and pet Toby. Besides playing with his cousins, this was the highlight of the trip for him; me. I'm not exactly sure how old I must have been, but obviously it had to be pre my memory cells retaining the information. Needless to say, it was fun hearing them reminisce about me as a mere tadpole; not to be confused with a former classmate of mine, Jimmy (Tadpole) Burdette. But to hear them tell it, Toby didn't end at Uncle Ben's and Aunt Dot's. Every horse I saw was a Toby. Apparently I was at the impressionable age, just expanding my tiny vocabulary.

If I saw a horse or horses in a pasture I'd alert everyone in the car of the Toby sightings. No one ever clarified if I used Toby plural and I never asked. I think I just hollered, Toby, jumped for joy and pointed, but that's just my assumption. Sometimes you just have to fill in the blanks. All of my toy horses were the miniature Toby versions. Cowboys and Indians probably rode a Toby. I'm not sure what breed Toby might have been. Uncle Ben is no longer with us but I suppose I could have asked Aunt Dot before writing this or maybe my older cousins might have a better memory than me.

I suppose it really doesn't matter now. The original Toby is long gone too. I don't recall at what age I actually stopped calling a horse a Toby. My elders didn't fill in these missing holes in my recall system. I never owned a horse but, if I had, I would have probably named it Toby. I guess I should count my blessings that Uncle Floyd was not in my life at that time or I could have been nicknamed Toby instead of Puth-up. Second thought…that might not have been quite so bad.

Most of my great uncles and aunts have passed on now. I should look up those long lost relatives still kicking and see just how many of them or their offspring still live in the country, and take one of those Sunday afternoon drives to visit them if any of then still live out there. No, on second thought, while visiting them would be special, not finding Toby in that pasture would be a disappointment. Sometimes nostalgia is best kept in the past, but now that I've put it to print, Toby will be immortal. I'm smiling right now, by the way, and will think of Toby the next time I see one. I'll try to refrain from shouting it out loud or maybe I will; then I can travel down the nostalgic highway with those who have not ever heard this childhood saga. See you on the other side, Toby, my four hoofed friend.

Get off your horse and drink your milk.
     - John Wayne

A Grade Full of Firsts

Childhood digression, we've all been there. We have those wondrous snapshots in our youth that jump out at us; some are fond memories, others not so. Besides that early stint in kindergarten, kids usually look forward to starting the first grade. It's our rite of passage, almost like growing up or something. Focus, think like a kid right now and how tough it is to explain the phenomena and put it into words. Hindsight, we had no clue how starting school would forever impact our lives. Beginning this journey would be the first step for us, forfeiting our freedom as we knew it. It would equate to us punching a time clock and others controlling our day; those weekday mornings of sleeping in, gone for the next twelve years, except for the brief reprieves during summer.

The back yard of our house on Hunter Street butted up to the fence that enclosed the Langley Milliken Grammar School yard. How little did I know then that once I entered those front gates, being inside would take on an almost penitentiary atmosphere. And yes, it was called a Grammar School, grades one through six and was located in L.A, Lower Abbeville, at the end of South Main, on the fringes of the textile mill community. The local mill was Milliken too. After completing the sixth grade we were bused to the opposite side of town, Abbeville High, where we merged with six graders from two other schools, Greenville Street School and the Sharon Community. Sharon Elementary School was west bound highway 72, towards Calhoun Falls, and was also the site of the one and only Sharon Drive-In. We were living large back then, having our very own outdoor movie theater. You were only as comfortable as your car's interior and the amount of people you piled inside; one single car price, your ticket to the big show. Greenville Street was where, as we called, the privileged North Main kids attended. It was the closest of the three schools to the town square and to Abbeville High.

Oh yeah, there was one more, Wright, where the colored folks attended. They kept us separated back then, blacks and whites; me starting the first grade in 1959. Wright had its own Grammar and High Schools located in an area where most black folks lived. Such was the way back then, right or wrong; as kids we never knew to question the arrangements. Not getting ahead of myself, I'll cover my upbringing and beliefs in another segment, entitled *My Black Mama*, Anise, a woman I loved dearly.

As a preschooler, I often ventured to the back forty of our yard and clung to that fence as I watched the children inside laugh and play during recess. Witnessing the happy, fun times, I had no inkling of what went on inside that brick building and behind those closed doors. Squatting at the fence, I could only envision what I was missing, with all that laughter and running here and there. A bell would ring and the kids would line up and vanish inside. I was mesmerized.

I could hardly wait to take my turn on that tall sliding board, the huge swings and monkey bars. Each dwarfed my tiny little jungle gym set. That's what we called our backyard combo, typically equipped with a pair of swings, slide, monkey bars and a two-seater swing, where you faced one another. The slide alone in the playground at the school was easily five times the size of mine. It looked like a sky scrapper, as did the endless rows of swings and the gigantic monkey bars.

One particular noon time I had taken up my usual position along the fence, drooling and imagining how it would be if I were on the other side. The tiny prickling sensations along my legs and inside my shorts happened seemingly simultaneously and out of the clear blue. I began slapping at my legs and those regions concealed by the fabric of my shorts. The pain became unbearable and soon I was screaming and crying. I had picked absolutely the wrong spot to daydream. I had planted my tiny butt slap down on an angry ant hill. The little buggers were having their way with me, biting, stinging or whatever ticked off ants do. For the record, these weren't the dreaded fire ants of today, but just the same, they were doing a number on me. At least a hundred and fifty or so yards of open terrain separated me from reaching Mama.

I tried to stand but the onslaught was relentless. I didn't originate the phrase, *ants in your pants*, but I certainly understood the meaning of the term that very moment. I'd run a ways, fall or squat and slap some more before trying to run again. Trust me when I say it; you can't outrun pissed off hitchhikers. I'd fall, I would cry, slap some more and scream Mama's name at the top of my lungs. I felt alone in the world, no one coming to my immediate rescue. Eventually I did make it to Mama's comforting arms. She had to doctor on the zillion bites on my legs and inside my pants where biting critters should never have access. I think it might have been a long time before I ventured to that fence again, if ever I did at all; daydreams transformed into nightmares.

My time did finally come when I was to start the first grade. Mama and daddy accompanied me my first day as did other parents; to dispel our first day jitters and to sever the umbilical cord, so to speak. Their babies were venturing out into the world for the first time, unsupervised by them, trusting others to take their place. Maybe this was more for them than us. After a couple of hours, all the grow-ups had exited, leaving us kids to become acclimated to our new world. Inside was much different from what I had viewed from the outside of that fence looking in. Eventually that bell rang, sounding the beginning of recess. This is what I had long awaited to experience. The yard full of various giant jungle gym monstrosities screamed my name; *come little Tommy and try us out.* And try I did.

   The swings were almost carnival like in my tiny eyes. There must have been a dozen or more of them suspended from larger than life A-frames. No wonder these were so popular. You had to wait your turn for a free spot. Six year olds are not noted for patience. I decided instead to tackle the beanstalk, the slide mounted at the top of the highest latter I had ever climbed. There were no ropes to restrain kids back then; everything was freestyle; no consideration apparently of just how far one could fall if one lost his footing. Safety was not of the utmost concern back in the day before OSHA and the regulatory movement. Still, there was a short line waiting their turn to slide. I think too many kids may have feared the sheer height of the slide. Not me, I was raring to go and go I did, over and over and over, until the bell rung signaling recess had sadly ended.

   Standing in line seemed to be the theme in school. We did it for everything; waiting our turn to test ride the fun stuff in the yard, lunch and even exiting and entering the building and classroom. As I lined up as instructed, laughter from those lined up behind me caught my attention. Why were the children having fun in line? What was all of the snickering; had I missed something? To my dismay, a girl directly behind me whispered the little secret in my ear. *Did you know you had a hole in your pants?* This is not something you wish to hear from the lips of a girl. Red faced, I felt the back of my pinstriped shorts. What I found was not a hole, but instead, the entire seat of my shorts was missing. A gap the size of the Grand Canyon occupied where fabric should have been.

Embarrassed, I had nowhere to hide. It didn't matter which way I turned, kids had a bird's eye few of my white underwear. While it was almost threadbare too, thank goodness it was not to the point that everyone could see my boney little bare hinny. The teacher caught whiff of what was happening and pulled me from the line and took me to the principal's office. There I waited for mama to bring me another pair of shorts. I can't believe she saved those pants as a keepsake, a memento of my first day. She just loved showing and sharing them with relatives, recapping the event. My classmates ragged me forever too; especially if they saw me even near that sliding board.

First grade, it makes or breaks us; often setting the tone for the rest of our lives. Mine was somewhat of a roller coaster ride. I'm sure others could say the same, unless they're suffering from traumatic mental blocks. Days passed but I had my list of things to do. Moving on from the slide to the monkey bars, my quest to quench my preschool fantasies continued. There is nothing more thrilling than climbing and hanging upside-down from the maze formed by what looked like left over plumber's pipes. While the exhilaration experienced satisfied my childhood acrobatics, another event loomed in the school year that would forever mark my stint in the first grade. Somewhere along the way I had actually noticed the opposite sex. Puppy love, first time infatuations, can be the best of times or the worst of times, all contingent on the opposite sex's reaction to you and your cravings; or so it goes most of time. Trust me, there are exceptions. I am living proof.

    Her name was Sherry Hall. I'm not sure what attracted me to her but attracted I was; swooning is more like it. I never even saw it coming; hadn't even known I could swoon. It was as if the fog cleared and there she was in all her wonder; a girl of all things. Boys will be boys and we will clumsily do what it takes to show off for the opposite of us; so was the case during recess on the monkey bars. There she was, sitting on the bars, the girl, luring me like one of those mythical Sirens. It was up to me to do everything I could to validate just how much *monkeying around* I could do on those bars. Hanging upside down, flipping from one bar to another; soon I had her covering her mouth and giggling as only a school girl can. Covertly I inched closer. She was never the wiser, or maybe she was. After all, girls are supposed to mature quicker than us.

    Eventually I eased very close, until a mere section of pipe separated us. We were soon face to face; both laughing and probably talking nonsense, but I can't remember anything about the conversation. Just before the recess bell rang, we sat side by side, inches apart, just she and I alone on those monkey bars. What did I really know about girls?

They were supposed to be yucky, creatures to shun and avoid; but Sherry was different. Why, I have no clue. Being smitten isn't a pretty sight at such a tender age. I didn't know I knew how to be smitten either.

What happened next was perhaps my first experience with spontaneity, and I didn't even know the meaning of the word. The bell rang signaling the end of recess. I don't know what came over me. It certainly wasn't premeditated. I leaned over and kissed her on the mouth; I mean puckered up and square on her wet ones. I had never done this before; didn't even know I knew how; but I did it. She smiled and scurried down the monkey bars. I think we were both probably red faced. I could still feel the sensation of heat burning on mine. For the first time I guess I realized we weren't alone in the universe. Two girls, second graders, huddled nearby, at the corner of the building and they were whispering and giggling, pointing at me; busted.

Sometime after lunch and maybe when we were lining up for our second little stint outside, our teacher separated the boys from the girls, aligned us. She had one of those foot long rulers in her hands and lightly slapped it in her palm as she walked past the assembled boys, looking us up and down. She resembled a prison guard on one of those television shows. This was certainly different from the rest of the times we waited our turns to go outside. She eventually spoke saying, *it has been brought to my attention that one of you boys was witnessed kissing one of these girls on the monkey bars during the first recess this morning. Will that boy please step forward?*

I made eye contact with Sherry, and then just as quickly stared down at my feet. No boy stepped forward, including the guilty party. She asked a second time. No one confessed. Why would they? I certainly wasn't going to volunteer. After the pants episode, I didn't need the publicity; even if it risked losing Sherry for good, by not admitting my love for her. What did I really know about love? I had only kissed a girl once in my entire life, and now look where that had landed me; in a police line-up. What next, were they going to bring in the witnesses to finger me? Innocent until proven guilty, right, and I didn't have my lawyer present. No one had read me my rights. I don't think back then we really had any.

Third time's the charm, and no one raised their hand admitting guilt to the heinous crime, the case of the girl and boy on the monkey bars, touching lips, innocence lost. I didn't even know it was unlawful to kiss in the school yard. Maybe it was just prohibited on the monkey bars because it was too dangerous; one could get all swimmy headed and plunge to your untimely death. I thought I was in the clear. I learned the meaning of don't do the crime if you're not willing to do the time. My innocent classmates didn't appreciate the lesson about to be learned. And now that I think of it, why didn't the teacher line up the girls and grill them. After all, Sherry's lips were a part of this too.

So this is the way it is going to be; palms up commanded the Gestapo. Each of my male classmates was given a hurtful swat with that one foot wooden ruler. This had gone from bad to worse. No way was I ever going to admit that I was the monkey bar kisser. After witnessing what had just happened, I just hoped Sherry kept our little secret. The two snitches had gotten what they had wanted and then some. Justice had been served, even to the innocent.

I never realized first kisses could be so traumatic. Not to be derailed, it didn't make me change my mind about the opposite sex. If anything, I now knew any reward was worth the penalty. I did shy away from those monkey bars for awhile; having still not seen the rules, dos and don'ts. I kept a watchful eye on those two tattling second graders often still watching me too. They were itching to turn state's evidence if I slipped up again. Sadly, Sherry Hall and I never came to be. We shared that one moment on the monkey bars, no more. I was a marked man, tainted and unworthy I suppose. Keeping her distance was the best policy. Fiction is normally based on fact and I did go on to use this little episode in my fiction novel, *The Perfect Spook House*.

Things surely did look different on the inside of that fence. Who would have ever figured little ole me would make such a splash the first day of my very first school year? There is still my dog and mama episode to come, those PTA adventures, but I'll save them for another chapter, *Me and Teco*. First grade, innocence forever lost, my first kiss and my mark on the boys, literally and physically. All these years later, I wonder where Sherry Hall is now and if she remembers that kiss on the Langley Milliken Grammar School monkey bars. Perhaps I wasn't her first, or just maybe I was. I'll just leave it at that.

> *"Wisdom is not a product of schooling but of the lifelong attempt to acquire it."*
> **- Albert Einstein**

Burning a Hole in My Pocket

A penny was actually worth something when I was growing up as was a nickel and a dime. When someone said something and then looked over at you and commented, "okay, put your two cents worth in now", you could unload on them guilt free. We had penny candy, penny bubble gum, penny cool aide straws, and penny wax figures with cool aide inside, jaw breakers, atomic fire balls and two cent bottle rockets. If you had a quarter to spend you could fill up a paper sack full of goodies. No, I never walked ten miles to school uphill both ways in the snow barefooted, but possibly my daddy or papa might lay claim to that feat. I didn't have any older brothers so I never had to wear worn out hand-me-downs either; a perk of being an only child.

On the square in downtown Abbeville stood Brown's Five and Dime Store and McClellan's where with a few nickels and dimes you could do some serious damage. Now we have Dollar Trees where everything can be bought for a buck. There are General Dollar Stores and Family Dollar Stores but don't be deceived, more than a dollar is required for most purchases. Before K-Mart, Wal-Mart and Target we had Sky City and Roses. Sky City is long gone but Myrtle Beach, South Carolina still actually has a Roses Store.

I preferred the ones within walking distance of Hunter Street where I lived. Take a left up South Main with a sidewalk all the way; it was almost like following the yellow brick road to Candy Land. Oz had no candy stores. The first stop on the mile long journey, William's Shell Station, a local hangout for papa and his cronies, the neighborhood clique. Pickings weren't the greatest there but we could buy a cold drink, ice cream and small assortment of candies.

If I was lucky, papa would be there and the round would be on him. Typically that would include an Orange Crush soda, possibly an RC cola and a chocolate moon pie, or papa's signature favorite and mine, a pack of salted goobers poured inside a bottle of coke. Bottles were made of glass back then. Take a swig first though before dumping the pack of peanuts inside.

Next stop, just up South Main from William's Shell and just under and past the train trestle, Tom Taylor's Store. Taylor's was sort of a very small version of the local grocery store. Mister Taylor catered mostly to the real consumer, not necessarily kids, but he did carry cold drinks, ice cream and a better assortment of candy than the Shell station. Pocket change could be spent there effortlessly if we didn't feel up to that last hill climb to our final and most prized destination, At the end of South Main near the highway 72 and North Main intersection, the first of only a handful of traffic lights in Abbeville was a honey hole. Two traffic lights anchored each end of the square and two others were on North Main and the last one was at the bottom of Penny Hill next to the Kum-Back, a fast food hangout with full curb service for automobiles.

The Holy Grail and worth waiting for and hording back our change, Busby and Cox General Store was the pot of the gold at the end of the rainbow in a young boy's eyes. They even delivered their goods; an older boy sporting a bicycle with a huge basket would deliver groceries. We never placed a delivery order for our stuff because we would have had to tip the delivery boy. Probably we never thought of it back then anyway. We liked carrying our stuff; made for easy access. Busby and Cox, partners, ran a very lucrative business and carried most anything anyone would ever want. If there was a demand, they had it or would make sure they kept it on the shelf, a typical dry goods store of the time.

If we showed up there with close to a dollar a piece, we would need a wheel barrow to carry our bounty. Both Mister Busby and Mister Cox waited on even us as valued customers. They would follow us from one display case to the next waiting for us to make our next selection. Usually my cousins Billy or Stevie accompanied me, each of us with that familiar jingle jangle in our flaming pockets; the coins burning like red hot fire coals against out thighs. Having it meant spending it.

Choices, there were simply too many. Taking a deep breath, I made my first move while Mister Busby stood there patiently, paper bag in hand. I blurted out; ten pieces of Bazooka bubble gum and it came not only with a big chunk of bubble gum but had a comic strip in the wrapper. I'll have another ten atomic fire balls and five jaw breakers; boy my mouth was going to be hurting from all that chewing and sucking. I pointed to the Tootsie Rolls, those six inchers and held up two fingers. I must also have a box of Cracker Jacks. Back then the box was much larger and had real prizes inside, our version of the Kid's Meal.

More bubble gum, I chose ten of the Monsters from Outer Space trading cards, each with a sheet of bubble gum. To accent my wardrobe I had to have a candy necklace. I counted out my coins as we went along so I'd know just how much I had left to spend and I would spend it all; I always did. You have to make the trip count to the outer reaches of South Main. I informed Mister Cox to add five of those Pixie Sticks to my brown bag. He smiled and said "what else", not "will that be all." Throw in three of those army wax figures with cool aide inside I proclaimed, doubling the value of my purchase because after I sucked the juice from inside, I ended up with a wax army man toy.

I still had scalding red hot coins in my hand so I continued wandering from one display to the next, making sure I had not overlooked something. I spotted one of my favorites, the Chinese hand cuffs. I wasn't exactly sure how they worked but by poking a finger in the ends of the fibered tube about the size of a finger, the contraption would certainly lock you into mortal combat with your friend or yourself, struggling to free yourself from its hold.

I stared at the ice cream freezer, opening each lid and looking inside. There were simply too many selections; banana popsicles, cream cycles, brown cows, push-ups, ice-cream sandwiches, and frozen cool aide pops. I sighed and decided to pass on an ice-cream this trip, figuring it might be too messy and tough to handle while carrying that huge bag of goodies. The day wasn't that hot outside anyway. I could catch the Pied Piper anytime I wanted an ice cream. The musical truck could be heard from blocks away playing its assorted tunes as it made its afternoon rounds through the neighborhood, the perfect kid lure.

I honed in on the comic books, just ten cents per issue but I had hundreds of them already in my stash that I had swapped with my cousin, and I hadn't read them yet. I counted the change one more time and made my final decision. I pointed to the fireworks and purchased ten two cent bottle rockets, two nickel packs of fire crackers and a penny box of matches. Yep, even kids could play with matches. It would be like the 4th of July on Hunter Street about dark thirty. My final tally, just a tad over a buck, no tax and my pockets were turned inside out, not a penny to spare. Mister Busby smiled and bided us a pleasant farewell.

We could hardy wait to get outside to bury our hand deeply inside the paper sack bonanza. From shopping frenzy to feeding frenzy we resembled sharks that had detected blood in the water. Our taste buds stumbled over themselves with the mixture of sweet and sour and hot combinations splattering our most favorite of our six senses. We would easily consume our fair share of the goodies on the one mile return walk. Try and see what a buck buys you now and save up extra to pay the tax on it. You can't buy anything for one or two cents and I'm not sure anything is even available under a quarter plus tax, so it really isn't a quarter.

Change no longer burns a hole in my pocket. I end up dumping it into a tray on the vanity or in a jar where we collect it. I look at the huge jar bulging with an assortment of coins and just imagine what I could have bought with it at Busby and Cox. Back then it would have represented a gold mine, a small fortune, but how could I have possibly carried all that change in my pockets without it pulling my pants down to my ankles. I guess I could have rationed it out for months if I was smart but it's tough to fight that burning sensation. Maybe I could have had that boy on the bike deliver it directly to my house. A pack of salted goobers and Pepsi would just about hit the spot right now. That would be about three bucks plus tax…oh well…the good old days are just that I suppose.

'Money never stays with me. It would burn me if it did. I throw it out of my hands as soon as possible, lest it should find its way into my heart.'
- John Wesley

The Red Camel Club

Growing up in the fifties and sixties with both my parents working second shift in the textile mill meant I spent plenty of time with my grand folks, John and Ruby Bowie from my mama's side. Papa, basically self employed, could pick and choose his times to go fishing and hunting, which typically included me tagging along. Let me tell you, no man loved fishing and hunting more than papa. I recollect that he tended to do more of both than hit a lick of work. Well, I guess that's how a young chap like me remembers it anyway. It put food on the table, his contribution to the household. Nobody complained about the good fixings. The menu often consisted of fried rabbit, squirrel dumplings, turtle stew, frog legs, fried catfish, crappie or brim. Let's not leave out our feathered friends, dove and quail to round out the wildlife cuisine. Even an occasional goat made its way to the table. Got your goat… right?

It's funny how a lot of folks will turn up their noses to wild critters while not flinching at the consumption of steak, pork or chicken. I'm sorry, a critter is a critter whether wild or domesticated. Now I'll admit, sometimes papa did push the limit by occasionally including raccoon, possum or eel in the menu. What can I say? He grew up in a time when pickers couldn't be choosey. Putting any sort of meat on the table could be considered a perk. If it could be caught and/or killed, it could be eaten. Guess it all tasted like chicken, even back then. Unlike some third world countries, neither dog nor cat was ever on the menu, but I suspect if papa had been born in one of those countries that did eat man's best friend he wouldn't have flinched at serving Fido as the entrée.

What was fishing and hunting without genuine fishing and hunting buddies. Mister Jim Creswell and Mister Ben Buzhardt were papa's cronies, his version of an entourage. I guess I was in the junior league, crony in training. Sometimes walking in that shadow is tougher than it seems. Just anyone can't pull it off effectively. What really caused me to standout from the rest; I had no Red Camels, a rookie curse. I'm not even sure if they made Red Camels back then to fit my size. I suspect they didn't or I would have had a pair. Papa and I would have been me and mini-me way before Austin Powers made the characters iconic in the movies.

Red Camels, I can see most of you squinting and scratching your heads. Time for a little history lesson, I suppose, or I could have just as easily told you to pause and Google again. It's time to visualize so hang with me. Picture a pair of denim trousers with a bib on the front and sewn in suspenders crossing over the shoulders and snapping onto the front. These were fondly referred to as bib overalls with riveted pockets, similar to those on conventional jeans. I was always enthralled by the metal buttons and fasteners and secret little pockets. As mentioned, if I would have had a pair I would have worn them proudly.

Rounding out the ensemble, a plaid flannel shirt, the true southerner's choice, often accentuated the wardrobe, especially during the winter months. Of course warmer weather prompted the wearing of a cotton short sleeved plaid shirt or a simple white tee shirt. Papa's wallet was stored in a snap down front pocket in the center of his chest and he always carried a white hankie in his back pocket. There was a special pocket for his watch sported by a chain. He wouldn't be caught without his trusty all purpose pocket knife. There was even a slot in the front for a pencil or ink pen. Red Camels were the perfect carry anything along with you clothing. The old adage, don't leave home without it held true as papa could have passed for Felix the Cat and his bag of tricks with what he carried in those overalls.

    Papa, Mister Jim and Mister Ben always smelled like real men back then. I'm not sure how to describe it. They did not have rank body odor. Instead it was a manly musky aroma, not offensive but identifiable. I smelled too much like a kid, odorless for the most part; occasionally with that salty sweaty non-offensive odor. The good thing about being seven or eight years old, we could rip and romp all day long and hardly sweat and if we did, it wasn't one of those "please stay away from me" stinky smells. Contrary to myth and lore, I did take a bath most every night and didn't just wait until Saturday. Now papa didn't necessarily do a sit down bath every day, but he did the wash off with a cloth at the sink and hit the most offensive extremities I suspect. Granny called it dobbing off. Mama called it dragging a rag through it. Visualize, you'll get it. Google won't help this time, trust me.

    Papa didn't shave every day and oh how he loved grabbing me, holding me up close, and then rubbing his sand papery twelve o'clock shadow against my face. I'd squeal and he'd laugh and do it again. It was sort of a ritual between us. As bad as I hated him doing it, I would have probably been disappointed if he had stopped trying. Chalk it up to that grandpa-grandson male bonding experience. Daddy never did it with me so it remained special between us two rugged men.

I don't remember papa ever wearing anything but those denim Red Camels during the week unless he had a painting job. An entrepreneur, he picked up side jobs painting stuff, typically houses inside or out. Papa had a pair of white overalls he wore when painting. These were speckled with a rainbow of colors that he wore proudly. Papa was in high demand because he was a bit of a perfectionist when it came to painting. Even though he used drop cloths, the paint always seemed to reach its intended target. Everyone knew they would get a first rate job at a reasonable cost. Unlike him, I didn't inherit this art of painting. More paint ends up on me and every where else it isn't supposed to be. That's why I hire out my painting jobs. It's good to now have a brother-in-law that paints. No bush fits my hand.

Just for a hoot once, when I was probably nineteen or so, I dressed in one of Papa's old fedora hats and a pair of his Red Camels, stuffing a pillow in front to round it out. Then I made a cameo appearance mocking the Red Camel boys. Granny Holmes and papa were my primary targets and luckily for me the episode was captured on a super eight soundless movie that I had reproduced on VCR tape; smart move now given the fate of the VCR. That's okay, I still have a VCR. I played it recently for an audience of one, me, and I sure looked stupid, but I wouldn't take anything for the smiles and antics from papa adlibbing along with me. And to just see my great grand mother, granny Holmes, ninety something young back then made me feel warm and tearful.

Papa passed on in 1990, at the age of ninety. He outlived Mister Jim and Mister Ben. I was only thirty seven. I didn't have him for nearly long enough. I still have a pair of those Red Camels and for a while I even had them hung on a wall in my house as an accent piece, a sort of shrine I suppose, accompanied by his fedora hat, a home made sling shot tucked in its side pocket, his pocket watch and a photograph with a poem I had written about him after he passed.

It was tough to let him go. I placed a 4-10 shotgun shell in his pocket for squirrel and rabbit hunting, before they closed the casket, along with an Atlanta Braves loyal supporter pin. It was my way of paying homage to a man I cherished and loved. I called him Papa. Others called him Papa John or Uncle John. He was the only papa I had ever known and I was his only grandson. Back in the day, we made a fine pair. Someday we will again.

'Opportunity is missed by most people because it is dressed in overalls and looks like work.'
- Thomas A. Edison

I'm Rooming with Papa so it must be Christmas

Santa Clause was the real deal back in my day. Sorry, Santa is the real deal. He ranked right up there with the belief that those teeth were exchanged for quarters under my pillow, the work of the Tooth Fairy. My Easter basket was left on the front porch each year by a rabbit. As a child, I clung to those beliefs. I would argue until I was blue in the face if you said they weren't real. How else can you explain that Santa knew exactly what day Christmas came on and that the Tooth Fairy knew when I lost a tooth and that I had put it under my pillow? I do believe some teeth were worth more than a quarter, but I guess that was the going rate. What did he do with all those teeth? That big rabbit sure stayed busy on Easter morning too, but what did eggs have to do with rabbits? Inquiring kid wanted to know. It was a wonderfully magical time to be a kid, so why look a gift horse in the mouth. I still don't know what that saying means. Where's Toby when I need him?

Believing in Santa did come with its challenges. How come every department store had a Santa? How could he possibly be in so many places at the same time or could arrive at that next location just ahead of me. He didn't always look exactly the same either? Simple explained my folks; Santa's helpers. At Christmas he couldn't be everywhere, so he had helpers to assist him in collecting that valuable information; the kid's name and what they wanted. It made perfectly good sense to me, at the time. I so believed it, that one visit to one helper was all it took for me. Just how did all these helpers cross reference the lists to make sure everyone was accounted for? I only question, was it the real Santa or was it Memorex, and did he really check that list twice to see who was naughty or nice? How many times did I show up on the bad list? I don't remember ever receiving that bag of coal so maybe I was in the clear.

Okay, so we know Santa lives at the North Pole, but where does the Tooth Fairy call home? And what about the rabbit and how does he carry all those baskets? Santa has a sleigh, The Tooth Fairy has wings, but what does old Peter Cotton Tail have? Oh yeah, is the Sand Man a distant relative of the Tooth Fairy? What's the difference in elves and those dwarfs that hung out with Sleeping Beauty? So many questions and not nearly enough answers.

One thing I learned, parents can be so cruel. At Christmas for many years I had to wait until all my grandparents arrived before I could see what Santa brought me. They kept the doorways closed to the Christmas tree in the living room, so I couldn't even sneak a peek. My grandparents didn't seem to share the same urgency in arriving as did I. I had two grannies and one papa, but it certainly felt like more when I was confined to the front room waiting for the bus to arrive. What's the point in getting up at the crack of dawn if you have to play the waiting game? I could have slept in.

A year or so later I don't know who came up with this wonderful idea of granny and papa doing a sleep over on Christmas Eve. First of all it meant I was kicked out of my single bed to provide granny a place to sleep. I had to share the couch's hideaway bed in the den with papa, which insured I remained captive, and far away from the living room and the Christmas tree. Did I mention how papa snores? And I still had to wait for my other granny to arrive, so what did this new sleeping arrangement really buy me except a bed buddy and change of scenery; neither of which were on my Christmas list?

Judgment time; finally all the likely suspects had

arrived and the doors were open for business. I'm actually allowed to see what Santa had left me under the tree. Soon I forget about all the circumstances and inconveniences leading up to that very special moment; at least until next year. Fire up my favorite Christmas song, *All I want for Christmas is my Two Front Teeth*, and I'm moved by the holiday spirit. Crashing through the dining room door, my gateway to the living room, there under the tree is my very first rocking horse, a Roy Rogers sing along guitar, boots and authentic sounding air rifle, and my very own Howdy Doody ventriloquist doll, and me sporting my footed pajamas with the signature rear flap; a trend setter I am.

For the next few years we had to play out this same scene, just like in that Bill Murray movie *Ground Hog Day*, wake up, torment me with the waiting, and finally allow me to collect my booty. That was all about to change and my world was about to come crashing down around my feet. Just a few short weeks before Christmas and while visiting my papa and granny, I was rolling around on their bedroom floor, playing with our pet dog, when I skirted underneath the bed. I came face to face with a boxed up race car track. Not wanting to spoil the surprise for my grandparents, I played dumb, figuring that's what they had bought me for Christmas. The surprise was on me when this ended up under my Christmas tree, supposedly left by Santa. I don't remember papa or granny filling in as Santa's helpers, but possibly they were volunteers. Papa had the belly for it.

No, something was badly wrong with this scenario. I was one devastated kid, if truth be told. I eventually confessed to my folks, that I had discovered that very package weeks earlier concealed under my grandparents bed. Their explanation; Santa had dropped it off early. The following year, with my perception of Santa's existence now shattered, my folks decided to allow me to receive and open all my gifts on Christmas Eve at my grandparent's house instead of Christmas morning. Without any of us actually admitting Santa's involvement, a new tradition had been born. I no longer had to be confined in a holding room on Christmas morning.

On my thirteenth Christmas, Billy, my thirteen year old cousin and next door neighbor, received a three speed bike, the first in our little world. Up until then our bikes had been one speed, as fast as we could peddle them. Both jealous and envious, I eventually coerced Billy into letting me have a turn riding the new fangled bicycle. Reluctantly he relinquished possession and allowed me to give it a spin, while he followed on my old antique. Barreling down the long sidewalk in front of Langley Milliken grammar school, I giggled like a little girl, zooming at top speeds never ever experienced previously on our conventional banana-seat bikes.

The paved sidewalk ends abruptly at the intersection, requiring the biker to slow down and take an extreme right turn onto a dirt path or end up in a deep ditch. We've often played chicken with that ditch, veering right at the last minute. As I approached, I reversed the pedals with my feet to brake for my turn. The pedals simply spun backwards, and I drove nose first into the ditch. Emerging bloodied and bruised and with the Christmas bike sporting a badly bent and warped front wheel, Billy's only concern and comment, 'why didn't you use the hand brakes, you moron?' Hand brakes I asked? That completed my last ride on the Christmas three speed, and I to deal with one very pissed off cousin, a specimen twice my size.

Fast forward to Christmas with the grandboys, some things don't really change. Before moving to the beach where the clan resided, we would spend Christmas Eve with my parents then hustle 4 ½ hours to spend the night with the grand's, so we would be there Christmas morning to witness them being surprised by Santa. Unlike my parents with me, they were allowed to enter the den harboring the Christmas tree as they woke from their slumber, whether we were ready or not.

Christmas Eve, after cookies and milk were left for old Saint Nick, and the boys were sent packing, I would covertly leave sleigh marks across the yard accompanied by an abundance of reindeer tracks. I deer hunted so I knew exactly how to fabricate authentic looking deer tracks. To set-up the illusion, the grandboys and I would scatter magical reindeer dust to attract them to the house just before bed time. I would follow that very exact trail to the patio to provide evidence that the magic worked to perfection. Inside I would turn over several items around the fire place to indicate Santa's clumsy arrival down the chimney. It worked like a charm. The milk and cookies would be gone, leaving just a few crumbs and one last swallow of milk. I'm not sure if the real Santa appreciated this joke.

Both have outgrown Santa but in our hearts we all still wish to believe. Sugar plums dancing in ones head have been replaced with songs on an IPOD, Smart Phone or IPAD. The Tooth Fairy now slides a buck under the pillow; inflation I suppose. The Easter Bunny no longer leaves baskets on the porch. Political corrective-ness has all but destroyed what was once sacred. Looking back now, waiting for my grandparents to arrive and sleeping with a snoring Papa, wasn't so bad after all.

'When we recall Christmas past, we usually find that the simplest things, not the great occasions, give off the greatest glow of happiness.'
- **Bob Hope**

Little Mountain

Abbeville, South Carolina, nestled between the state capital, Columbia and the Piedmont of Greenville, is rich with history. Being a kid growing up there in the fifties through the seventies, I didn't exactly appreciate the significance of my heritage so to speak. I had more important fish to fry, enjoying life, taking risks on the wild side and creating my very own tiny town theatrics. Sure, the old home town was the birthplace and deathbed of the confederacy, but what did that really mean to me. What did I really know or care about the southern states seceding from the Union; Secession Hill signifying the meeting place where the premise evolved? The most important event in my life had to be the end of another school year and summer adventures tugging at my faded cut-off jeans. I was barefooted and ready to take on what life had to offer.

To put things in perspective for the generation of couch bound, video game, savvy kids lacking imagination, vitality and the gumption to venture outside and embrace what life has to offer, we mostly invented ways to entertain ourselves. The current generation will have lost all social skills with texting and social media robbing them of being a kid. Don't get me wrong, baseball, basketball or backyard football could only hold our attention for so long during those long summer days, before we were bored and yearning for that dare factor, to go where no kids had gone before us. It was always outside for us; don't even think about making us come inside. We'd fight our parents tooth and claw for the right to push the limits of dark thirty. Sorry, dark thirty is that time of the day just before darkness falls. It can't be found on the face of a clock but trust me everyone back in my day knew the significance of the setting sun. The second book I published is titled *Dark Thirty*.

One of our favorite summer pastimes had to be quenching the oppressive humidity any which way we could. Sometimes this was accomplished via the oscillating sprinkler watering the yard connected to the hose pipe. Sorry, southern slang, hose pipe is garden hose to those not privy to the lingo of my time. Running though the fan tailed spray, the water kept us quite satisfied and momentarily entertained. The Slip and Slide was the ultimate adventure. The long roll out of durable plastic, affixed to the hose pipe, with water spurting from tiny holes; all one would have to do is get a running start on the grass then belly or butt flop on to the slick surface and ride it to the end.

Sadly, one cannot live by sprinkler or Slip and Slide alone. Water cost money and the meter was running as long as the water was flushing through that hose. Money doesn't grow on trees; our parents would constantly remind us. What that had to do with staying cool lost something in translation for us. Swimming pools, other than at the recreation center, were virtually unheard of back in the land before time. A few legendary paddle pools existed so I've heard. I had one, once upon a time, maybe 8 x 8 feet and two feet deep filled to the brim, but even this was a big deal for the gill-less fish we were. Granny Winn had a concrete pool at the bottom of the hill in her backyard. It required clogging the drain with a rag or whatever we could find to plug it, filling it up with a hose pipe and then enjoying the water until it became too filthy. Then you drained it.

Not to worry, we had Little Mountain Lake, just down the Cedar Springs Road from Hunter Street where I lived.

The actual name was Parsons Mountain, the highest point around, peaking at 832 feet. It was a little mountain, thus that's how we came to call it. Our mountain was originally named after Mr. James Parsons back in 1772 and gold was even discovered there in the 1800's. It's now part of the Sumter National Forest. For our purposes, it had a lake that was constructed there in the 1940's. If we were fortunate and with a tad of luck tossed in, our parents, grandparents or some family member would load up a slew of us kids in a vehicle and take us to our swimming hole. We thought this water paradise was enormous and in a kid's eyes it was. Visiting there as an adult, it more resembles an oversized pond now. The eye is in the beholder and back then, we were beholding to the adventure and time spent there.

Hiking the winding dirt and gravel road to the top of our little mountain highlighted many trips there. It was our very own Mount Everest. There on the top rested the ranger's lookout tower, but I'll get to that shortly. Along the way, on the opposite side of our lake's designated swimming area was the dam and spillway. No, this was not of Hoover proportions, nowhere close as a matter of fact. Heck, none of us had seen a real dam so again, eye of the beholder. Our adventures were perfect. They only required an imagination and willingness to toss caution to the wind. We possessed both.

Further up the winding road, Lost Lake was a place of interest, maybe not for us, but the teenagers were drawn to the secluded mud hole like flies. It was a favorite parking spot for making out and making ones fantasies come true. It would grow on us later and we too would eventually appreciate its significance. A similar place existed closer to town, just off the 28 bypass, 'The Beach', a place where fill dirt was excavated down the end of a secluded road. Well, not too secluded, because everyone knew where it was located. It was a make-out destination.

Before reaching the tower, we had to pass the old gold mines. Yes, these were genuine gold mines, three of them long ago deserted. They weren't clearly marked so you had to know where to go. We did. Two were surrounded by a fence and the third was a slanted hole into the ground, the entrance caved in with no opportunity for spelunkers. Each visit was marred with dares. Climb the fence and see how far you can go. We were all daredevils back then but none of us were quite that stupid. An obvious entry way didn't exist so climbing the fence really served no purpose. Sure, we talked up gold prospecting, but what did we really know about generating our very own gold rush. Just the same it was fun going there. Now they are marked as part of the Tower Trail.

The tower, now that was our Holy Grail. Negotiating the long incline to the lookout on stilts to us was like ascending Mount Everest. Once we arrived, there rested the ranger station at the top, resembling our very own Eiffel Tower. Next dare; who is going to the top of the tower? Really there was no risk, steps extended to the ranger platform. The doorway to the inside of the station was padlocked so you could only ascend to the section just below it. From there the view was breathtaking. We were on top of the world, standing there at the highest point of our Little Mountain.

Etching our names in the metal framework at the top was mired in tradition and marked our territory, our testament that we had completed the climb. You could always count on one scribbling; *Kilroy Was Here*, a bald-headed man, sometimes depicted as having a few hairs, with a prominent nose peeking over a wall with the fingers of each hand clutching the wall. The doodle supposedly originated during World War II and was graffiti associated with GIs. You could find it on most any bathroom wall or in out of the way places. Of course other inscriptions contained profanity and brought about bursts of laughter from us, taboo as it was.

Little Mountain was not just reserved for kid adventures. Some involved partnering up with adults. If you have to, you have to. One particular excursion was our version of a hayride. Papa or daddy always needed pine needles. What better place to collect this bounty than the pine forest of Sumter National Park. It was free after all and child labor laws weren't enforced in Abbeville County. A bunch of us would pile into the bed of papa's 1961 Apache 10 Chevy pickup truck, securing the rakes and we were off to collect pine needles. This was yet just one more game for our wild imaginations. Like I've said, we were the creators of our little universe.

Raking was not fun but the real fun hinged on us filling the bed of that truck. Once it reached the height of the cab we were done. We then became kid tarps, brought along to secure the load. We embraced our job seriously; well, maybe not seriously, but mashing down those needles and wallowing in them brought sparkles to our eyes. Let the hayride begin. Okay, it wasn't hay but it sounds better than pine needle ride. We weren't hard to please. We were boredom fighters after all.

In a less stressful time, no one ever considered that riding in the back of pick-ups certified the passengers as human projectiles. This was life before seatbelts or other restraints. A kid had the freedom to roam anywhere in a vehicle, unrestricted, often landing in the lap of the driver and helping them navigate. My favorite spot when I was small enough was stretching out on the platform in the back window. Cars had child size shelves just above the back seat in the day when you could tell a Chevy from a Ford. Life was good and tailor-made for kids.

    Sometimes we would venture to Sumter National Forest in search of an elusive plant. We became medicine men in the Amazon jungles, seeking some sort of magical cure for what ails you. Actually we had no idea why we were looking for this plant. My black mama, Anise, my second mama, the one who kept me in check while my parents worked the second shift at Milliken textile mill, required this plant, so enough said. Looking back, I think this was some sort of Ginseng. She supposedly made tea from the reddish root, it having some sort of healing and curative properties. As an adult, one of my coworkers referred to it as Bo-hog root and he said it was used for sexual enhancement purposes; home remedy Viagra maybe. Either way, it was a game of see how many we could find. It secured us another ride in the back of papa's Chevy as he would bring her and us to forest.

    Further down the Cedar Springs Road stood what we considered to be a genuine haunted house, the octagon shaped Frazier-Pressley House. It loomed in the shadows of the old oaks and was deserted for most of my life in Abbeville and used in my novel, *The Perfect Spook House*. As teenagers, dares would prompt us to venture inside under the cloak of darkness. We did our fair share of spook house investigations back then. We never had an eye witness encounter with a ghost but we always scared the crap out of each other, waiting around the next corner to jump out and yell. Old ancient cemeteries rated high on our close encounters list; the spookier the better.

We definitely upped the ante as we reached our adolescence, becoming more creative, our innovation peaking new levels once we could now drive. No longer handicapped by someone else getting us to where we wanted to go or possibly places we should never go; we took many a peek inside Pandora's Box and for the most part survived our experiences unscathed. It wasn't from lack of effort, pushing the envelope. Parents don't need to know everything, right? And for those parents reading this, let's just call this fiction, made up stuff...

'It is my desire to be a great writer. I know that I still have a mountain to climb to achieve that.'

- Guy Johnson

Let's Make d Deal, Monty Hall

Innovators, always, and back in the sixties we didn't have the zillion television stations or video games to occupy our bored little pre-teenager minds. We had to devise our own little distractions to break up our otherwise mundane existence. We seldom fell short on creativity and most of these distractions from the ordinary wouldn't necessarily kill us. No risk, no gain, no fun could have been our mantra. It could have been but none of us had ever heard of the word, *mantra*.

Game shows were the mainstay for daytime television. They rivaled only the numerous soap operas clogging the three stations. I saw very little of either except during the summer months when school gave me the time off and away from the world of the forced education system. Shows like *To Tell the Truth* or *Kids Say the Darndest Things* and *Truth or Consequences* were innovation at their broadcasting best. Each of these could have represented chapters from my life. Come to think of it, they did.

Those game shows certainly ruled in my day. Now they have a cable network specifically devoted to new game shows as well as replays of the ancient ones. My mama, rest her soul, kept her TV dialed into The Game Show Network. She loved reruns of the Match Game and Newly Wed Game. In real life I flunked both until I found my true love of the past nineteen years.

Can you say WHEEL…OF…FORTUNE; undoubtedly mama's all time favorite. She watched it in primetime and savored all the reruns as if seeing them for very first time. I hated that game show. Just the sound of WHEEL…OF…

FORTUNE made my skin crawl. I was so over Vanna White and she was an original South Carolinian; go figure.

Who wants to be a Millionaire? Bless mama's heart; Regis snookered her in too. I guess the fortune thing and having millions coincided. The Game Show Network always playing on the television at mama's house turned me against game shows in general. In my adolescent days they just seemed to be entertaining; the stars appearing on them so much larger than life. I guess that was before tabloid television and before we knew everything about every famous celebrity. Scandals have replaced the *warm and fuzzy* stories.

I suppose I may as well confess. As I kid I was quite fanatical about many of the game shows of my time. Marketing not to be outdone, transformed the more popular ones into play at home game versions. I still have my original *Pass Word* game; have had it now for probably over fifty years. I also have my original *Snap Judgment* game. I had the *Concentration Game, Match Game, Family Feud* and the *Newly Wed Games* for a while, but I think they've all been trashed. One can only be so much of a packrat. You must remember these were not video games but instead a combination of card and board type versions. I do still possess the home version of *Win, Lose or Draw*. I loved Bert Convey as host of that game show and it actually aired after I got home from school or was that work; same difference?

Everyone remembers Bob Barker as the emcee for *The Price is Right* but do you remember him as the host of *Truth or Consequences*? I suppose the *Bachelor* and *Bachelorette* reality TV series replaced *The Dating Game*. After the *Newly Wed Game* and an unsuccessful marriage there was always

Divorce Court. Yep, game shows have certainly evolved. I still gravitate to the old original versions.

Who could ever forget Monty Hall and *Let's Make a Deal*? Halloween attire and gimmicks equate to let's make a fool out of ourselves. Do you want the two hundred and fifty dollars or what's behind door number three? Take the door; no take the money! I'll take door number three. What if I give you another twenty instead? How about another fifty; another one hundred? No, I'll take door number three. Show me what's behind door number three. There stands a dusty old miner with a jackass and cart full of rocks. You should have taken the money!

Like I proclaimed, innovators we were, so how could we improve the gaming? How could we possibly embellish on a game show already highly acclaimed as a winner? From the minds of babes anything is possible. Cousins Billy and Stevie, come on down. With my kitchen as our backdrop we were about to give it a spin; *Truth or Consequences* meets *Let's Make a Deal*.

Allow me to set the stage. We have two contestants, same age, ten years old; supposedly one just as smart as the other. Having no audience present such as parents improved the games integrity. I am the diabolical host and believe me, host is the best position for our little game. That being said, I had to take my rotation as a contestant too; my turn in the barrel so to speak, but for now the host I am.

To play the game we only required a strategically located pantry. Our two contestants were seated so that they could not see the contents of the deadly little vault; a treasure strove of hidden ingredients; the nightmare of Pandora's Box. Premise of the game, very simple; each contestant would take their turn. The host would place his hand inside the pantry on an item of his selection and would ask the contestant, "do you want this or not?" Two choices, answer yes or no. No meant you passed on the item and yes meant you had to taste the item.

We typically played this in the afternoons after school and after we had built up an appetite. Each contestant had been allowed one quick look inside the pantry so they would be assured various candies and cookies and other yummy snacks did indeed reside on the shelves. They also had the opportunity to assess the evil nasty things that lurked there. One rule, the host could not place his hand on potentially deadly items. Of course a ten year old's perception of deadly is somewhat skewed.

Second rule, the honor system was in place which meant you could not switch items after the item had been selected and either chosen or passed over. Is there really true honor among ten year olds? I suppose that depends if your peers have ticked you off or not, or if you have a favorite cousin or are just feeling devious. Remember, I am the devious one so I'll just leave it at that. I hoped the other hosts were honorable when I sat on the hot seat. Who could really ever know the answer to that one unless you were the one always ending up with the nasty selections? Let the game begin.

"Stevie, do you want this item or not?"

Taking a deep breath he finally said, "Okay, I'll take it."

I extracted a sleeve of saltine crackers. Stevie sighed relief and ate one saltine. Now it was Billy's turn; truth or dare time. Billy, although the same age as Stevie and me was like that cartoon duck character, Baby Huey, twice as big as us; so one had to handle him with kid gloves. Making him too angry could be kid suicide and remember we had no adult supervision or intervention of an old fashion butt whipping.

"Do you want this one or not Billy?"

"Okay," he answered.

To build up the anticipation and climax to the perfect show stopper I slowly removed my hand to reveal a bag of ruffled Lays potato chips. Billy smiled and elbowed Stevie as he plucked a handful from the open bag. Both contestants were happy so far and I remained alive and kicking; both good signs, but how long could this theme last? All was not tasty inside that pantry. Your gut should tell you that the wise thing to do is always say no, however, what's the fun in that?

This was about gamesmanship, taking the dare and trying to outdo your opponent and outsmart the pantry host. None of us knew how to spell strategy then much less embrace the concept. We did know that there were cookies, candy bars, chips and other good stuff in that pantry. The other crap wasn't supposed to kill us. We didn't fathom getting sick. Besides, this was supposed to be fun; at least to a point. The thrill was agreeing to risk it all and taste what lurked at the end of the host's extended arm. The chances of getting something good grew slimmer as the game progressed.

"Stevie, do you want what I have in my hand?"

Another deep breath as Stevie attempts to read my poker face. They didn't call me Stone Face for nothing. Stevie rationalizes that both he and Billy have successfully survived round one but what is in my hand now? Another rule, you pass and your opponent has to taste what you forfeited. Stevie decides to pass. Billy gives him the look and then watches as I reveal his fate; marshmallows. Steve exclaims, "Darn it!"

Billy receives the goody and now has his opportunity to accept my choice or pass it to Stevie. He smiles and passes. I produce a bottle of vanilla extract. It could have been much worse. A teaspoon full and it's over; Stevie's turn again.

I now mess with them. "Are you sure you want his one?" I stick my second hand inside. "Or would you rather have what I'm touching with my left hand? Right or left or pass?"

"I pass," says Stevie.

"Right or left hand," I question Billy as he playfully punches Stevie in the shoulder.

"Left," he boasts and I produce a can of shortening.

Billy exclaims, "I'm not eating that!"

I remind him. "You know the rules. I had raisins in my right hand but you picked my left."

"You can't make me eat that junk."

"Come on Billy," says Stevie. "Are you just a chicken?"

Now those were verging on fighting words where I came from, but Billy cursed under his breath and dug the spoon inside the lard can as we sometimes called it. He took his medicine but not without a hitch. "Now, it's my turn to man the pantry. It's you against Stevie."

I hate this game. This is where that revenge thing comes into play and if I really trust where Billy is placing his hand. I passed this first three times and Stevie received treats every time. Billy just smirked at me, daring me. No one dares me and gets away with it, so I nodded I would take what he had. He withdrew his hand exposing my fate and I said I quit, but a man has to do what a man has to do and I reluctantly took my medicine. Puking is allowed but you don't receive bonus points. The pantry game, it never killed us but don't try this at home; the family pantry is not what it used to be.

Next time I think we'll just play the phone game. Randomly dial a number and say something stupid to the person on the other end and hope you didn't call someone who recognized you and snitches to your parents. Innovators, yes we were. We had to be, had nothing better to do. We really enjoyed ever single moment of life without cable TV or video distractions. Our minds were our most powerful tools. Possibly that's why I still have a vivid imagination. I wonder if Billy and Stevie would be up for a friendly round today.

'I'd say that, to be a good deal maker, you have to have 3 basic characteristics - timing, timing, and timing.'
- **Richard Armitage**

My Black Mama

Growing up in the fifties with both my parents working the second shift in the local textile mill, I had to rely on my grandparents and night time sitter to mold my young impressionable mind. They filled the void left by my parents working the four to midnight shift. They didn't choose to work the second shift, it just happened. It was called making a living. Providers couldn't be choosey. Entitlement programs hadn't ruined America yet. People actually wanted to work and earn their own way. It grew character. While they did this, I sat at home on the sidelines doing what I was good at, being a kid.

Mama and daddy made the most of it to make sure I had a normal life. Normal didn't necessarily match up well with my peer group. When other kids were in bed, I stayed up and watched the first part of the *Tonight Show with Johnny Carson*. I knew everything about Ed McMann and Doc Severinsen when other kids were sawing logs. "Heeeere's Johnny" greeted me each and every night at 11:30.

I may not have understood all the jokes and one liners but I laughed along with the audience or sound track when Johnny's many characters performed a skit. Art Fern, Carnac the Magnificent, Floyd R. Turbo American, Aunt Blabby and El Mundo were part of my life. It was difficult sharing them with my friends. Most had never seen the late night king of comedy. They didn't know what they were missing. I was only missing sleep, so what.

I blame my folks for me being a night owl, only requiring five or six hours of sleep to this day. If my folks were alive they'd be the first to tell you they never had to call me a second time when it was time to rise and shine. I've never pressed a snooze button in my life. Yep, it was me and Carson ending each night on a funny note. So you ask, how on earth two responsible parents would allow their child to stay up so late. They really had no choice. I had a sitter while they worked. Television shows called them nannies and most of those depicted were Mary Poppin stereotypes. Mine, Anise Ray, a portly black woman, was 'My Black Mama.' She had a family of her own, but week days three to after midnight, this scrawny little white boy belonged to her.

Mama got off work at midnight and I accompanied her to take Anise home, and then we waited for daddy at the mill until about 12:30 for his shift to end. I always missed the last half of the Carson show. Most of time it was nearing 1 AM before my head hit the pillow. Anise and I made the best of it until time for her to go home. Not to worry, she'd be back again tomorrow. She had weekends off.

Anise loved telling this one particular story that became a defining moment in our relationship. Sitting in the tub, me about three years old, she bathed me and gave me what she called a quickie bath. She said I looked up at her as she sponged me off and asked her, "Will your black come off on me?" As only she could tell it, she answered, "Lordy no honey child, my black won't rub off on you and your white won't rub off on me." That was the end of that. Satisfied with her answer, I never asked the question again. Color was no longer an issue and to this day still isn't for me.

Janie, from the household of Anise, was a member of a record club. Many of us got trapped in those record or eight track tape clubs. Getting snared by one was comparable to being the owner of a timeshare. Once in, you couldn't get out. Janie received a Jan and Dean album. What was she going to do with a Jan and Dean record, not exactly her taste in music? I brought it off of her for probably a couple of dollars and still have it fifty some odd years later. Same goes for a Four Seasons '33'; I was sort of an unofficial member of her record club, buying those she didn't want. Records came in 45 and 33. The 45 had one song on each side of the record. The 33 was larger with five or six songs on each side. I still have the Four Seasons album. I recently saw Jersey Boys and had no idea how Frankie and his cohorts skirted crime and mafia connections.

Lila, Anise's daughter actually worked for daddy for many years at Milliken. Our families had all sorts of ties. Daddy was notorious for his whooping yell in the mill, a way to get attention of those who otherwise wouldn't have heard him over the loud equipment. A whoop and waving arm was his trademark. I had to listen to that imitation more times than I could count from classmates that worked for him after school. I'm sure Lila heard it more times than she would care to admit.

Anise was often the target of my ambushes and practical jokes. I would catch her in compromising positions, taking her photo if she napped on the couch. I did that to a lot of people. Heck I could make one of those coffee table books of the many family members I've captured sleeping in photographs. I'd stage all sorts of surprises for her. Open a closet and a rubber flying bat affixed to a string would swoop at her. Rubber snakes were hidden in drawers and cabinets. All was in good fun. She'd chase me about as if she were going to catch me and beat me within an inch of my life. We'd both have good laugh afterwards.

I grew up on buttermilk and cornbread. I think buttermilk was in my baby bottle and in my baby formula. Several times a week Anise would cook us up a skillet of cornbread. If we were real hungry, she'd take a short cut and cook us a batch of quick cornbread. Instead of pouring the cornbread batter in the skillet and placing it in the oven, she would heat up oil in the skillet on the stove eye, and plop spoonfuls of batter in the hot sizzling grease and fry up cornbread fritters. I still occasionally cook it that way today and think of her when I do.

Fast forward to January 22, 1972, my daddy's birthday, and he was best man at my wedding. I could feel pride oozing from his every pore as he smiled on his long haired, brown eyed, toothpick skinny eighteen year old son with the pork chop side burns, preparing to tie the knot, always looking cool in his cream colored 1970 Monte Carlo. My wife to be was a little bit country, and me, a little bit rock and roll, way before Donnie and Marie laid claim to it. She loved Donna Fargo, *The Happiest Girl in the Whole USA* and I was taken by Don McLean's *American Pie*, listening to WBBQ on the radio, out of Augusta.

Anise, my black mama was escorted into that Pentecostal Holiness Church on that blessed day along with our parents. She sat proudly on the first pew, dressed to the nines. She beamed with pride watching me take that big life altering step. After all, she was my mama too. She had given me the gift of color blindness, when she herself had grown up in a time where color mattered and racial notions existed.

Life's lesson for me, I never saw things in black or white growing up, not while attending school or to this very day. To me, using the "N" word is just as bad as taking the Lord's name in vain. It was just something you didn't do. I consider myself very fortunate to have had a second mama in my life. Both of my mamas are gone now, but in heaven they are treated as equals for God, too, is color blind. I bet she has whipped Him up a skillet of quick cornbread time and again with her heavenly cast iron skillet.

'Truth knows no color; it appeals to intelligence.'
- **James Hal Cone**

A Dollar a Day is All You Pay

For any of you who have already read my memoir, *The Caregiver's Son, Outside the Window Looking In*, you'll recall my love for my papa and how I shadowed him on countless fishing and hunting adventures. If you haven't, I'll pause long enough for you to go on line and order you a copy, or just jump on it the first opportunity you have. I'm not sure which one papa loved more, hunting or fishing. Personally I was better at fishing. Fish more times than not hooked themselves. It didn't involve aiming my 4-10 shotgun and being a Cracker Jack shot to bag a squirrel. Both do take patience though; something I was absolutely not good at as a kid. I'm not much better at it now, come to think of it. I broke the ice when I landed that five pound cat all by my lonesome. This is where you need my memoir; it recaps that boy versus the whale incident. I'll stay away from spoilers and won't recap it now.

Most of papa's fishing holes were close by. I think he knew where every pond was located in the county and pretty much had permission from their owners to fish them. Heck he had probably done painting jobs for most of them; his way of getting his foot in the door. With his old 61 Chevy Pick-up as our chariot, we homed in on them at record speeds, matching the minimum posted speed limits. Papa was not a speedster for sure but eventually he got where he was going. Time seemed to be something he had plenty of so why worry about it. I can't ever recall him getting in any sort of hurry; maybe twice. He attempted to chase me down a time or two, especially that time I had been chunking rocks at passing cars. The other time was when that Tom turkey had him in its sites during the great goat caper; a story left for another time.

Fishing was fishing and anytime they were biting, a good time was to be had. Heck, we had good times even when they weren't. Papa had this knack for knowing when it was right to fish for whatever kind of fish. According to him it had something to do with reading the signs. These were only visible to him apparently because I certainly couldn't see any signs that said today the brim are biting but the catfish aren't. Crappie and brim were notorious for being on the bed when the moon was right (one of those signs), but I never heard that reference made about a catfish. That's why I just wet my hook when and where he told me to. I just left the mumbo jumbo to the professionals. Just like bait selection, knowing when to use worms, crickets, minnows or mullet and for which species of fish just wasn't my thing. I'd use whatever Papa brought to the fishing hole. And yes, I did bait my own hook. That was the fun part.

There were plenty of ponds, rivers and lakes to fish from and we did our share of wetting our hooks in all of them. Still, there was one place papa so loved to visit and it didn't rely on the signs being right. It all hinged on when the fish were being stocked. It was located near Fork Shoals, with no short way to get there. The honey hole was nestled somewhere between Honea Path and Williamston and required creative zigzagging some forty miles from Abbeville through Due West, Donalds, Honea Path, Ware Place, skirting Princeton, making that last right turn at McKelvey Crossroads, just past Lickville to reach our final destination. This was a far piece for papa to drive but we made an all-dayer out of it, stopping in Princeton for breakfast along the way.

You see, this was one of those pay a dollar a day to fish

holes. For Papa it meant forking over two, one for me. Back then they didn't have those kids get in free under a certain age. If you could handle a cane pole or rod and reel, you paid the price of admission. There was no money back guarantee if you didn't catch any fish. It was a dice roll but not to worry, we never left empty handed. Papa somehow knew when they were trucking in a new load of fish so he planned our visits accordingly. You heard me; the fish didn't live in the three ponds; hadn't been spawned and raised there. The proprietor of this little enterprise paid to have them hauled in. He made his living charging folks like us to fish, plus he also had a little store on the premises, selling an assortment of bait and fishing supplies, drinks, sandwiches and plenty of junk food. He'd rent you fishing equipment or fold up chairs if you didn't bring your own. The man was quite the back country entrepreneur.

Sometimes my cousin and uncle would accompany us, all piling inside the cab of that old truck; pre-seat belt days. As I got older papa let me ride in the truck bed. As long as it was warm weather this was the next best thing to a carnival ride. Arriving at the pay to fish destination, my first objective was to talk papa into buying me something from the shack located at the first and largest of the three ponds. Most of the time he was a push over because he liked the same sorts stuff that I did. Where do you think I learned these eating habits in the first place? A Coca Cola and salted peanuts were usually a given before the day was out. There's a technique to consuming this combination though. You dumped the contents of the peanut sleeve into the bottled coke, but only after that first swallow. Remember those Busby and Cox visits. There is no way to describe the taste of those salted goobers floating in the neck of that bottle when you turned them up; a delegacy of sweet and salty. I think southerners invented this; possibly even papa originated it to hear him tell it.

A Moon Pie and RC cola was another special combo. No, you didn't crumble up the Moon Pie in the RC cola bottle, but I bet it would have been good if we would have thought about doing it. Of course no roadside shack would be complete without having fresh salty boiled peanuts on hand, cooking over an open fire inside a black cast iron kettle. There would be an assortment of sandwiches available, usually deviled egg or maybe pimento cheese. Did I mention ice cream? Yep, any proprietor worth anything would stock ice cream sandwiches, black cows and orange sherbet push-ups. This was indeed one of my favorite fishing spots, the honey hole and Holy Grail all wrapped into one. Fish, who really needed them, but he paid a dollar for me to be there so I had to drown a few worms.

The first pond was stocked with mostly catfish, even though we might occasionally catch a brim. Papa deemed it a lucky day if any of us caught an eel. This was basically a snake looking critter. Papa thought of it as a fresh water delegacy. The next pond had a mixture of brim and carp. Mullet was used for the carp. These were sucker-mouthed, funny looking scaly fish. They weren't the best for eating but they were usually large and thick, would fill a frying pan. Brim would bite worms or crickets mostly. The third pond was for the avid bass fisherman. Minnows and various artificial lures were used to land the largemouth bass. Papa typically shied away from that third pond. He wasn't a sport fisherman enthusiast. It was further down the hill and looked snaky, as papa called it. The first pond served his purposes just fine, filled with cats.

Red worms, dubbed wigglers for a reason, were the primary bait and Papa raised them in his backyard. When these store bought catfish were really biting, you could hardly keep your hook baited. It wasn't unusual for the four of us to catch a hundred or so keepers. There was no limit. Good eating size averaged around six or seven inches long. I did only cork fishing; meaning papa strategically affixed a red and white cork to my fishing line to regulate the depth of my sinker and hook. A bobbing cork meant you had a nibble or bite. The cork disappearing beneath the water meant you had a strike. If the cork didn't come back up then you had hooked the cat. Pretty simple, even a kid could do it. Don't get me wrong; doing this time after time, with little breathing room, will take it out of you. Kids require a little goofing off time. We're not cut out for endless grabbling with critters. After awhile the fun sort of wears off and it seems too much like work. It didn't take me long to earn papa's dollars' worth. An orange sherbet push-up could have as easily entertained me.

After the hard fought battle, came the ride home. Worn out from dragging in one cat after the other, I'd often give in to fatigue and nod on the way back. Too often when I'd close my eyes, I'd see a red and white cork bobbing, just before it went under the water. I'd blink, open my eyes, and nod again, only to replay the same scene. I think I virtually relived the event for the entire return trip. The day was not complete though. This bounty had to be cleaned; and in this case it doesn't mean washed. Cleaned is a fisherman's term for dressing the catch. No, we didn't cloth the slimly little devils. Dressing is another term for beheading and gutting them; quite graphic but a necessary evil.

Techniques vary, depending on the types of fish that lined up on the stringer. A stringer is basically the rope that holds the caught fish. It has this long sharp metal end that you slip through the gills of the first fish caught and loop it through a ring that anchors the rest of your catch. Each fish thereafter is butted against the first and the stringer remains in the water until you are ready to go home. It keeps the fish alive and wet for the most part. PETA would see it differently but the Lord provided us with fish to eat so we really don't pay them much mind. Catfish are cleaned by whacking off their head and skinning them. Yep you heard me, skinning the cat, pun intended. Scaly fish have to be de-scaled with this special little hand held scaler. Skinning is a much cleaner process. Scales are popping off and sticking to everything but you have to do it because they're not too tasty if left on.

There is really just one way to eat catfish; deep fried southern style, tails on. A buttermilk and egg dip is prepared and then you just roll them around and coat them before introducing your catch to the cornmeal. Batter up, drop them in a deep fryer or black skillet, already preheated, popping and snapping grease at you each time a new fish makes contact. It doesn't hurt to add hushpuppies, French fries and coleslaw to round out the perfect meal. Let me get one thing straight though. Southerners love their sweet tea, but we don't want our slaw or our hushpuppies sweet. Just like cornbread, Jiffy Mix will never be found in the pantry because it's like eating cupcakes; especially those in the little muffin shapes. I digress, sorry. You northerners can ruin traditional dishes; I'm just saying.

Okay, the spread is laid out before us, a platter piled with catfish, another with hushpuppies and the third with fries; not the store bought crinkly kind, real potatoes with the skin still attached, and good ole dill pickle and cabbage slaw, perfected with Dukes Mayonnaise. There is only one real mayonnaise, Dukes. Don't be snookered by the others. Real men don't use catsup either by the way; pass the Texas

Pete, please. Bless the food we are about to receive and have at it. Those crunchy catfish tails are a piece of heaven and the piles of skeleton remains on everyone's plate is a sure sign that the fish fry was a success. I just hope there are a few hushpuppies left. Next to cornbread, nothing goes better with a bowl of buttermilk, all crumbled up, with a little salt and pepper, a slice of onion, or better still, fresh spring onions, and just stay the heck out of my way as I've already doody-clared. My parents and grandparents are to blame for me being obsessed with cornbread and buttermilk.

And to just think, a dollar a day to fish all day is responsible for all this. For the low, low, price, I bonded male style with papa. On top of that I parlayed that dollar experience into a day of consuming ice cream, goobers, coke and plenty of other junk I would not have normally gotten at home. I even caught my fair share of fish, drowning a few red wigglers. I witnessed a true master prepare the catch, skinning those cats as sure as a skilled surgeon. Family fellowship, sitting around the table, actually enjoying one another's company, swapping tales, some possibly stretched, but good stories just the same; not something many families experience today. The mere price of a dollar, one hundred cents, I'd say priceless, wouldn't you?

I was in hog heaven, elbow to elbow with the real fishermen. Some things you just never forget. It's important to capture these with pen and paper, on tape or camera. Remember, sometimes the old hard drive crashes and burns and with them it all goes poof. I'm not talking computer. I'm talking the old brain cells. We get old. We forget. Sometimes it's just our age, other times much worse. Happy times deserve to be told. Those kicking and screaming while we tell them will get over it. They just need to learn patience and compassion for their elders.

I did forget one important thing though, an excerpt from My Caregiver Book; papa singing to the fish, those little nonsense songs, all for good fun and always bringing a smile to my face. It goes something like this…

> Have you ever been fishing on a hot summer day
> watching the little bitty fishes
> As they jump and play.
> With your hands in your pockets
> And your pockets in your pants
> Watch the little bitty fishes
> Do the shimmy, shimmy dance.

Tell me you're not smiling after that. Good times deserve sharing good memories. I miss you Papa. Are they biting where you are? Tell Mister Jim Creswell and Ben Buzthart hey for me. I bet all of you are decked out in your Red Camel overalls. I'd give a dollar to see that one more time.

> *'I worry about kids today not having time to build a tree house or ride a bike or go fishing.*
> *I worry that life is getting faster and faster.'*
> — **John Lasseter**

BFFF

In my day, mom and pop joints ruled. I grew up in an era I refer to as BFFF, *Before Fast Food Franchises*. Most places that sold burgers, ice-cream or other specialty food items were owned and operated by the local families. This was before McDonalds, Hardees and Burger King or all the many that would follow that basic format. We were having it our way before they made the promise of fulfillment. We hurried on down when hurry wasn't something we had to do. A whopper was a whopper because those running the joint believed in giving you what you paid for. No one asked you if you wanted fries with that. Fries were a given. You substituted onion rings if that was your preference or got half and half. These were real fries, not the crinkled kind. For burgers, you simply said all the way and they knew what you meant.

In Abbeville, we had Cream Land, the Kum-Back and the Rough House, although the Rough House back in my youth was still a real pool hall so only the adults were allowed to venture inside to purchase the famous hotdogs sold there. Today it is family friendly and not a place you might receive a butt whipping if too much beer consumption riled one of the patrons.

While the Rough House was known for its hotdogs, the Kum-back was famous for its roast pork sandwiches. Owned by Jasper Davis, carhops took your order directly from your vehicle and returned it to an affixed tray mounted in the window on your door. You dined in; your car was your personal dining room.

Cream Land had great shakes and ice-cream but their cheese burgers were heaven. Of the three, only the Rough House still stands today on the Abbeville Court Square in its original location. It is owned and operated by hometown resident, Shelley Reid, our very own renowned actor. We eventually got a chicken place called the Bantam Chef. It had the usual burgers and dogs, but good ole southern fried chicken was its specialty. Later it was sold and transformed into Lee's Fried Chicken.

In ancient times, those days when I grew up, a drive-thru meant you drove up to a window, were greeted by the attendant who took your order and you waited there until your order was completed and handed to you. You were made to feel special. Your business was appreciated. Those taking your order greeted you with a cordial smile and they thanked you after they took your order and again when the food and money transaction had been completed.

While innovation has made these vehicle lines move faster, those dreaded speakers are a pain to communicate with the unknown identity on the other end. Plus, too often I feel I'm having a conversation with one of those adults from a Charlie Brown cartoon. At least that's what the muffled voice sounds like to me. I find myself either asking them what they just said or they ask me to repeat what I just told them. I miss that friendly face to face contact, those servicing you actually being sincere and understanding the value of true customer service.

In our little world, Abbeville didn't have the market cornered when it came to burger joints. When we were lucky enough to travel to Greenwood or Anderson, others awaited our arrival and a chance to serve us our way. Greenwood, just less than twenty minutes away via highway 72 offered up some humdingers. Name your poison. The Ranch and the Dixie were on opposite sides of the roadway from each other, located on Montague Avenue. Both offered curb service, carhops ready to take your order as you sat comfortably in the confines of your vehicle. The Dixie had the best cheese burgers. The Ranch was the better teenager hangout but only if you were from Greenwood. Abbeville and Greenwood teens were like rival gangs. The Shirley brothers owned the turf so enter at your own risk. Instead of fries with your order, you could receive a royal butt whipping. The Dixie was much safer and more family friendly.

Then there was Mister Quick, also located along Montague; flame broiled all beef patty served with ketchup, mustard, pickle and onion on a toasted bun. The main attraction was the manager, Melvin, wearing his oversized black rim glasses and paper Mister Quick hat. He had one of those unique voices that added entertainment value to every visit. Melvin we miss you.

On Saturdays I often took road trips with Granny Winn, Aunt Cornelia and Uncle Jerry to the Emerald City, Greenwood. The routine always included dinner at Mister Quick. We'd visit Roses department store or attend the uptown walk-in movie theater when an Elvis flick was playing there. Granny never missed going to the latest Elvis movie. But be assured, Mister Quick served us our meal on most occasions. One exception, we sometimes really splurged and went to Lee's BBQ on Highway 10, an all you can eat place.

On the south side of Greenwood was the Caravan, another one with curb service. It seemed like most paces had curb service back then. It was perceived a perk, not to have to leave your car and have the food brought to you. We didn't venture to the Caravan much because Granny considered it just a tad too far; far meaning three or four miles further. Greasy food awaited your digestive system there. In my day, greasy was a good thing, expected and the more the better.

Anderson was a little further from Abbeville, maybe 30

or so minutes, via highway 28. There we had Besto. It was basically an ice-cream place that sold burgers and dogs, fries and onion rings. Anderson was the home of Pete' Drive-ins. Pete's were numbered; Pete's 1, 2 and 3 and so forth. There was also one of those little roadside markets close by, one that sold boiled peanuts and fresh produce. These were convenient open market one-stops with dirt and/or sawdust floors before Seven-Eleven burst on the scene. In Abbeville we had the equivalent, the Orange Spot. I loved those places. They carried an assortment of toys and comic books, my meager allowance burning a hole in my pocket as we parked out front.

A visit to the Electric City, Anderson, with granny, my uncle and aunt included a stop by John B Lees, just off the court square on North Main. There we'd peruse the 45 records and cash in on those ninety nine cents purchases per 45. We had a card that was punched each time and we got one free after buying our fifth. No food was served there but just thought I'd mention it. They did have good customer service.

The ultimate burger place had to be the Beacon in Spartanburg. It was a far piece to visit regularly. Placing an order there was very simple. Just tell them you wanted the half and half cheeseburger plate. A black man yelled your order to those preparing it, scaring you half to death, even when you knew what was coming. A half and half was half fries and half onion rings, pounds of them stacked on a plate and somewhere underneath the heaping helping was your cheeseburger. It was a grease-burger in paradise. Add a cup of sweet tea and you were knocking on heaven's door, the angels trumpeting their approval. Afterwards you just wanted to loosen your belt, unfasten your pants and kick off your shoes. Nodding and napping on the drive home would be in your future. I was a kid, a passenger, not the driver. Napping was a given.

When my parents really wanted to kick it up a notch and pull that occasional splurge, we'd load up one or two cars of family and friends and headed to Hartwell, Georgia to Swamp Guinea or over to Lincolnton, Georgia to Soap Creek Lodge and Restaurant. Both were family style restaurants. That meant everyone sat at the same table and they brought food out in abundance. Fried catfish was my favorite fixing at Swamp Guinea. Of course they served chicken, country ham, Brunswick stew and who could forget those frog legs. Georgia must have been the family style state.

Soap Creek had the best shrimp and an assortment of other seafood picks. Cousin Bob and I embarrassed our party during one visit, challenging one another to a boiled shrimp eating contest. We left a couple of twin peaks in our wake, the shucked shrimp peelings piled mountain high on the table. I think the contest was a draw and I'd dare risk estimating just how many dozens of shrimp we put away. I don't think we made a return trip anytime soon; not sure if we were banned by the owners or if no one wanted to take us back. Eventually the Bowie's, relatives of mine, opened up their version, The Fish Hook, an all you eat feast. Family style had arrived in Abbeville.

I was a teenager when Hardees burst onto the scene with their then scrumptious roast beef sandwiches and charcoal broiled burgers. I can still hear that tune playing in my head, 'Hurry on down to Hardees'. There menu included hamburger 15 cents, Cheeseburger 20 cents, Fries 10 cents, Apple Turnovers 15 cents, Milk 12 cents, Coffee 10 cents, Coke, Pepsi, Root Beer and Orange, 15 cents and 10 cents, and Milk Shake (Chocolate-Strawberry-Vanilla) 20 cents.

Hardees had those famous characters in their television

advertising campaigns in the early 1970s, Gilbert Giddyup, and his nemesis, a purple-coated villain named Speedy McGreedy. One of my best friends was named Speedy so he just simply loved this theme. Anderson had the first one and when my pals and I traveled there, it was a must stop; cheap eating. The roast beef on buns came wrapped in colorful tinfoil. We ate our weight in them. The fries were pure gold.

Of course there was Burger King, Home of the Whopper, with that little king as a mascot. McDonald's had its golden arches and this insistence on tracking how many customers had been served. Their theme, you deserve a break today... at McDonalds. These new fancy burger places came with their fair share of gimmicks. McDonalds paraded out the Filet-O-Fish, something beyond the basic burger. Each had their version of giant burgers, beyond mere mouthfuls. In ancient times, the product sold itself and word of mouth and a satisfied tummy did the rest. Besides, pickings were slim so we really had no other places to go to get good take-out food other than the homegrown establishments.

Abbeville held onto tradition for many years, apparently refusing to allow the franchises to infringe on family operated businesses like Burger Town, The One Stop and Rough House. Eventually Hardees splashed onto the scene and is still going strong to this day. That opened the floodgates for the likes of McDonalds, Burger King, KFC/Taco Bell, Pizza Hut and Subway. Still, the hometown mom and pop's managed to hold their own, The Village Grill, Doolittle's, the Dutch Oven, Yoder's, Trainer's, Lynn's, Cold Springs and Cherokee Trail to name a few, have taken their spots as mainstays.

It is tough to beat the mom and pop spots. When traveling that's what we look for, not the franchises. I'm craving something greasy and sloppy right now, one of those hard to get your mouth around burgers, juices flowing freely down my wrist to my elbows while I double clutch it. I wish I had a time machine and could zoom back to those blasts from the past, cut the square, make my rounds to all the favorites. Not to sound corny but I really do miss those good ole days, cruising with friends and just acting goofy and silly. Next trip to Abbeville, I'll just have cut the square before parking in front of the Rough House, last man standing so to speak. Thanks Shelley Reid for keeping old times alive for the rest of us. Save a couple of those famous hotdogs for me.

'Man who invented the hamburger was smart; man who invented the cheeseburger was a genius.'
- **Matthew McConaughey**

Counting Cows
Road Warriors Post Apocalypse

Double lane roads, behemoth automobiles, family packed shoulder to shoulder front seat and back on Sunday afternoons, was life just too perfect back in the day. Remembering back when can certainly curl up the corners of my mouth. A tradition back in my day, Sunday afternoons, after the usual Sunday spread at Granny Bowies and a quick nap by the men folk, Daddy would pile us into his car for that afternoon drive to destinations unknown most of the time.

In the late fifties to mid sixties the luxurious Chevy Impala had been our chariot and the best selling automobile in the United States. Then in 1966 we graduated to the Chevy Caprice, it breaking onto the scene in 65 to replace the Impala at the top of the Chevy food chain. These classic vintage rides would have held their own against today's family vans and SUVs. Make no mistake; we were strutting in high cotton. Calling shotgun when I was usually the only kid on board seldom guaranteed me a window seat. Often I'd settle for climbing over the backseat rest, stretching out in the back window; no seatbelts were required to prevent me from becoming a human projectile. Bouncing from front to back seat, I could even sit in daddy's lap while he drove and help him man the wheel without fear of incarceration by the police.

To escape boredom on long drives we had to become creative. Counting cows served as one venue. Someone picked the right side of the road and the other inherited the left side. The game was simple, count cows in the pastures on your side of the road. If they were a lot of cows, you had to count fast; guessing mostly at how many speckled the horizon. If you passed a cemetery on your side of the road you lost your cow count and had to start over. To this day I don't understand the cemetery-cow correlation, but I didn't come up with the game.

Another deviation from cow counting was car counting. Pick a make and identify and count them as you met them on the highway. Makes and models were easy to identify back then. You could tell a Chevy from a Ford, an Oldsmobile from Pontiac or Buick. Today I can't tell one from the other because everyone makes a knock off of everyone else's. Even a Chevy and Ford don't look like a Chevy or Ford.

The Chevy and Ford usually got first dibs back in my simple world because more of them were on the highways. If you came to a garage on your side of the road, you lost your cars and had to start over. That made much better sense than the cow-cemetery rule. Who ever heard of burying cows in a cemetery? On the old Tarzan movies, elephants had a graveyard but not moo cows.

My grandson did a deviation on this with VW Bugs where you'd call it when you saw a bug and you kept a running tally on how many you identified first. Unlike ours, the rules tended to change every time it is played to sway the count in my grandson's favor. If a VW dealership shows up on your side, say bye to your count. Plus, he could identify every make and model of any vehicle from ten car lengths away. I still don't know how he does it. He can't explain it to me either except he's a car fanatic.

The Pop Eye game left a sore spot I must say. This game could only be played at night. The first person to spot an automobile with a missing head light shouted Pop Eye and was granted an opportunity to punch his opponent in the shoulder. A deviation to this was when riding with female companions where you could opt for a kiss instead of a punch. I liked that version much better. Sore puffy lips beat an aching shoulder every time. It was even more legal than the monkey bars.

Sunday afternoon drives weren't always preoccupied by fun and games. Often it included a drive out to Culbreth's Garage to view wrecked vehicles, those often resulting in a fatality. I still don't understand the fascination and lure to view a crashed up automobile that might have caused someone to die, but it was sure a big deal back then. We might even ride to the scene of the accident if daddy knew the location. Local accidents, especially those that resulted in death, dismemberment, or near death were the talk of the town, so first hand observations made for good conversation I suppose. Sirens and ambulance alarms always perked daddy's interest. I'm certainly glad I didn't inherent that trait.

To continue the morbid trend, our afternoon drives might just include a ride to the local cemeteries; Long Cane or one of the others nearby. The clan would wander through the grave sites identifying and visiting the dearly departed, some new, and others long gone from this world. Swapping old stories and fond memories ensued, followed by tears and nose blowing. This exercise reminds me of another weird attraction; people visiting the funeral home and gazing into the coffin, stating how the person doesn't look like themselves. Of course they don't; they're dead. Dead doesn't look like the living.

My take away from the cemetery visits besides

climbing on the stones and being yelled at was seeing the gigantic yellow grasshoppers that seemed to reside there. These monsters were three or four inches long, red winged and formidable. I called them cemetery grasshoppers because that was the only place I ever saw them. They were huge, winged and hissed when you grabbed them. I was fascinated by these marvelous creations. Maybe they were reincarnated lost souls; those who hissed in real life.

Sometimes we did actually have a predetermined destination like visiting the kin folks, most of them being brothers or sisters of my grandparents. We might end up in Iva, Anderson, Greenwood, Level Land, Due West or Ninety Six, all good ole southern South Carolina small town venues. Running joke when mentioning Due West, an actual college town showcasing Erskine, was due west of what? They even have bumper stickers stating just that.

Speaking of kin folk, going to see Granny Holmes was almost guaranteed at least once a month. Granny Holmes was actually the mama of my Granny Bowie, my mama's mama. She was indeed the stereotype of an old southern woman. She was about five feet tall; extremely bell shaped, and wore her hair in a little bun behind her head. Granny Holmes sported an almost to her ankles dress, accented by an apron that appeared to be tied under her arm pits. She was toothless except for two ragged upper canines off to one side of her mouth.

Like a nomad, she moved about living most of the time with one of her children, never ever working anywhere that I can remember. We'd always take her the Sunday newspaper and she'd read it out loud to us even though it had previously been read. Funny thing, she could read but neither of my grand parents could. In return we were usually served up a meal of hot cornbread and fresh buttermilk or biscuits and gravy, sometimes served with greens or butterbeans; good eating makes me want to slap my mouth. Granny Holmes lived into her 90's.

My particular favorite thing about those traditional Sunday afternoon rides had to be the pit stops at places like Cream Land, The Orange Spot, The Dixie, The Caravan, Mister Quick, Besto, the Come-Back, Bantam Chef or Pete's Drive-In, all contingent on what area of the county or surrounding towns we ended up. I had to make choices. Did I want an ice cream, a root beer float, milk shake or boiled peanuts or maybe a comic book or toy if my parents would cough up the doe? And if I so chose an ice cream, would it be a soft swirl in a cone possibly with a hard layer of chocolate, a cream cycle, a banana pop or my favorite, a push-up. Unlike the cemetery, I had landed in heaven on earth. Being a kid was a wonderful thing just for those special perks.

The afternoon concluded by us returning to granny and papa's house and eating a supper's portion of the Sunday meal. Back then almost all the fixings were left in the original cooking containers and stored back inside the oven. Lids were placed back on top of the assorted pots, tin foil protected everything else. Only the potato salad or left over freshly cut tomatoes and cucumbers were placed inside the refrigerator.

No one ever seemed to worry about food poisoning, salmonella or any of those dreaded inflictions that people worry about today. I don't remember anyone ever becoming sick from eating food left out for half the day and my grand parents' house was not air conditioned. A fan in the kitchen widow blowing outwards sucked in the outside air through other open windows supplying the ventilation for the entire four room mill house.

Now at the ripe old age of sixty one, I've lost touch with those traditional Sunday afternoons. After early church and a sit down bought breakfast on the way home, my Sundays are typically spent dozing and watching sports on television in couch potato mode while my wife reads her book. Occasionally we'll go out, mostly to shop or I might play a round of golf. We never just hop in the car and ride to destination unknown, exploring roads we've never traveled or sites we've never seen. Just maybe we should.

Living in a tourist town, Myrtle Beach, automobile accidents occur hourly so we'd never keep up with viewing the wrecked cars. Besides, with so many garages, we'd never know where to go to view the carnage. As for cemeteries, that one never caught on with me any way and today's cemeteries are just flat acreage with no tomb stones. Grave markers are affixed flush to the ground. They don't hold the same charisma, and I bet they don't have those gigantic grasshoppers. Quick stops are on every corner now and don't hold that same appeal as visiting the Orange Spot open market or the old timey ice cream shop with the outside walk up window. Our ice cream comes from the grocery store and never in a cone.

I didn't realize how badly I missed those days until writing this. When one gets old one tends to look back on stuff one took for granted. Simple was better. No hustle, no bustle, care free and loving it, too bad I don't have that time machine. To my deceased mama and daddy, granny and papa, and great grand and all those kin folks alive and kicking or not, I wish you were here and we were there. Back then was a good then. No stress, no fuss, just breath in the world and go with the flow. Those who never experienced those times have only us to bring them back to life. Sadly the generation of today couldn't care less. A second without a smart phone affixed to their hands is unthinkable.

    We talked. We didn't text. And you better think twice before you bring gadgets and distractions to the dinner table or church. I'll take counting cows over counting on a text any day. We were sociable, not living and breathing for the social media. Catching grasshoppers was fun. An afternoon drive to nowhere in particular was priceless.

'A good traveler is one who does not know where he is going to, and a perfect traveler does not know where he came from.'
- Lin Yutang

Fall is for Fairs

Fall always ushered in the return of the county fair, guaranteeing the arrival of the traveling variety show coming to a town near you. You must remember, back in the late fifties and early sixties predated the likes of Disney World. While Disney Land did exist in California, that offered very little in the way of entertainment for most kids living on the opposite coast in South Carolina. Unlike most children my age, I actually visited Mickey World when my folks did a cross country trip to the west coast. I celebrated my sixth birthday in California, but that soon became a distance memory in a young boy's mind. We have short retention abilities.

Disneyworld in Orlando opened October of 1971 and my parents and I were there along with an assortment of uncles, aunts, grandparents, cousins and my then wife to be, arriving in a caravan of three vehicles. Just say it's a small world after all and that tune will forever haunt your waking thoughts. Unfortunately, it being located nine hours driving distance from little old Abbeville didn't offer many frequent opportunities to visit the magic kingdom.

Before Disney World, theme parks crashed onto the scene offering some relief. Six Flags over Georgia made its 230 acre debut in Cobb County of Atlanta in 1967. Less than a three hour drive, this still didn't offer an annual trek. Forced family fun to Atlanta once every half dozen years or so was plenty for most parents. Still, the reward was worth the wait. I'd take them where I could get them.

South Carolina finally made its mark in the theme park arena in 1973 offering up a much smaller 122 acre version of its rival, Six Flags. Just over two hours away you would think going to Carowinds would be a yearly rite of passage, but parents are not quite so taken in by these money sucking venues. Remember, kids who don't fork over a dime for vacations. Parents have that *been there, done it* attitude. Kids don't tire of a good thing. Pouting and whining can only get you so far. You can't over use it.

So that leaves us with the ever reliable county fair and if we're so fortunate we might even venture into the bordering counties, Anderson and Greenwood for their versions of the county fair. On a grander scale, there was always The Upstate Fair in Greenville and The State Fair in Columbia, but slim chance we'd ever see either of those. I think only once did I ever attend the Upstate Fair and I did that as an adult, hindsight realizing like my parents before me that maybe fairs were just money magnets; this time luring it from my pockets. I liked it much better when I didn't have to pay for it. Holes don't burn in adult pockets.

Nothing packed more punch though than the Abbeville County Fair, not in the eyes of an impressionable little tike like my self. It was bigger than life with spills and thrills a plenty. Often we'd receive complimentary tickets at school and with those in our hands, our parents had a moral obligation to hold up their end of the bargain and take us. For the sake of argument and to just randomly pick a year at the fair, I'll choose 1960; me a mere seven year old, naïve with wonder lust eyes for the big lights and musical atmosphere. Life was a circus; or in my case a fair.

One of my first memories of the fair had to be that of Willy Wire Hand. Typical county fairs have tents or buildings set up for local venues to strut their stuff and wares. The Little River Electric Co-op, the local power company, used a life sized metallic robotic figure as their spokes person. Picture the Wizard of Oz's tin man wearing a lineman crew yellow helmet, wiry arms with huge work gloves and a bottom half that resembled the plug in on an electrical cord, and there you have Willy Wire Hand. His eye's lit up and jaw clicked and moved as he greeted people approaching the display.

Willy would carry on a conversation with the passersby, giving youngsters like me the impression that this mechanical marvel might actually be alive. Truth be known, someone concealed behind a curtain with a view of the audience instigated the interaction and conversation, another Oz like coincidence. That hidden person operated the mechanics and spoke into a microphone attached to an equally concealed speaker. Pre-terminator and Star Wars, Willy was ahead of his time. Sadly, Willy disappeared from the format within only a couple of years. I'm not sure why.

My next favorite thing at the fair had to be Saboo, the wild jungle boy captured in Africa or some far away place. Wearing something similar to Tarzan's loin cloth and sporting long wild frazzled and tangled black hair hanging down over his eyes, Saboo roamed aimlessly in his confinement, a fenced in area with a sawdust floor located inside a tent. He chanted and lurched at the onlookers with this wild eyed and drooling snarl. He scared the *you know what out* of me, but at the same time I was mesmerized by his antics. I'm still not quite sure why he didn't leap over the four foot high fence. Even I could have pulled off that feat.

The introduction of a live chicken to Saboo's confined space highlighted the performance. He captured and then fondled his new feathered friend for awhile as the crowd remained transfixed on the wild boy and his attraction to his new pet. Without warning, the seemingly docile lad clenched the unsuspecting fowl in his canines and promptly bit off its head. A gory mess ensued as the wild boy dismembered the bloodied mess that had once resembled a chicken before our very eyes; his version of finger licking good I suppose.

The crowd went wild as feathers flew; no pun intended. He held and plucked at the remains of the chicken, feathers and blood glued to his mouth and face as he sat in a corner and eyed his audience; how else, but wildly. Sadly, as had Willy Wire Hand before him, Saboo had a short stint as a fair attraction. I suppose there's just so much raw chicken one can devour. I figured he just became too tamed while in captivity. God forbid if we would have had PETA back then.

Another of my favorite expos to visit had to be the livestock building where all the blue ribbon winners were housed. An assortment of awarding winning cows, bulls, hogs, pigs, sheep, goats and every imaginable feathered fowl were assembled in pens for the gawkers. Farmers demonstrated the art of cow milking, sheep shearing and pig calling. Cute little pink piglets would compete in races too with everyone cheering for their chosen favorites. I suppose that's where they got the chickens for Saboo; from the loser's pen. I'm sure glad he didn't have a fondness for beef.

Then there's the midway; games and rides for one and all. I targeted the fun houses and haunted houses first. This one particular haunted house, a ride through one, had to be the best ever because some unknown and unseen entity would jump onboard your car from behind. It would then proceed in touching your head and shoulders with hairy hands before it would just as suddenly disappear. The next year my cousin and I took sharpened pencils with us and intended on stabbing the perpetrator. Luckily for it and us, no one boarded our car.

Rides, oh yes, there were plenty of other rides to challenge our bravery; the ferris wheel, the scrambler, the wild mouse, the toboggan, the octopus, the Himalaya express, the swings, the merry-go-round, the round-up, tilt and whirl, roller coaster and the zipper. I never understood why there were age and height restrictions for the bullet and bumper cars and not for some of the others. My goal, to ride them when I could and I did, over and over and over.

The midway had their assortment of games to challenge our skills and deplete our meager allowances. Large stuffed animals and other enticing prizes lured us to the challenge. After all, what could be so difficult in tossing a few rings and bean bags, throwing darts and baseballs or shooting hoops? Once the last ring had been tossed, the final baseball had been thrown, the third basketball had skirted off the rim; we stood there bewildered and empty handed; no stuffed animals or other valuable prizes in our possession. Resourceful kids will not leave empty handed.

I turned my attention to the midway game I always dominated; the pick up ducks with a prize always guaranteed. No, I never won a giant stuffed teddy bear or any other fluffy animals, but I did walk away with such items as Chinese handcuffs, frog clickers, police whistles, decoder rings and magical kaleidoscopes. among other assorted tokens for my time and effort. Prizes are prizes and I won them fair and square. I'm a skilled duck picker upper. I was *Duck Dynasty* before it quacked onto the scene.

Then there were those side shows; the ones displaying freaks and oddities like the bearded lady, the alligator boy, lobster man, the giant, the fat lady, the tiny people, the thin man and so forth. I'm still not sure why Saboo didn't share the tent with these folks. Maybe it was his bad table manners. Seven years old would not get me inside these venues unless accompanied by an adult. Even an adult in tow couldn't get me inside the girlie shows. I didn't like girls back then anyway, so it wasn't a big deal. Why would I want to pay to see girls when I could see them everyday for free? Some people thought otherwise because men sure lined up to go inside.

Did I mention the food at the fair? Carnival cuisine is the best; cotton candy, snow cones, roasted and boiled peanuts, French fries and funnel cakes, all for that perfect belly ache. Our fingers would be sticky and our lips would be stained multiple colors. We wore these colors and substances with pride. Wash our hands; certainly not as long as we had our tee-shirts and pants legs. And the good thing about a fair, it would return again next year, the same time at the designated fairgrounds. I would be willing, raring and able and one year closer to riding that confounded bullet. Be assured, I would not loose my uncanny duck selecting ability; the gift of duck calling.

> **Life** *is like a carnival.*
> *The cotton candy is all of the sweet things in your life.*
> *The carnies are the unwanted junk.*
> *The rides represent all of the diversity and choices.*
> *And then there is the dunk tank a place where you can get all of your angry out just like your friends when you vent to them.*

Talking out the Fire

Either you believe or you don't. I for one believe. History tells us that certain people throughout time have allegedly possessed remarkable healing powers by either touching the inflicted or speaking to them to cure what ails them. I'm not talking evil witches who toss out curses or backyard doctors bleeding you dry with leeches. These are honest to goodness decent folks that have a God given gift for talking out the fire of a burn, making warts disappear or even ridding kids of their itching and tormenting poison oak or persistent poison ivy.

In Abbeville, up the hill about a mile and at the end of Hunter Street from my house, we had Cousin Jenny Martin. No, she didn't hang out a shingle advertising her services. People with the gift rarely do or even brag or boast they have this unique power. Back in the day it was even unheard of for special people like Cousin Jenny to even accept money for using their God given powers. If truth be known, she would be the first to give credit where credit was due. Word of mouth, tales of her ability and testimonials from those cured were better than a televised infomercial back then. Mama and Granny Bowie fully believed in Cousin Jenny's abilities and they easily convinced me after my very first visit.

Cousin Jenny, a short little modest country woman living a meager life style, would never stand out in a crowd or would she ever want to but, when you met her, you instantly sensed she was special and simply a wonderful loving person. In my earliest recollection of her at probably around five or six years old I never feared her or her abilities. I knew that neither Mama nor Granny would ever take me to a person or place where I would be harmed and scared out of my wits. I trusted them and I trusted her even before I understood the meaning of trust.

The majority of my visits to Cousin Jenny were prompted by me being highly allergic to poison oak and poison ivy, and having been inflicted with the itching, oozing curse from some excursion in the wilds. Back then, Calamine Lotion only came in this pinkish version and by the time mama or I applied it to all the patches of rashes I looked like a Comanche warrior ready to do battle with an unsuspecting wagon train. They should have sold this in a more concentrated variety, and then I could have been dipped in a tub the same way they do dogs and cats for fleas and ticks. Fortunately, it did temporarily relieve the tormenting itching and prevented me from scratching myself bloody. Now they have a clear version and they've modernized the brand name.

Doctors say that the rash doesn't really spread but instead it's just a delayed reaction due to contact with the plant. I'm not so sure I buy into this. I know the more I scratched the more it spread and it could spread with a vengeance. These same professionals say it's not contagious, but my friends often avoided me like the plague. With all the welts and Calamine Lotion I resembled a pinkish refugee from a Leper Colony.

As a kid, I learned quickly to be able to spot the wicked weed, recognizing the leaf shape and its most prone places to grow. What was the old saying? "Leaves of three, beware of me." Each of the leaves of my attacker has three smaller leaflets. The middle leaflet has this longer stalk than the other two sides, and if you've been stricken by it, you quickly learn how to spot it. Even so, you could count on me getting nailed by it several times during the summer. I think I just had to be in the general proximity of the plant and it transmitted its evilness to me either airborne or via mind control.

If mama deemed dousing me in Calamine Lotion ineffective, and it seemed the more I scratched the more it spread, then a Cousin Jenny visit would be on slate. Later I caught on to this and requested a visit at the first signs of a rash. I figured, why paint me up when we could cut to the chase and have her work her magic. I often rode my bike to her house unsupervised by an adult. I knew a good thing when I saw it.

When adults did accompany me, the typical visit went something like this. There'd be a brief mention of why we were there, and then it would transform into a basic social call. The adults would catch up with family matters and social events, who's who and what's what in Abbeville. Usually Cousin Jenny would place a hand on me very discreetly, not necessarily even touching the rash, and she wouldn't quote any biblical term or spell breaking incarnation. After anticipating something a little more spectacular, it turned out being very uneventful from a theatrical perspective. Oddly enough the rash would cease to itch and within the next day or two, the rash would miraculously go away. To this day I still don't understand what exactly she did or how her power worked. It doesn't really matter I suppose; it worked, enough said.

Cousin Jenny could also talk the fire out of a burn. I

read somewhere that the ability to do this goes back some thousand years or so and the fire talker usually chants bible verses while touching, rubbing or blowing on the burnt areas. I never witnessed this one, but my daddy burned his hands badly once and paid her a visit. He swore by her just like the rest of us. He didn't say what she actually did but the healing process began immediately after his visit.

My cousin and next door neighbor, Billy, afflicted often with warts, visited her to rid his hands of those ugly knots. I accused him of playing with frogs but we know that warts don't really come from frogs, or do they? It didn't really matter because she managed to make them vanish. Before then I seem to remember Billy doing something with a potato and burying it in the ground. That sounded too much like witchcraft to me.

Rumor has it that these gifted folks can pass their powers on to someone else, but if they do they might forfeit their own ability to do it. I've heard this was limited to non-kin and the opposite sex. I guess I should have asked her to teach me, since she really wasn't a cousin and I was definitely the opposite sex. I wonder if a person can treat themselves. Maybe I would have had immunity to poison oak and ivy by possessing the power. I suppose there's too much water under the bridge for me to ponder what if.

Luckily as an adult I don't seem to be affected as often by the wicked little weed. Maybe I just don't play those childhood games among the woodland where it lurks. And thanks go out to John Franz who invented Roundup in 1970. It works wonders in eradicating the invader. Too bad it hadn't been invented fifty years ago. It would have worked much better than discoloring me with Calamine

Lotion. Then again, we did have Cousin Jenny Martin, didn't we? Bless our hearts.

'Since ancient times, certain people have practiced healing simply by using touch and speech.
The tradition came to the New World through both indigenous people and European colonists.
It still exists today, carried on by healers who talk the pain out of burns, stop bleeding, cure thrush or remove warts without using medicine.
Nearly all healers say God is the source of their power, which is why they don't accept payment or advertise.
People learn about them by word of mouth.

Speaking in Tongues

Ruby Holmes Bowie, my mama's mama, my grandmother, was a perfect candidate for sainthood, but then again I'm partial I suppose. Ten years younger than Papa, who was born in 1900, she had that old as dirt thing going too, living to the ripe old age of ninety four. She wasn't perfect by a long shot but she had this connection, sort of a direct line to the heavens. Often I wondered if she had one of those concealed red phones at her finger tips like the Presidents have, enabling her to dial up the Lord direct, no call waiting of course.

Granny had not been blessed with the best of health but she persevered under the worst of conditions. A large hole in the shin of her left leg, more like a trough dug out with a large spoon, always fascinated me as a child. Best I can remember this had resulted from a diseased bone when she was young. That leg was stiff and would not bend so that posed challenges for her in tight spots, especially getting in and out of a vehicle and driving her 1969 Chevy Impala. She didn't learn to drive until she was around sixty years of age. She claimed she had attempted to get a driver's license at an earlier age, but papa made her too nervous when she was behind the wheel. Finally she completely gave up after a minor fender bender.

Of Pentecostal Holiness faith, Granny didn't believe in wearing pants, make-up or cutting her hair. She wore her dresses at near knee length and her hair tightly in a bun. I can remember spending the night with them as a kid. She would look like one of those witches from a bedtime story when she took her hair down and combed it before bedtime. It would be frizzy and shoulder length and very un-granny like. She actually never cut her hair for the first time until she reached near ninety years old and mama convinced her it would be easier to take care of. She looked quite pretty without that bun. Her face was smooth as silk, free of any wrinkles. She professed using her Oil of Olay and used it religiously; no pun intended. Somebody once told her it was oil of old lady; whatever works.

Granny tried to keep a tight rein on mama, her only child, but Mary Elizabeth Bowie Winn didn't fall off a turnip truck and was astute at playing the game too. While she didn't think they were intentional or even fabricated, Granny would have these convenient nervous spells, causing breathing problems. They would all but make her bedridden. We thought some of them were her attempt to disrupt mama and daddy's lives, especially when she knew they were going off on vacation. Sometimes it worked, most often it didn't. Mama could quickly baby and nurse her back to normal by just being there, and then she would get the heck out of Dodge.

Granny couldn't read but that didn't mean she didn't keep her bible near by. As modern technology evolved she soon learned the way of the tape player and had the entire Bible on cassette tapes. She could play the scriptures at her leisure, even if she was incapable of selecting the verses. This often resulted in her replaying already played verses. It didn't really matter to her; the good book was the good book and listening to the gospel no matter how many times was the righteous thing to do.

She loved those Sunday morning gospel singing shows before going to church and swore by Pat Robertson and the 700 Club when he and it emerged on the scene. Nothing beat that old time religion. She even followed Jimmy Swaggart until his big sinful debacle. Old Jim Baker had his hard times too, but Granny, solid as rock, kept the faith and prayed for them all. Sinners deserved forgiveness.

I remember as a wee tike, gospel singers traveled from one venue to the next. Mama and daddy would take the family to the Greenville Memorial Auditorium to listen to the likes of the Blackwood Brothers, Kinsgsmen Quartet, J. D. Sumner and the Stamps Quartet and the Oak Ridge Quartet. Often some of these same gospel groups would visit the local churches. I recall that several of the Pentecostal Holiness Church's big draws were the Singing McCloud Family and the Happy Goodman Family, old time gospel crooners belting out the tunes. Granny would be in hog heaven, taping her foot, clapping his hands and paying witness to her faith.

Most folks don't realize the impact the Pentecostal Holiness Church had on the sanctified movement. Some people instead think the holiness church dealt in snake handling and frenzied whooping and hollering. The last part was probably right, but I never witnessed anything reptilian in our church. One thing for sure, you could most certainly count on the church service to be filled with twanging guitars, possibly a tambourine and country-fied piano with the congregation belting out The Wings of a Snow White Dove or How Sweet the Sound from the hymn book. Cousin Pete Bowie would be leading the congregation in the hymns.

Pentecostal preachers knew how to cut to the chase. Their sermons struck directly to the point and did typically include shouting, an element of frenzied excitement and a lot of amen's. Let's set the record straight right now. These were preachers, not pastors or reverends or priest or clergymen. Preacher Reese held my fondest memories as a child. He and the church went hand in hand in my boyish eyes. I guess you always remember your first preacher.

Let me lay the groundwork for how I remember the typical Abbeville Pentecostal Holiness Sunday church service. Of course there would be plenty of rocking the church singing and the eventual passing of the plate, tithe and offerings. Cousin Pete Bowie, larger than life, led the choir, peppered with more Bowie's and an assortment of other kin folk. Papa and Granny anchored the second pew, center stage and let no man or woman even attempt to occupy that spot, ever; it was their assumed assigned seating. Uncle Neuffer and Aunt Sally Lou Bowie anchored the opposite end of that very same pew. Two brothers had married two sisters and that made for a lot of double first cousins. They often book ended Aunt Nellie Compton, another sister.

I believe the Pentecostal Holiness church must have invented the art of fire and brimstone style preaching. Most preachers were very passionate and vocal in their delivery. They became more revved up the longer the sermon ran. Like a baseball game, forget watching the clock, it would be over when it was over and more times than not, it would go extra innings. That led to a lot of squirming on my part. I dreaded the part when Preacher Reese called on the youths of the church to come to the Alter for sanctification. I wasn't sure what that meant but I didn't particularly like the sound of it.

The youth were expected to open up their hearts and receive the Holy Ghost. I associated the Holy Ghost as being an entity of the Holiness church. It made perfectly good sense to me, but what did I really know back then? Preacher Reese upped his game, began shouting louder, prompting many of my peers to be swept away with the spirit. This in turn impacted many of the adults of the congregation, launching them towards the pulpit. Granny would be one of the first. Being only seated two pews back had its perks. This next part is what really freaked me out.

The adults hunkered down in the faces of the youngsters

gathered at the Alter, placing their hands on their heads and encouraging them to feel it, allow the spirit to cleanse their souls and wash away their sins. I drew Granny in the lottery and she now laid her hand on me and began gibbering in a language I had never heard or could understand. The Holy Ghost held her firm in its grasp and she now attempted to channel that energy into little old me. The process known as talking in tongues was up close and personnel and scaring the crap out of me.

Like someone possessed, Granny directed her barrage of odd sounding syllables and sentences at me. Rather than be pulled into this web that furiously tugged at my soul, I instead held fast and fought it. I was a hard head that way; I still am. The more I resisted, the more Granny's vocabulary seemed to expand, the louder she shouted and her eyes rolled back in their sockets. I was a boat rocker and a non-conformer. This was just way too weird to me. I'm still like that to this very day. I just didn't feel it and faking it didn't seem the right thing to do. That probably explains one of the reasons I sort of have a church-phobia.

There's nothing wrong with talking in tongues and feeling the Holy Ghost. Granny being touched and practicing it is proof to me that it was real and worked for those who believed. I believe in God and the church but for what ever reason I just couldn't wrap my brain around that phenomenon. I no longer attend a Pentecostal Church as we've opted for Methodist. Believe me, there is no comparison.

Granny talking in tongues there might just be a show stopper in the Methodist arena, but it would be worth the price of admission to watch the congregation's reaction. They'd probably be peeping under the pews in search of snakes. I can't say I could blame them if seeing this for the very first time. Either way it wouldn't deter Granny. When the Holy Ghost knocked on the door, you let it in; except if you were me, then you'd fight to maintain control. Sorry, I was naïve back then.

Keep them straight up there, Granny and I'm sure you are. Down here, I love you and miss you, but back then you did literally put the fear of God in me, even if I refused to let the Holy Ghost enter my little world. One shuns what one doesn't understand.

New Testament Acts 2:1-4:

*"When the day of Pentecost came,
they were all together in one place.
Suddenly a sound like the blowing of a violent
wind came from heaven and filled the whole house where
they were sitting.
They saw what seemed to be tongues of fire that separated
and came to rest on each of them.
All of them were filled with the Holy Spirit and began to
speak in other tongues as the Spirit enabled them."*

The Backyard Grocery

Innovation, not a word I was familiar with back in the days before time. We, speaking of the kids of my world, were quite innovative when it came to foraging. Survival of the fittest had nothing to do with it, and we weren't exactly starving. Foraging in my world before there were convenience stores and fast food joints on every corner meant just what the words say, the backyard grocery; we could find all sorts of goodies in nature's backyard. Sure, we had store bought food and could raid the frig or pantry, but what's the fun in that. The Lord had provided man the means to live off the land. We weren't exactly men but we would have made excellent pioneers.

There was just something special about a bunch of us hunting, picking and gathering edibles; something that today's kids can't do with a couch strapped to their butts and a video game controller, cell phone or Ipad glued to their hands. It took effort and teamwork and actual exertion, sometimes even sweat to shop in nature's backyard grocery store. To us it was fun and time well spent, but then again, we loved the outdoors. We would never be happy cooped up inside when daylight was still burning. Summers were the best, no school and dawn to dusk to do anything that pleased us. Often we played outside well beyond dark thirty and enjoyed every minute, barefooted and shirtless all summer long. Well, the girls weren't shirtless, too bad now looking back.

Our food sources were seasonally controlled. Luckily for us, most were in abundant supply during the spring and summer, with a few exceptions. Two of our favorites to gather were plums and blackberries. Both grew wild.

You just had to know where to look for them. Now I'm not talking about those huge red or purple store bought plums. I'm talking the real deal, nickel to quarter sized red delicious delights. One of our honey holes for gathering plums was at the top of the hill, above Hunter Street in L.A. (Lower Abbeville), the mill side of town. Sometimes multiple visits were required because they weren't ripe yet. We were undaunted by the extra ventures to the outer reaches of the neighborhood. It equated to fun for us, exploring and horsing around.

We could strip those plum bushes clean when the red ripe fruit was in abundance, eating most as we picked them. No, washing them was not a concern. Pick and pop them in your mouth. We didn't think anything about it. One flaw in our system was eating them when they were still just a tad too green. Consumption of green ones usually resulted from a dare. Green ones were bitter-sour. The dare came with a price; potential belly aches or as we called it back then, a bad case of the squirts. These complications usually just lasted for a day. What did we care, the plums were free and we were willing and able.

Seeking out blackberries required about the same strategy. One difference, the blackberry bushes were equipped with prickly thorns. We called these locations briar patches for good reason. It was not uncommon to be scratched and bleeding from our arms and legs. We were kids. We were always cut or bruised, or had skinned knees or elbows, a way of life. Our wounds would scab over and heal soon enough. We'd wear our battle scars proudly.

The real danger in picking blackberries didn't come from pain inflicted by those nasty briars, but instead from a critter no one could even describe. The dreaded chiggers lurked there, using the berries to bait us close enough so they could attack. No, you never saw them or felt them bite, but the aftermath was always evident. I can hear my mama saying, 'You're eat up with chiggers.' Now chigger bites can be most anywhere but their prime target seemed to be our privates. We'd look like we had been attacked by a vicious swarm of mosquitoes. We'd claw our itches until they bled. Home remedy applied by our parents was finger nail polish over each of the little festered bites. Glad most were concealed by our shorts, but still, nail polish isn't exactly meant to grace tender areas. The idea, so said mama, was that the chigger is alive and burrows and continues to spread and the nail polish kills them by suffocating them. Today, doctors say that chiggers, a kind or mite, inject proteins from their spit into our skin when they suck our blood. The bite causes itching, redness and sometimes blisters, because we're allergic to their spit. Who am I supposed to believe now?

Nectar from the gods, honeysuckle vines were in abundant supply. The sweet scent of blooming honeysuckle is a fragrance that is common in the southern spring. I'm sure you *green horns* have no idea how to enjoy honeysuckle. It's really quite simple and requires very little skill. Think sort of like a bee, except we don't have the ability to flitter and fly from flower to flower and suck in the juice at the bottom of the cone shaped bloom. Not to fret, it can be done never the less. Merely pluck the entire honeysuckle blossom, bite the funnel end and suck on it like a straw. Repeat these steps as many times as you wish and enjoy the sweetness. Again, we never were concerned with germs or any other contamination. Life was simple and quite enjoyable. None of us ever died from what we ate. A kid today would be caught dead doing what we did.

In most backyards other plentiful seasonal bounty

awaited our greedy little hands. Apple and pear trees were prime targets. There was nothing more fun than to climb an apple tree and shake the limbs, raining on those below in a meteor shower. It was better to give than receive, a shaker not a mover or dodger. Fig bushes were out there too but figs are an acquired taste. One particular hazard in gathering apples, pears and figs was winged things with stingers. Yellow jackets and wasp frequently feed on the fruit. Unlike chiggers, these puppies delivered a punch. Finger nail polish wasn't going to help you here.

Cleanliness wasn't a concern. A mere wipe on our cutoffs, if we so chose to take the time, was all that was needed before taking that very first bite. Too much of a good thing could equate to belly aches or those dreaded squirts though. Pepto-Bismol had not burst on the scene yet. We simply suffered through the ordeal and went back for more, never actually learning the value of the lesson. The squirts built character and prevented sneezing, coughing and the hiccups.

Cooler weather brought on the nut crops; no not us. Pecans were our favorite both from at edible stand point and for gamesmanship. Repeat after me, *P-Can*, not *Pa-con*. While impossible to shake an old pecan tree, some were accessible by climbing. Same technique, shake what you could to pellet those below in the hail storm. Better still, toss projectiles into the air and through the branches to dislodge the clusters. This added a tad more danger to the game, not only having to dodge falling nuts, but also the broom handles or bats or whatever else was being tossed wildly skyward. What goes up must come down unless it becomes lodged in the tree; and then targeting it became the new challenge. Everything we did we seemed able to make a game of it. Imaginations were a terrible thing to waste.

Walnuts upped the ante. Larger than golf balls, you really didn't want to take a shot from one of them. A world of hurt would be the result. Tactics were a little different. Strategy, throw the projectile and then run as quickly as you could from underneath the tree's canopy. Surprisingly no one ever became impaled or seriously injured from these antics. I don't recall any concussions. Once the walnuts were grounded and gathered, then came the next challenge; cracking the black steel-like, tough husks to get to the hardened shell inside. A hammer or a good sized rock was the tool of trade for cracking the nut so to speak. Rocks did come with consequences though; poor judgment leading to mashed fingers and a tearful ending. More times than not we would give up after wearing ourselves out for too little gain.

With winter, foraging became slim. While winters could be cold in our neck of the woods, snow didn't fall every year. When it did, it would usually be melted by the next day if not the same day. Once in a blue moon we would have a good'un as papa would often say, five or six inches to maybe nine or ten. If any significant amount of snow blanketed the yard one thought came to mind beside snow ball fights and building a snowman; we're making snow ice cream. Now if you have never tasted good old fashion snow ice cream then you don't know what you've been missing.

The recipe for our brand of ice cream was simple. Locate a collection place like the top of table, an automobile, a roof top, somewhere isolated and free from people or animal contamination. Avoid any yellow stained white stuff and refrain from collecting it from the ground. Place the snow in a large bowl. Add vanilla extract and sugar, a tad of milk and you had it, perfect snow ice cream. Today there are all sorts of taboos about eating it. Sometimes you just have to throw caution to the wind and live on the wild side. That's what we did but we were fearless.

For us, all was free and fun. Today nothing is free and fun, and it has been all but forgotten. We ate all this stuff with reckless abandon, never concerned with cleanliness or becoming lard asses. We burned off our calories doing stuff outside, not sitting in front of the television, computer, video games or thriving on the personal media devices as is the curse today. Heck we had only three television channels and a land line for our phones. It was boring to be inside.

The great outdoors was a playground and supermarket; combing the two was a given and rite of passage. Sadly, today it is difficult to locate wild plums or blackberries. Pecans can be had but rarely do you ever see anyone gathering walnuts. Grocery stores and super box stores have made it too easy. Kids and adults alike would cringe with the mere mention of sucking on a honeysuckle blossom. That's okay. I have my fond memories and no one can ever take that away from me. Like all dinosaurs, the backyard grocery has become fossilized. This ole dog will never bury it for good. And please don't get me started on hand sanitizers. Five seconds was a good rule.

'The landscape belongs to the person who looks at it.'
- Ralph Waldo Emerson

Walk-Ins and Drive-Ins

First one must admit that one has a problem, right? Okay then, I will raise my hand, state my full name and own up to my addiction. I, Thomas (Tommy) Allen Winn am a movie-holic, always have been. I know I should take full responsibility for my actions, but I will again throw my parents under the bus. Lay the blame where it belongs. Heck, while I'm at it, I may as well back the bus over Granny Winn too. She is not without fault. Okay, you got me; I'm not a product of bad parenting or terrible grand parenting, but still, I do believe at an early age, they influenced that path I ventured down. They led me to my obsession with full length features.

In the fifties and early sixties, family night often meant a Saturday trip to the drive-in movie. Yes, we actually had bonding moments with our parents; where they went, so we went. Clarification, yes we did drive to the movie and once there, we actually drove into the outdoor cinema in our automobile. Comfort was based on the condition and size of your vehicle. Yes, in this case, size did matter. There were no vehicle restrictions, except if you were in a van, you had to park on the back row. Most teenagers in a van were going to park back there anyway, if you catch my drift. Drive-ins were the perfect make-out places back in the day.

As we pulled up to the collection booth, the huge marquee outside spelled it out in large letters, the feature being presented. If we were lucky and often we were, the one price would include a double feature, mostly in the winter months when darkness fell earlier. Family friendly choices were a must, and back in my early days of addictive behavior, most drive-ins featured flicks for the entire family. Disney was rolling out good wholesome family fun. The studios actually focused mostly on G rated movies. To set the record straight, the rating system had not been envisioned yet. Risqué movies could be found. Simple rule though, you saw what your parents allowed you to see, unless you were sneaky; guilty as charged. This is a confession, right?

Timing was everything, daddy preferring to arrive just before dusk, and in plenty of time before the movie started. There's nothing more aggravating than those late arrivals, headlights glaring and shinning on the gigantic two story sized screen, or blinding you as they searched for a parking spot. Yes, parking spots were a critical part of the process, just like selecting your seat in a walk-in theater. Daddy liked parking in the middle row, the one adjacent to the concession building and restrooms. Every other parking spot had a post mounted in the ground, speakers hanging from the left and right. Depending on how you parked, the speaker was hung on either the driver's side or passenger side window.

Daddy, as did most men, selected the driver's side, a man thing even back in the day. It's in the male's genetic makeup to have complete control over the volume knob, closest thing to a remote control we had back then. Weather played a large part in the decision to go or not. You certainly didn't want to have to run your windshield wipers or heaters during the feature. If you were dating it didn't matter. Those vans parked in the back eventually used their defroster to un-fog the windows, even in the best of weather conditions.

We were in, parked and now waiting on it to get dark enough to start the movie. There are priorities and protocol. A trip to the concession building must be organized. Drinks and popcorn were a must. Candy bars were creature comfort food, typically on the menu. Most drive-ins had playgrounds for the kids; an assortment of amusements, slide, swings, teeter-totters, etc. Playgrounds were located underneath the elevated big screen. I assumed there had been strategically placed, putting the kids as far away from those hoping to enjoy the movies and placing us up front so our parents could keep us in their sight.

While Abbeville did have a drive-in back in the early days, near Sharon School, West Highway 72, I don't really recall any trips there, too young or maybe it was already defunct when I came of age. Most of my memories were of the Highway 25 Drive-in over in Greenwood, now long gone and presently occupied by the K-mart and surrounding stores at the intersection of highways 25 and 72. I was devastated when they did away with the drive-in. It was just un-American.

There was another drive-in also on highway 25, the opposite side of Greenwood, The Auto Drive-in but we didn't go there as much. Ironically it still stands to this very day and in recent years reopened. I have different fond memories of it as a driving teenager and young adult. It has more to do with making out and getting lucky, not so much for movie viewing. I fogged up my fair share of windows there. I think my parents preferred Highway 25, not only for the movies and closer location from Abbeville, but because they always had bingo night when they had double features, the caller announcing the card spaces during intermission time.

While I saw tons of movies at the Highway 25, the titles I recall more were when I visited as a budding young adult, ones I would never have been able to attend with my parents. George Romero's original *Night of the Living Dead* scared the 'you know what' out of me. The feature was in black and white, but gory just the same. I remember seeing the campy and almost x-rated film, *Myra Breckenridge*, with Rachel Welsh, Mae West and Rex Reid. Then there was *The Graduate*; "Are you trying to seduce me, Mrs. Robinson?" I'm sure as I kid I saw every Disney movie ever made, as well as Elvis. We'll get to The King shortly.

There were four drive-ins in Anderson, The Fox, Highway 29, Skyway and Viking but these were a little further drive than Greenwood. One of these eventually catered to adult movies. My parents never visited any of the Anderson ones, but once I was calling the shots, I did venture to Anderson, along with some buddies, and yes, on dates. Who could forget the dusk until dawn all nighters? The *Planet of the Apes* marathon was almost too much monkey business for one night. I recall one triple feature, *Patton, Mash* and *Vanishing Point*; each is an iconic classic to this very day. Yes, we did visit the adult version upon occasion. A couple come to mind; Russ Meyers: *Cherry, Harry and Rachel* and *Beyond the Valley of the Dolls*. Huge ta-tas was Meyer's featured draw, so obviously impressionable types like us were drawn to his cinematic spectaculars, covertly of course.

As a kid, we vacationed in Daytona Beach, Florida quite often, typically two weeks in July, coinciding with the Daytona race of course. My dad was a huge fan of car racing. We still did that family night at least once while there, having one particular favorite drive-in we visited. I said weather was a factor. No place was more impacted than in Florida during the summer. The oppressive heat and humidity could be brutal with as many as four adults and me in the car, all the windows rolled down to ventilate. With those warm muggy nights came the blood suckers, the Florida vampires, enter the relentless mosquitoes.

When paying, the attendant handed the driver a complementary 'coiled snake' to burn during the movie. This was a coiled citronella incense contraption secured on an aluminum tray. It was strategically placed on the dash and then lit with a lighter or match. They came two to a pack. If you were lucky they would last until the movie was over. One never forgets that scent. They do still sell these by the way. I have used them recently where I live on the Carolina Grand Strand.

I have one movie memory in Daytona, *Li'l Abner*, the musical production, 1959. I would have been six. We always picked up Krystal (10 for a dollar) burgers or Del Tacos (4 for a dollar) before heading to our Florida night out. We didn't have either one of those eating places back home so splurging we did. Sometimes the drive-in offered 'dollar nights', meaning cram as many people in a car for the one low price. Luckily this was before the introduction of headrests. I sat up front anyway so I had no obstructions.

Then there were those walk-in theaters. That's what we called them, drive-ins or walk-ins, so that there was no mistaking what you meant. Before the Abbeville Opera House was converted back into its historical roots, it subbed as a walk-in movie theater. Conveniently located on the south corner of the square, for fifty cents or a quarter and two bottle tops, it was every boy's fantasy.

Like most walk-ins in the south, the downstairs was reserved for the white folk and the balcony for the colored folks. That's what they called black people back then. I so wanted to sit in that balcony. I think they were the best seats in the house. I didn't understand the whole colored-white people divisional lines and practices, but as I kid I had no right to question it. Our schools were kept separate too, a society divided so it seemed.

I remember seeing the original *Lone Ranger* there featuring Clayton Moore as the Ranger and Jay Silverheels as Tonto. Western serials were in steady supply for Saturday matinees, often leaving us with the dreaded cliff hanger until the next time. Tarzan movies were another major feature. Two others stand out in my brain, *Around the World in Eighty Days*, and *The Seventh Voyage of Sinbad*. It's funny how one remembers this stuff. Disney features were a given there too.

After the Abbeville walk-in bit the dust, we had to rely on the State Theater over in Greenwood on Main Street. Granny Winn, my daddy's mama, never missed an Elvis movie. Most every Saturday I accompanied her, My Aunt Cornelia and Uncle Jerry to Greenwood for shopping at Roses, either eating out at Mister Quicks or Rick's Barbeque; and if lucky to an Elvis flick, if one was playing. Granny was a groupie if ever there was one. Elvis did the unthinkable in her eyes in his movie, *Stay Away Joe,* when he smoked cigars and actually said a curse word. What had the world come to?

My greatest adventure of all times had to be when Stanley Price, Stevie Culbreth and I went to see Clint Eastwood and Lee Marvin in *Paint Your Wagon*. Clint and Lee had always been stereotyped as tough guys in the movies, often dark and edgy. *Paint Your Wagon* was a musical. We didn't know that or maybe we wouldn't have gone. I'm personally glad we did. It was by far the most fun I have ever experienced in a movie.

Something just struck our funny bones about this one. Maybe it was Clint and Lee who had no business singing or possibly the various gold miners interacting with the sinful whores and other folks of the mining town, but it triggered something unimaginable in the three of us. Stanley is a loud laugher and this particular movie unhinged his funny bone, the likes the world has never experienced. The more he laughed, the more and louder we laughed, contagious volleying back and forth. Lucky for us there were very few patrons present. Maybe the general public realized that the movie stunk to high heavens. We laughed until we physically hurt. I think I was sore for days afterwards. I still don't know to this day why we weren't booted out. Possibly, our laughter was interpreted as an appreciation for the finer cinema arts. It was one heck of a hoot, I'm just saying. I wonder if my pals remember this episode as vividly as I still do.

Anderson had its walk-ins too but we opted more for the drive-ins there, except this one particular time. Coloring outside the lines and doing things you're not supposed to do is a rite of passage for young teenage boys. I think that is written somewhere in the growing up rule book. Stanley, Speedy, Larry, Pete and I decided to try and see Marquis De Sade, historical research let us just call it. It was depicted as an adult film, x-rated before x-rated was clearly defined. Actually by today's standards it would have maybe been an R or NC-17, but even back then, one had to be at least sixteen to enter these types of movies. By months, I was the baby of the group, but looked older for my age. I fretted about the ID check, if they asked to see ours.

We lined up waiting our turn to purchase a ticket, the attendant asking to view each ones' identification. I was screwed. They'd go in and I'd have to wait in the car. Lastly, I stepped up to the booth and I was the only one he didn't ask to see an ID. I was strutting about like the barnyard rooster, cock of the walk for quite some time there afterwards. The movie was too sadistic for our taste, such was ole Marquis, but we did see some female flesh so all was not wasted on the buck, fifty tickets; and we had popcorn and a coke, another fifty cents spent, the camaraderie, priceless.

There are many more adventures I could share about drive-ins but I'd have to apply parental restrictions and disclaimers to this release. Many firsts for me happened at the Auto in Greenwood, the best money I ever spent for not watching the movies. And then there were those guys' nights at the movies, not ever to be confused with family night, us experimenting with underage adolescence, applying innovation and work-arounds to bend and break the rules applicable for those our age. Did we live recklessly and on the edge? Certainly we did. Elders refer to it as sowing ones oats. We considered it a rite of passage but I bet we sowed an impressive field of oats too.

The drive-ins served us well, the perfect gathering, seclusion and confinement behind the protection of those car doors. The vehicle of choice each visit was our convert chariot to promiscuity. And guess what, we're all still here and are not sitting around whining about how our past somehow ruined our lives. Maybe my wife and I should plan to visit the Auto in Greenwood the next time we visit Abbeville. She and I have never shared a drive-in movie. Anticipation is a terrible thing to put off.

'Drive-in movies, comic books, and blue jeans, howdy doody, baseball cards, and birthdays. Please take me back to the world gone away.'
- The Band, Chicago

Here's a little Drive-in Google Trivia:

The drive-in theater was the creation of Camden, New Jersey, chemical company magnate Richard M. Hollingshead, Jr., whose family owned and operated the R.M. Hollingshead Corporation chemical plant in Camden. In 1932, Hollingshead conducted outdoor theater tests in his driveway at 212 Thomas Avenue in Riverton. After nailing a screen to trees in his backyard, he set a 1928 Kodak projector on the hood of his car and put a radio behind the screen, testing different sound levels with his car windows down and up. Blocks under vehicles in the driveway enabled him to determine the size and spacing of ramps so all automobiles could have a clear view of the screen.

Following these experiments, he applied August 6, 1932, for a patent for his invention, and he was given U.S. Patent 1,909,537 on May 16, 1933. Hollingshead's drive-in opened in New Jersey June 6, 1933, on Admiral Wilson Boulevard in Pennsauken, a short distance from Cooper River Park. Rosemont Avenue now runs through the prior location. It offered 400 slots and a 40 by 50 ft (12 by 15 m) screen. He advertised his drive-in theater with the slogan, "The whole family is welcome, regardless of how noisy the children are."

Win, Lose or Draw

I know what some of you are thinking; that game show hosted by Bert Convy in the late 1980's. Well, while I'm already here, I may as well toss out a little trivia before moving on to a sort of related topic. Did anyone know that the popular game show was co-produced by Burt & Bert Productions (Burt Reynolds and Bert Convy)? The set was actually modeled after Burt Reynolds' living room. That's a little nugget even I didn't know. Google is a powerful research tool. The closest to Google back in my day was Cousin Claude Newton, a book worm who was an endless resource.

The premise of the competition was rather simple. There were two teams, men versus women, each composed of two celebrities and one contestant, taking turns guessing a phrase, title or thing that one teammate was drawing on a large pad of paper with markers. Visualize a flip chart. The drawer could not speak about the subject in his or her drawing and could not use letters, numbers, or symbols. If one of these illegal clues was used, any money won in that puzzle was split between the two teams. However, if a non-drawing team member mentioned a word that was part of the answer, their teammate at the sketch pad was then allowed to write it down. There were several rounds before declaring a winner and then one last chance for the team to up the ante, but you get the gist of it.

The Milton Bradley Company, the famous board game company, founded in 1860 created its version of the show in 1987. It could be played like the TV show or a variation of the game with pawns and a game board. Party, Junior, and Travel Junior editions were produced, plus a Refill Pack for the game. Milton Bradley was taken over by Hasbro, Inc. in 1984. This is the end of the trivia round. How did you do, old timers? If you Googled, you cheated; shame on you. Heck, some of you probably have no clue; board games you ask. That's why I refer to this as nostalgic nonsense.

Getting to my point; Papa and Granny Bowie, my grand folks of course, my mama's parents were born in the early 1900's. Papa was actually born in the year 1900, making it easy to remember his age. He was about ten years older than Granny. They married their gals young back in the day. Life wasn't easy for either of them, but to use their words, 'they got by.' Priorities were much different in those forgotten times.

Providing meant working hard. The provider had options; buy, barter or utilize hunting and fishing skills to put food on the table. Papa was an excellent hunter and fisherman and not so bad at wheeling and dealing. Money didn't always change hands. Swapping out favors or chores worked just as well. Papa was a painter, interiors and exteriors, and in high demand, known for his excellent workmanship. He preferred cash for his trade, but that was often negotiable.

Growing up in the south, working in the cotton mills, as they were called then, provided a living for many in Abbeville. Papa and Granny lived in one of the mill houses built on many of the streets located close to the Milliken Mill, referred to as a textile industry now. Milliken's premise; provide the workers with an affordable place to rent, close by, to ensure they were within walking distance of their jobs. If you didn't work in the mill, you didn't live in the mill hill community. Those living on the north end of town were often considered the more privileged and uppity folks.

Both grandparents, living the hard life, mostly in the rural sections of the county, meant things came with a price. Education wasn't high on the radar screen; at least not 'book learning' as it was so called. Possessing common sense, some sort of trade and working your fingers to the bone was more important. Children were expected to put in their time and pull their share of the load, whatever the chore might be. Laziness was not tolerated and your time on the clock was governed by nature, sunup to sundown, the weather for certain situations and the signs came into play if planting crops. I'll get more into signs in another chapter.

Book learning, so just how does this really impact a person? Reading, writing and arithmetic are essential tools, wouldn't you agree? If you can't read, the world can be a difficult place to survive. And if you can't read, you most certainly can't write. Math, well you have to figure out how to manage a budget, buy stuff, and pay those bills, so it sort of comes in handy. You certainly don't want to over pay, short change or get snookered by someone untrustworthy making change.

Neither papa nor granny attended school; not uncommon during their upbringing. Schools weren't always located close by, so getting there and back often consumed much of the day. There is some merit to those stories many of us have been told by that generation; 'I had to walk five miles in the snow, one way, barefooted, to attend school.' Most of us are spoiled and blessed today.

Dilemma, if granny and papa couldn't read or write, just how did they survive in a world that depended on one being educated to cope with the day to day tasks? Remember, common sense is often the most powerful attribute. Challenges, however, did prevail. In a world before cell phones, texting or even answering machines; something the youth of today could never fathom; just how did granny and papa pull off the feat of communication. Schedules change. Conflicts arise. For much of their adult life, papa painted or found other ways to make a meager living while granny toiled away in the mill. Passing ships, sometimes they didn't see each other after sharing early morning breakfast.

Innovation, what a wonderful tool for overcoming insurmountable odds and they were quite the innovators. Pencil and paper is not just for writing notes. This is where the Win, Lose and Draw analogy plays into my little story. Eventually I do get to my point. Sorry, southern upbringing equates to milking a story. I learned from the best, Papa. He could string you along spinning a tale or just making foolishness. Many never had the pleasure of seeing this side of him. I did.

Let's lay out a scenario. Papa completes his painting job earlier than expected, the one he had told granny about that morning over breakfast. Granny is still at the mill when he arrives home. With daylight to burn, papa decides not to waste an opportunity, and he hankers to wet his hook, drown a few red wigglers and go to one of his favorite fishing holes. The signs are perfect. The brim are on their beds, just waiting for him to come along and snatch them from their watery haven with his baited hook. I'm just giving you good ole fashion visuals. Squint your eyes and use your imagination, or not, if you don't quite get it.

Papa utilizes the pad and draws his best picture of a fish, a cane pole and a hook. That relays to granny where he has gone, but to better explain, he adds one final touch. He draws the face of a clock with the hour hand indicating the time he should be back. Upon granny's arrival from her shift at the mill, she sees the note on the kitchen table. Simple, papa has gone fishing and should be home around seven. His actual location is of no importance to her. Some things are tougher to draw. Regardless, she can now plan supper around his proposed return. Hopefully tomorrow they will be having battered and black skillet fried fish for supper.

Papa draws his best depiction of a squirrel or rabbit, and a long gun, when he's gone hunting. Granny seeing the note; she wishes him happy hunting, almost able to taste squirrel dumplings or fried rabbit, whichever is his chosen prey. The critters basically look the same except a long furry tail means squirrel and cotton tail means ole Peter Rabbit. He sometimes adds a bird to the mix when quail or doves are on the agenda. A bird is a bird in granny's interpretation. Remember, papa is a painter and the scribbling pad is now his canvas. As a kid, seeing them do this, I thought it was just too funny. Looking back, I have a fonder appreciation of their skills and work around to overcome the handicaps they faced.

Granny, as many women do even now, sent papa to the grocery store to pick up a few needed items. Sending the men folk to the store for anything comes with challenges. Take it from one who knows; what they say and what we hear don't always align properly. Don't bother arguing afterwards; it's a lost cause. You'll only be accused of not listening. We never listen according to them. We can often return with a unique variety of items. Sometimes we get lucky and buy the correct stuff or brand.

My daddy was the perfect example. Mama would say, 'We need a dozen eggs and no buttermilk.' What would daddy do; return with buttermilk and no eggs, seemingly honing in on the last thing he heard mama say. This was forever a battle between them, even before he came down with Alzheimer's, when he finally had a legitimate excuse for his actions. Even then, she ragged him about it. (Shameless plug: Read my published memoir, *The Caregiver's Son, Outside the Window Looking In*, to learn more about these adventures.)

So how would granny ensure papa picked up what she needed? You got it; the ole pad and pencil, drawing it out. But wait, grocery items can't be as easy as drawing a fish or rabbit, a gun or a fishing pole. Not to worry, granny and papa were gifted and quite talented. I'm sure there was trial and error moments until they perfected their routine, but they did the best with what they had to work with. Methods require madness.

Granny could portray a milk carton, a stick of butter, eggs, sack of flour or meal, using the first letter of each, or a can of shortening. A can is a can so how did she differentiate? She would draw an ear of corn and various beans, tomatoes, etc. beside the can. They developed artistic dialog and they got by the best they could. Granted, usually papa's runs to the grocery store were for a small handful of items but their system worked. Granny did the main shopping for the most part, no list of sketches required.

Still it is amazing how two people cheated of proper schooling found a way to make it work. There was always food on the table and a loving environment to be found in that old mill house. Mama assisted them with their monthly bill paying, like writing checks, when they finally had to break down and open a checking account. Still, those little scribbling moments existed, artwork for the heart and from the heart.

What I wouldn't do to have a few sheets of their fanciful communication dialogue now. It would be simply priceless. I can envision that fish, hook and a pole; makes the corners of mouth turn upward. It was simple times but they weren't simple people. I dabbled in drawing off and on over the years. I guess I inherited it honestly. I miss them dearly but memories are precious, and passing this along makes sure it lasts forever. It is that time long ago forgotten for many and never realized by the young pups of today's generation. Technology at our finger tips, one tends to forget that back in the day you did what you had to do to get by.

'This world is but a canvas to our imagination.'
- Henry David Thoreau

But You Doesn't Hasta Call Me Tommy

Allow me to begin with a clarification before I go any further. The title of this chapter was derived from a character (Raymond J. Johnson, Jr.) created by Bill Saluga in the 70's. His shtick as Ray J. Johnson is to become annoyed when addressed as "Mr. Johnson", exclaiming in a loud voice, "My name is Raymond J. Johnson, Jr. Now you can call me Ray, or you can call me J, or you can call me Johnny, or you can call me Sonny, or you can call me Junie, or you can call me Junior; now you can call me Ray J, or you can call me RJ, or you can call me RJJ, or you can call me RJJ Jr." ultimately ending with, "but you doesn't hasta call me Johnson!"

Names, name calling, nick names, real names, sometimes we answer to anything or ignore all but our parental given one. As kids, taunting and name calling is part of our world. Some are unjust, often brought on by the way we look and act or from maybe accidental or unfortunate circumstances pegging us with the title we'd like to forget. Some adults look at a little kid and say stuff like; you're cute as a button. What's that supposed to mean? I've never seen a cute button, have you, really; think about it. Or, what a cute little monkey you are. I resemble a chimp; please ruin us for life. Adults can be unintentionally cruel, even with chosen God given names for us. Making jokes and nicknaming us is rarely appreciated. Kids usually do it with a purpose, name calling being part of our game.

One of my first so called nicknames that come to memory involved me meeting a great uncle I never even knew existed. I was five, almost six. My folks decided to take this cross county trip and when I say cross country, it doesn't go much further across than from South Carolina to California. The road trip participants included my parents, my grandparents, an adult cousin and me, crammed in one car, road trip America, two weeks to get there and back.

Uncle Floyd, my papa's brother and his wife, Aunt Jane lived there. The year, 1959, May, and I would celebrate my 6th birthday on the west coast. Even to this day I can still remember snippets from the vacation; stuff you wouldn't expect a kid to remember. It was my first of two times to visit Disneyland, the second coming when I was fifteen. While vague, I do remember riding the old train that encircled the theme park and I remember the grand entrance, the flowers shaped like the head of Mickey Mouse. I even met Mickey and some of those other characters that were larger than life. I thought they were real, still do. Most of the rest is sort of a blur.

Uncle Floyd, with his signature bald head, prominent for the Bowie males, spoke words that would make a sailor cringe. He spewed curse words and dropped 'F' bombs with reckless abandon, but he was my newly discovered uncle just the same. He even acted sort of like an uncle, and along with Papa, took me to a local California mom and pop grocery store to purchase some goods for the night's supper. Papa told me I could have an ice cream so I opted for one of my favorites, a Push-up, orange sherbet in a cylindrical tube on a stick. You pushed the stick end like a plunger towards your awaiting mouth.

At this particular time in my life I was missing two front teeth. Pronouncing Push-up was a challenge and came out more like 'Puth-up.' Ah yes, Uncle Floyd zeroed right in on that pronunciation blooper and thus dubbed me *Puth-up*, affectionately so I assume. From that day forward *Puth-*

up is all he ever called me. I think he forgot my name was really Tommy. I was so thankful he lived on the west coast, far away from any of my friends and family back in the Palmetto State.

We eventually trekked back to Abbeville, me the young and budding six year old, soon to be a full fledged first grader. I left that awful nickname thousands of miles behind, never ever giving it another thought. Low and behold, Uncle Floyd and Aunt Jane decided to move to Abbeville. My past caught up with me way too soon. I was forever *Puth-up* now, the cat out of the bag. Friends and family thought it was a hoot. Adulthood brought no escape or relief. *Puth-up* I was until the day he died.

I suppose one of the next names to grace my humble existence happened during a church Sunday school class Christmas party. I was a young lanky pimple faced teenager, must have been around 1966. The girls decided spinning the bottle would be a marvelous idea. We boys openly protested, most really wanting to play but not willing to admit it. You know the drill. Boy, girl, boy, girl form a circle. A coke bottle is placed in the center, each person taking a turn spinning it. You spin the bottle and if it lands on a girl you're required to kiss her on the lips of all places. No, you don't have to kiss the lucky boys, although today that might be an acceptable practice in many circles or even preferred in others.

As luck would have it, my turn arrived and I gave it a spin. It pointed directly towards Beverly; possibly an omen of things to come. I didn't know it at the time but I would eventually take her hand in marriage. We didn't even date until our senior year in school, even though I had known her all my life. A first grade me never hesitated kissing

Sherry on the monkey bars, but now, some six or seven years later I wasn't so confident. Possibly in the back of my mind I remembered where that first kiss had gotten me.

Everyone vocally encouraged me to oblige my commitment and kiss her. I needed a safety net, those monkey bars. Barbara Ann spoke the loudest saying, "Kiss her, Tommy Toothpick." She repeated it several more times, me cringing more from that name than from locking lips. "Kiss her Tommy Toothpick," the others chimed in. So I did, square on the lips too. January 22nd 1972 I'd seal the deal for real.

You got it. Tommy Toothpick became my Sunday school class name. Later they dropped the Tommy and just called me Toothpick. I fit the build, what can I say? I was five eleven or so and skinny as can be, somewhere in the one hundred twenty soaking wet category. Toothpick is not a flattering nickname. I guess it ranks a tad better than Puth-up. At least I didn't really have to explain Toothpick, but boy I had to back pedal my way out of the orange sherbet. Puth-up took on a life of its own as I got older and my pals had other explanations far worse than ice cream. I remained Toothpick in that circle of so called friends. I'm not exactly sure just how much weight I had gained before losing it. I weighed one hundred fifty five at six feet, two inches when I graduated.

Let's fast forward to the seventies, me now married to my spin the bottle target, working at Flexible Technologies in Abbeville. I was twenty one years old; the year 1974. I worked the third shift, 11:30 PM until 7:30 AM. A small group, six or seven of us, sort of bonded and were always looking for something to do after work. We tried bowling in Greenwood for a while. We even took up tennis, all buying tennis rackets and playing either at Erskine College in Due West or at Hickory Knob State Park.

Tiring of that, we formed a chess club, having chess tournaments most weekends. This was during those Bobby Fisher days. We were obsessed with the checkered board. While chess challenged us mentally, it lacked in physical endurance. So what did we do, we all bought dirt bikes and went trail riding through Curl Tale or Parson's Mountain. Like anything we attempted, it wore out its welcome and appeal.

Golf was next on the list of sports to try. I didn't own a set of clubs and had never even considered playing golf. To me it was for rich kids or the privileged upper crust. Persistent, my third shift buddies talked me into venturing to High Meadows Country Club one morning after work. It was and still is a nine hole course located on the outer reaches of Abbeville on highway 71. They armed me with a driver, a tee and a ball, no practice, we just launched into play mode. You'd think it would be easy to hit that ball off that tee. It was just sitting there. I whiffed three or four times, making contact with nothing but the air I breathe.

Finally I actually struck it or should I say I struck the ground first and then pounded what they called 'a worm burner' down the middle of the fairway. At least it went straight for a change. Hitting the ground loudly first became my signature swing. It made a thunderous whomp sound when I banged the head of the club on the turf. I lost count just how many times I hit that same ball on the first hole. They hadn't exactly explained to me the importance of keeping a tally. Chippy goaded me, yelling, "whomp it again." Whomp I did, over and over and over. I was a loud golfer.

We finally reached the ninth and final hole and I was about whomped out. I was lying who knows how many strokes in the center of the fairway, a location I had rarely been all morning, about one hundred fifty yards from the green. Beulah was standing in the fairway, midway between me and the green, propped against his golf bag pull cart. Walking was much cheaper than riding so we all walked. He encouraged me to hit the ball, knowing I hadn't hit a ball straight or off the ground for eight holes.

"Whomp it," he yelled, waving me on. Okay, so I did. I hit the perfect line drive towards the green. Beulah spoiled my shot by blocking it with his shoulder, dropping him to his knees. That night when we reported to work, our little clique recanted the events of the morning, dubbing me with my new name, Whomp. A short time afterwards, evolution ran its course and I became known as Whomper. An elderly Whomper, still known by that name to my original golfing buddies and new golfing pals made along the way, I never lost the gift to whomp the ball. While working at Kemet Electronics in Greenwood in early 2000, we even dubbed our Wednesday afternoon golf group the Wednesday Whompers, none of us very good at the game of golf. I remained the Original Whomper and founding father.

I'm sure there have been other not so memorable names along the way for the one christened Thomas Allen Winn. My dad was a Thomas too but mama feared I'd be called Junior so instead of naming me Thomas Jefferson Winn the second, she tagged me with Allen as a middle name. Instead of Allen, I grew up as Tommy. I remained Tommy for thirty eight years. All the good names ended in 'y'.

After working at Flexible Technologies for almost

twenty years, I left to go work as a Quality Manager for a friend and former boss, Kirk, at Greenwood Plating and Fabrication. Mel, a third generation electro-platter and one of the owners of the business asked me what he should call me. I shrugged and told him whatever. He began calling me Tom, thus everyone else at the facility knew me only as Tom.

My favorite, Papa just called me Hun. He'd ask me, "You want a Coca Cola and pack of peanuts, Hun?" He said, "reel him in, Hun." "Let's go sit on the front porch, Hun." "Don't tell your granny, Hun." "Don't cry, Hun." I don't ever remember him calling me Tommy. Hun was just fine with me.

Little Tommy Toothpick had vanished, sort of. When around old friends, new acquaintances called me Tom, to the snickers of the old guard. When family or old friends called me Tommy in front any of my new friends and coworkers, the snickers erupted from them. Some still called me Whomper. Thankfully none called me Puth-up. Tommy became a name of the past except for those who had only known me as Tommy. Likewise at my fortieth class reunion, a former classmate who had always been Billy was now called Bill. I'd yell to him, Billlllllllll and he would return the Tommmmmm.

Final chapter, I stumbled into the life of writing and eventually becoming a published author in 2011. What name should grace the cover of my first novel, Road Rage? I certainly never considered Puth-up, Toothpick or Whomper. Tommy just didn't have that worldly author ring to it. Tom seemed so common. I considered making up a fictitious name to go along with my fiction writing. Many authors write under a pen name. Me an author, it still sounds a little farfetched even at this very moment, I've now published four books.

Then it hit me; why not go with T. Allen Winn. I repeated it over and over. It rolled off my lips, T. Allen Winn, bestselling world reendowed author. Oh well, the name guarantees nothing. I'm far from world famous and can't even land on the hundred best seller list of Aynor, South Carolina. All I can really say is, "You Doesn't Hasta Call Me Tommy, you can call me Puth-up, or Toothpick or Whomper; you can even call me Tom, or T. Allen, or TAW, or TW, but you Doesn't Hasta Call Me Tommy...unless you want to, Hun.

*'Nicknames stick to people,
and the most ridiculous are the most adhesive.'*
~Thomas C. Haliburton

Everyone probably has an Uncle Floyd
Puth-up, The Expanded Version

I don't know if Uncle Floyd had a nautical cell in his body but he could certainly cuss like a sailor. Floyd Bowie, one of my Papa's brothers, unknown to me until that first trip to California in the summer of 1959, would forever impact my future. Neither I, nor he could ever have possibly imagined the significance until after that west coast encounter. I was five years old when we began the east coast to west coast journey, but I would be six on the return trip west to east. Who would have thought a two week cross country car trip would age me so? I suppose having a birthday while in California did affect that outcome.

I don't remember what exactly prompted this spring time vacation in late May; being a five year old, they didn't exactly ask for my input. I did know that the trip would include visiting an Uncle Floyd and Aunt Jane but, other than that, I wasn't privy to much. I wasn't even sure where California was and certainly could have never imagined such a long journey lay ahead.

Let me paint this picture for you. Envision this, five adults and one kid, their belongings, food and drink, on a two week trip from South Carolina to California via the back roads of American in a four-door fifty something Chevrolet with the only air-conditioning being how many windows you rolled down.

You heard it correctly; no air conditioning and you actually rolled down the windows by hand with a turn crank mounted on every door just below the window, no push buttons or automatics on those babies. This was pre-SUV and before seatbelts and we had only an AM radio with limited channels. The road trip, truly the fun filled family bonding experience, was part of the American culture. While these same trips are still dubbed FFF, the acronym has changed to forced family fun. National Lampoon had nothing on us. We were the Griswold's before anyone knew who they were.

Daddy and Mama, Granny and Papa, Cousin Leila and I left the Palmetto state behind us and trekked towards California, not as part of the gold rush but, instead, in search of more of the Bowie clan. I must admit, much of the actual trip still remains a blur to me but I do remember seeing cacti for the first time, lemons growing on trees, the desert and some small town in New Mexico infested with mountains of unfamiliar dead bugs. They had been swept up in piles in every nook and cranny. And there was the heat, hotter than blue blazes and relentless. I think it took the better part of that first week for us to cover the distance to Pasadena or its suburbs, but I was a kid so what did I really know about time and distance.

Time to meet Uncle Floyd and Aunt Jane and there was nothing southern about either one of them, but why should there be, they lived in California. Uncle Floyd sort of looked like Papa; bald, heavy build, dark complexion but he wasn't wearing Camel overalls and he chain smoked. Aunt Jane was even of darker complexion, almost Hispanic looking and she was quite the smoker too. They greeted us warmly and then introduced us to Teco, the tan little Chihuahua and Bob-A-Lou the green parakeet. Apparently they were best of buddies because Bob-A-Lou was allowed free rein of the house and preferred hanging out with Teco, even riding on his back. What an odd couple I thought; Uncle Floyd and Aunt Jane too?

Very early into the going I heard language my young ears had never heard before as Uncle Floyd had quite the vocabulary and apparently had no qualms about spewing them at will in mixed company, kids or women present meant no never mind. I do believe that it had to be the first time I had ever heard the F word spoken and there were plenty of "Hells and Damns" thrown in for good measure. I had not actually witnessed it being done, but he would have been the perfect candidate for having his mouth washed with that bar of soap. One thing for sure, he could not be persuaded to clean up his act. He was what he was; deal with it.

I don't recall how many days we stayed with them in California, but here's what I do remember about the stay. I did have my sixth birthday party there. Of course my guest list included only adults, no kids. I remember receiving my first bow and arrow. The arrows had those red suction cups on the ends and I lost them several times, shooting them over the neighbor's high wooden fence. Uncle Floyd would have to retrieve them for me. I think he quickly grew tired of this task because mama relieved me of my weapons. Happy birthday to me, I'm saying.

Being the tourists that we were and none of us having ever visited California before, Uncle Floyd, our tour guide, made sure we had an opportunity to see the sights. I'm sure we saw plenty of neat stuff and places but here's what stood out in a six year olds mind. We visited a Hollywood set and it just so happened to be one of my favorite shows at the time. I think my new uncle may have been tipped off by someone. Irregardless, I found myself on the production set of Circus Boy.

For those of you too young to know or too old to remember Circus Boy, here's the basis of the plot. The title sort of gives it away but here goes. Young Corky played by Mickey Dolenz, the same of the Monkeys fame, had lost his parents, The Flying Falcons, in a tragic trapeze accident. Uncle Joey the Clown, played by Noah Berry, Jr. basically adopted Corky and he remained a member of the Burke and Walsh Circus. Corky became the circus's water boy and quickly bonded with Bimbo a baby elephant. The two were inseparable, Corky often riding on Bimbo's back while dealing with all sorts of adolescent situations episode to episode. Two other main characters were the circus owner, Big Tim Champion and Pete who put up the big top tent. It aired from 1956 to 1958 in primetime, eventually rerunning on Saturday mornings.

They were filming an episode so the set was closed. We could see the activities in the distance but I never actually laid eyes on Corky or Bimbo. The best thing I could do at the time was have my picture taken while I rode a motorized stationary elephant for the price of a quarter. To even be that close to the real Circus Boy still sent chills down my spine. I often pretended to be Corky riding my imaginary Bimbo the baby elephant. Childhood memories that you actually remember are priceless.

The California Uncle took us to Disneyland. One of my favorites, Walt Disney Presents had introduced me to Disneyland, Mickey Mouse and friends. I had a crush on Annette Funicella of the Mickey Mouse Club. My folks even bought me a Mickey Mouse hat equipped with ears and I felt like an honorary Mouseketeer. I would sport those ears and march around singing "Who's the leader of the band..." knowing all the words to The Mickey Mouse March ending with. "Now it's time to say goodbye..." I lived and breathed in Fantasyland.

A five year old, just turned six, can only retain so much information fifty some odd years later, but what stands out to me is the huge Mickey Mouse head formed by flowers at the main entrance to Disneyland and riding the train that encircled the park, and of course, Cinderella's Castle. Meeting all of the costumed characters parading around held special meaning as did riding on the Dumbo ride. Uncle Floyd came through for us again, even though I'm not so sure Walt Disney would have approved of his language.

He took us to an orchard where they grew lemons. I had never seen a lemon tree before. I should have never mentioned lemon tree because now I have that catchy tune running between my ears that will be tough to shake. "Lemon tree, very pretty, and the lemon flower is sweet, but the fruit of the poor lemon is impossible to eat." My mouth turns wrong side out when thinking about sucking on a lemon.

My Cousin Leila had a pleasant surprise. Her husband flew in from Hawaii to meet us on the west coast. Billy Joe, a true southerner originating in the Level Land community of Abbeville County, had that signature two name first name. No one ever called him Billy; he was Billy Joe. I'm glad I didn't get hung with Thomas Allen. Tommy worked just fine for me. I did know a Tommy Joe though.

Uncle Floyd through conversations with papa discovered I had a fondness for orange sherbet so they took me to a local hot spot to buy me an ice cream. I pointed to exactly my brand, a Push-up, a cylinder of sherbet accessed by pushing a plunger to force it through the other side and into your awaiting mouth. You've already heard this story in the previous chapter. Unfortunately with two missing front teeth I pronounced it puth-up, no matter how hard I tried to not say it that way.

Now Uncle Floyd got a real hoot out of my little speech impediment and laughed like there would be no tomorrow. Unbeknownst to me at that very moment, I had branded myself; a curse that would haunt me for the next thirty or so years. Uncle Floyd affectionately began calling me Puth-up. Do you realize how embarrassing it is to be called Puth-up. It opens up Pandora's Box with a flood of questions concerning the origination of my alias. Luckily for me we would soon be heading back to South Carolina and I would be leaving this nickname far behind.

As luck would have it, Uncle Floyd and Aunt Jane later decided to move to Abbeville. They even stayed with us until they located and bought a house. While Teco and Bob-A-Lou were most entertaining and fun to be around, I couldn't say the same for good old Uncle Floyd.

Without hesitation and whether it be family, friends or complete strangers present, he called me Puth-up. Do you know how traumatizing it is to be called Puth-up in front of your peers? It just sounded plain filthy and forbidding and I always had to explain why he called me this. Oh yeah, and when I began dating, he couldn't wait to call me Puth-up, just to see how my girlfriends reacted. Well, all these years later and after Uncle Floyd has longed passed, I have front teeth and still love an occasional Sherbet Push-up. While I can pronounce it correctly, I can't help thinking back to my days as Puth-up. It doesn't seem quite so bad looking back now.

A nickname is the hardest stone that
the devil can throw at a man.

Cowboys and Indians

We all grew up playing our versions of silly games from the traditional favorites like hide and seek, tag, chase, dodge ball, London Bridges, and Simon Says. I always liked playing Red Rover where you and your playing partners picked sides then locked hands beckoning for someone from the other side "Red Rover, Red Rover, send Billy right over" and if Billy was successful in running through and breaking a human link, he could pick someone to take back to their side. If unsuccessful, you kept Billy. The game was over when all of the kids were on one side or the other. You were only as tough as your weakest links.

We didn't stay inside watching TV or playing video games. First of all, television only had three channels, ABC, NBC and CBS. Video game technology would not be invented for another twenty years and I remember my first in the early seventies, Pong. Our parents had to threaten us to within an inch of our lives to make us come inside at night, especially during those long summer nights when darkness didn't fall until after 9 PM. The outdoors was our world.

Most of the games we played didn't require props or accessories. Hide and go Seek for instance; all the kids but one hid and that lucky loner would seek out the others. The last boy or girl standing unfound won. Neither tag nor chase required anything more than willing and running bodies. Simon Says consisted of commands from Simon, the gatekeeper. The designated Simon would bark out, "Simon says Tommy, take ten baby steps or Stevie take three butterfly twirls." Two game objectives; always ask May I or forfeit your turn. Always take advantage of your maneuver and move forward as far as possible. If you failed to say May I, you had to return to the starting spot, but if you reached Simon first, you won and then became the new Simon. Simon too often got accused of showing favoritism and justifiably so.

If you had enough kids you could play any of these games with nothing else needed. Life was quite simple back then. We played this version of chase-tag where you couldn't touch the grass. Objective, stay on walkways, driveways, ledges, wooden planks, anything that could make way your escape, ensuring you didn't come in contact with the grass. Some of us were much more creative than others. I was one of them.

That being said, we were quite the innovators. Give us any kind of ball, basketball, beach ball, soccer ball and we could parlay the round object into a game of dodge ball. Simple, if you were hit by the thrower, you were out of the game. We pitched pennies, jumped rope, tossed horse shoes and threw darts. We learned to be creative and we had fun. Some of the best games were the ones from our wild imaginations.

Who could not love playing army? With pistols and rifles firing caps or just mimicking gun fire with our mouths, we would play war, picking sides and going into battle. Neither laser tag or paint ball had made their way onto the scene in my day of the gun. We had to rely on the bang-bang I shot you gamesmanship rule. Often the shooter and victim disagreed on the kill. There were no wounds or paint to mark the kills. All you had to go on was your opponent's call that they got you and the honor system. We had no referees so disputes were settled by those who shouted the loudest or were the largest and more intimidating.

Innovation intervened when we didn't have the weaponry, ammunition or other components to wager a decent battle. Sticks often served as guns and as already mentioned our mouths provided the sound effects. Some of us were better than others at sounding authentic. When playing Cowboys and Indians, if we were lucky, we had those stick type horses with actual fabricated horse heads on them. If not, we more resembled witches playing cowboys and Indians riding those broom sticks.

Sometimes we got really creative and brought fireworks into play. My cousin and a neighbor friend fabricated homemade pistols out of piping scrap. They'd take a piece of 1 ¼ inch steel pipe, saw it off to length, bend it in a vice to form the shape of a pistol, pad the grip to prevent stinging of the hands, then load a firecracker in the end and light her up. The gunsmith came in all ages as did gunfighters, Indians and soldiers. There were no laws saying we couldn't play and have fun.

As for these new fangled weapons, the fire projected from the barrel and the explosion did look more real than anything else we ever had in our possession. It created fantastic sound effects. Innovation led to even trying bottle rockets in the homemade devices. Those of us on the receiving end of these assaults didn't appreciate the missiles being launched in our direction. Luckily, parents intervened and halted this practice before one of us lost an eye or some other body part we needed.

Never to be bored or outdone, we deviated from the norm and developed our own version of Cowboys and Indians. We introduced a hybrid to hide and go seek to the scenario. Rules; simple, the Indians were allowed sufficient time to hide and then the lone Cowboy hunted them down. The twist, everyone was fair game. Fastest draw eliminated the other. Claimed shots were debatable. So picture the lone Cowboy stalking cautiously around corners, looking behind shrubs, under and around parked vehicles, inside sheds, garages or any other obstacles large enough to conceal an avenging Injun. The Indians did have the upper hand most of the time so the Cowboy had to be a true gunslinger to prevail. I liked playing one of the Indians. I was good at ambushing.

It is funny how there are those moments in time you never forget, even a zillion years later. I'll never forget the classic confrontation, David versus Ann; no, not David versus Goliath, but just as good. In this case, David, the next door neighbor, would be Goliath, the designated Cowboy, while my cousin Ann would be the David and a way too sneaky Indian. Setting the stage, David was four years my senior and five years older than Ann, my visiting seven year old cousin. Ann, Billy, Stevie and I were the hiding Indians and David would be hunting us down. He's the Cowboy who invented the pipe gun but he wouldn't be using that fire power for his particular game; not that it could have saved him anyway.

Completing his count down to a hundred from the front porch, David now began his hunt for the hiding Indians. He made quick work of Stevie, Billy and me, but old paleface had not been able to locate the squaw of our tribe. Rules, game ends when the Cowboy has been shot, all Indians have been found and gunned down or the Cowboy finally claims he or she gives up and forfeits the win. David was not one to forfeit. He would find her and bring her to justice so to speak. The only good Indian was a dead Indian in our backyard frontier. We were light years from political corrective-ness.

We stayed our distance, watching David meticulously search every nook and cranny, checking many of them a second and third time, but no cousin Ann. She was good. We had never had a game go this long and to think it was being dominated by a girl; unheard of and just a tad embarrassing to the mostly all boy tribe, even if she was on our side. But then again, all the boys were dead. The girl was still alive and well out there somewhere. None of us knew where. We watched and waited.

None of us wore or owned watches so I'm not sure how long the game actually lasted, but by our standards it seemed like forever. We were tiring of David's hunting and tried several times to get him to say uncle. Nope, no little girl was going to outsmart him he remarked. His face lacked confidence. We all sort of began conducting our own private searches for Ann; curiosity was getting the best of us too.

David checked inside an out shed for the zillion millionth time, but there was no sign of her. He stood there puzzled and contemplating what was left to search, when less than five feet away Ann popped up like a Jack in the Box from her hiding place, a fifty gallon metal drum, commonly used for trash cans back then. She yelled bang, bang, you're dead. The expression on David's face was priceless. We whooped and we hollered at the sight of her emerging from that trash barrel.

While none of us appreciated being outsmarted by a girl, give credit where credit is due. Ann had proved to be the best Indian that day. I bet if I asked Ann and David right now, they'd both be able to recall that event. I can still see her vividly, popping from that barrel, a slow motion replay. I think on any given day she could have taken down the likes of Clint Eastwood or John Wayne, but in the summer of 1960, David had taken a bullet for all of us. Yep, I'm smiling about it now, partner. I'm thinking about riding the broom around the house before my wife returns, but maybe that would be a bit too much, especially if I got caught. Best leave it to memories. Bang, bang, you're dead; got to just love it, cuz.

> *'To tittle-tattle is like playing poker;*
> *you win from time to time but in the end are*
> *ensnared at your own game.'*
> ~ **Judge Roy Bean**

Me and Teco

A boy and his dog, there's nothing new about that bond. It's been written about and appeared in movies countless times so I suppose one more story couldn't possibly hurt. It should be a rite of passage for every child, boy or girl, to pick out their very first puppy, man's best friend. A dog would say they deserve a boy or girl of their very own.

For me, it happened in 1959. We had returned from a two week cross country automobile trip from east to west coast on the back roads of America, five adults and one boy crammed inside the big four door Chevrolet. I had celebrated my sixth birthday in California, meeting an uncle and aunt for the first time, my papa's brother and his wife. My newly discovered aunt and uncle had a little tan colored Chihuahua named Teco. What a great name for a dog.

After seeing how I had reacted to their dog, my parents decided it must be the right time for me to have my own. My whining and pouting might have influenced their decision. I had perfected this sure fire technique. Plus, it was my birthday now wasn't it, so I played that card too. The stars and planets were aligned perfectly to bring me good luck; at least that's my story.

We drove down the curvy Cedar Springs Road to a house at the end of a long dirt drive. A new litter of pups had just been born. My daddy called the dogs Boxer Bulldogs. They were all so tiny and cute, had not even opened their eyes. He told me to pick one so I did, but then I couldn't take it home yet. There were too young. Now do you know how difficult it is for a six year old to rationalize just getting a puppy but then not being allowed to take it home? Take a kid in a toy store and tell them to pick out their most favorite toy then leave the store empty handed. That should be against the law.

What I didn't know is that Boxers must be docked and cropped when they are old enough. These hadn't undergone the extreme dog make over, so I ended up waiting weeks before we returned to pick up my dog. Kids don't do this week thing very well. Parents don't always make the best decisions. I'm sure they regretted prematurely springing the surprise on me. I constantly asked when we were going to get him; sort of like, are we there yet?

Finally the day came for us to retrieve my puppy. He was the last puppy in the litter to be picked up. I peered in the box and thought this couldn't be my dog. Its tail was gone and its ears were ragged and painted purple. Boy did I cry. What had they done to my puppy? Docking and cropping had happened to my puppy's tail and ears. Daddy tried to explain that my puppy had been operated on to make it look like a Boxer Bulldog. He had already told me on the first visit that it was a Boxer Bulldog so why did they have to do this to him? I didn't understand or buy it, but eventually I accepted the mutation as my very own.

My parents told me I had to name him. What did a six year old know about naming a puppy? I had never had a puppy. I only knew one dog name; Teco. I liked that name. I hoped he would too so I held him up and called him Teco. He licked me in the face. That sealed the deal, sort of like a handshake. We took Teco home. Boy and dog, dog and boy, the perfect match had been made. We became best buddies. He understood me or at least pretended to. He was an accomplished actor even as a wee pup. That was my best summer, a pup transformed into a dog.

Teco had those boxer trademark teeth protruding from his lower jaw making the cute little puppy into a force to be reckoned with. His toughness ended at those teeth's roots.

The big bad mean looking creature was just a big old pussy cat, unless someone tried to mess with me. Two words transformed him into an attack dog; "sic'um!" He would charge and tackle whoever I pointed toward. His attack resembled a mauling but he never bit a single person. Those being wrestled to the ground weren't so sure until I laughed and called him off of them.

All summer we traveled as a herd of two, thus evolved the curse. Teco would not allow me out of his sight. Often I played hide and seek with him. I'd sneak from the house and somehow he sensed my little covert operation. Nose to the ground the boxer turned bloodhound. He always got his boy.

Summer over, I found myself starting the first grade. Langley Milliken grammar school bordered our back yard, separated by a mere six foot chain link fence. By way of the flying crow, I could be in my classroom in mere minutes, especially if I crawled under the fence. My parents drove me there instead; two left turns and one block later we were parked out front. I was an official first grader.

How he did it without my foot prints to follow I'll never know. I sat there in my class room at my desk style table for two; Teco entered the doorway, sniffed a couple of times and then zeroed in on me. He was by my side slobbering all over me. Let me tell you; the teacher didn't appreciate it one little bit. I was definitely ahead of the game for show and tell day. We could see Spot run but Teco was not welcome.

My parents arrived. We loaded the tracker in the car and took him the short drive home. Teco had to be locked in my daddy's shop until I returned from school or he would end up there with me again. Once Mama attended a PTA meeting where the teachers would be all chummy and talk about us. Guess who made a cameo appearance? You got it; Teco. Mama didn't find anything funny about his surprise visit. A slobbering Boxer Bulldog doesn't quite fit in at a meeting meant for people.

Over the years, the hide and seek blood hounding became my personal challenge. A friend would close him up in the shop while I zig-zagged, climbed trees, hid in weeds, or crossed creeks to outsmart that dog. Nose to the ground he found his boy every single time. It defied explanation.

Teco hated firecrackers and but yet he was terrified of thunderstorms. He would foam at the mouth and attack firecrackers with them often exploding in his mouth. We had to lock him in the shop when we shot them off for holidays. He almost chewed through the door. I can't think of any particular incident that made him this way. It couldn't have just been the loud sound or he wouldn't have feared thunder so.

When the thunder rumbled he headed for high ground. He scratched and slammed against the door until we let him inside. If we weren't home he would travel the mile from Hunter Street to South Main Street to my grandparent's house seeking refuge. Papa and granny would let him inside until the storm had passed. Then they would bring him home.

The funniest thing I ever did to Teco was dress him up in one of Daddy's army shirts. I had found it a duffle bag in the attic. I even tied one of Daddy's old army caps on his head and staged the scene with a toy rifle. I photographed him dressed like GI Joe. The pictures didn't quite do it for Daddy though and he told me to stay out of his army duffle bag. He had been in the Korean War but would never talk about his tour of duty.

I'm not sure if Teco hated cars or their tires or what, but he chased cars passionately. He actually caught a few but automobiles are not easily brought to a screeching halt by a boxer clutching their tires with his mouth. If doggy insurance had been available back in the 1950's and 60's I'm sure Daddy would have purchased it, because Teco had a wing named after him at the animal hospital. Cars wrecked him more times than I can count. He had nine lives like a cat.

One particular time we were in Daytona on vacation for two weeks and Teco landed in the hospital after tangling with a car. He had a really close call that time. Papa told my parents but they decided not to tell me. We lived in Abbeville and Doctor Rogers, the vet, was in Greenwood, twenty or so miles away. Houdini pulled off an escape. Teco ran away while the pen was being cleaned. He was now lost in another town. My parents didn't tell me that my dog had vanished either.

Papa and granny drove all over the place trying to find him. One afternoon they stopped and asked an old black woman had she seen a Boxer Bulldog? She scratched her head and said, 'Lordy mister, how come ya'll got a dog in a box in the first place?' Days passed and no Teco. Papa was trying to figure out how he was going to break the news to me when we arrived home from our vacation.

Just before we returned from our vacation, one of Doctor Rogers helpers was cleaning out the dog pens outside again when out of the blue Teco walked back in the gate. He had been missing for nearly a week. My parents eventually told me what had happened but only after they had made sure Teco was okay and we had been happily reunited.

Cars weren't the only thing that Teco apparently chased. David, our neighbor, the one who got ambushed by Ann from the trash barrel, was riding his bicycle full speed down Hunter Street. Teco broadsided him, sending David over the handlebars, face first onto the pavement.

It knocked out a row of his top front teeth. His mama was none to happy and wanted to have Teco put down. Those were David's permanent teeth she kept saying. They couldn't have been too permanent I thought. Somehow my folks convinced her otherwise. Maybe they paid for his replacement teeth.

All those car and Teco encounters and my dog just kept on ticking like some sort of super dog. He defied all odds, almost. I was in the eighth grade and that would make Teco eight years old or fifty six in dog years. Daddy had taken him to Doctor Rogers, not from a fender bender this time. He had a sore on his tally-wacker that wouldn't heal. He was having a tough time controlling his peeing. Daddy told me he had cancer and was going to have to be put to sleep. Saying bye to a friend is not easy, even for a bulletproof teenager.

Me and Teco sure had our times. It seemed like way too short of time. I cried a lot, when I was alone in my thoughts. The seemingly indestructible Boxer had succumbed to a disease and not a Buick. It's not always easy to rationalize a loss, especially when it's a family member. Somehow I coped and survived. We did have a house dog at the time, Tippy, so I latched on to him to ease the pain. When the thunder rolls, so do the memories. He's on cloud nine now, and I just bet he's not letting the Lord out of his sight.

'If there are no dogs in Heaven,
then when I die I want to go where they went.'
- Will Rogers

Breaking an Arm Ain't That Hard To Do

It's not so unusual to see a kid with his arm, hand, leg or even a foot in a cast. I certainly remember growing up, taking risks and dares, untrained acrobats we were, a time before tuck and roll. Possibly children are just stuntmen in the making. Hey, we may have invented the concept. Seriously, take a moment and think about the stuff you did and survived, unimaginable feats, those only envisioned by dreamers and daredevils. Double and triple dares validated our pecking order in the adolescent food chain. Stupidity reined. Chickens became our world's bottom feeders.

As we grow older, the bones apparently harden, unlike those early days when we're almost rubberized, only capable of succumbing to mere scraps, scratches, bumps and bruises. It must be God's plan to bring us into this world with skin and body oblivious to major damage from tumbles and falls. Think about it. Children first learning to walk do seem to fall all the time, very seldom incurring major injuries. It's almost like they have a memory chip that ensures that they fall backwards on their padded butts. As we grow older, we apparently undergo some sort of rewiring process, often accident prone and more seriously injuring ourselves. By the time we reach ancient, we've totally completed the metamorphose cycle, and all bets being off. We fall and we can no longer get back up, our hips, seemingly becoming our weakest link and prone to break.

Physical inadequacies aren't our only challenge in the trip to adulthood. My childhood was bombarded by tiny invaders, those no see-ums awaiting a chance to transform our ever changing little bodies. Too young to remember, but my parents said whooping cough was first to take a swing at me. It was a formidable foe back in a time before medical miracles had all but wiped it out. Then there was the measles, not just one, but at least two varieties. Thank you. I'll have another; I had both German and what they called back then, Red measles or the regular kind. These were contagious. If one kid got them, mark your calendar, others were sure to follow. Both cause skin rashes. German measles lasted about three days, the other one about a week. We looked polka dotted and played the sympathy card to our advantage one can be assured.

Then there was the dreaded chickenpox. This one was beyond simple rashes and polka dots. I do remember having them. The pockmarks were on my body and in my head. My mama warned me not to scratch them and they itched terribly. That's like telling a kid not wipe his hands on his clothes during a meal. Don't take the Vegas odds that it won't happen. Her warnings were persistent, especially when the marks became scabbed over, a sign that we were just about out of the woods. Scraping off those scabs came at a price, scars. Sadly, I have a few blemishes, the pox last parting shots and an itch that just had to be scratched.

Like the measles, expect other kids to join in on your fun before the epidemic subsided. The good news is you only got the chickenpox once. Unfortunately, having had the chickenpox, I have recently discovered that it saves the best for later. The sneaky culprit apparently remains dormant in the body, battling the immune system attempting to keep it at bay. Later in life, which would be about where I'm at now, it can be reactivated as the shingles. No, this is no mere roofing material. I've watched both my granny and a next door neighbor each suffer through a bout of this dreaded disease. The pain seems unbearable, even the mere touching of clothes can hurt to epic proportions. Oh joy, joy, just hope the ole immune system wins this battle.

Finally, the last one on the childhood check list is the mumps. This one was a common humdinger back in the day before vaccination. My next door cousin got the mumps and he looked like a chipmunk that had crammed his cheeks full with every nut from the tree. This one is painful, so I'm told, swelling up the salivary glands, but that was not the worst fear. As it was told, you didn't want the mumps to so called drop on you, especially if you were a boy. Painful testicular swelling could occur; your nuts would hurt like heck.

My mama sent me next door to play with Cousin Billy daily, wishing this painful disease on me. Her explanation fell on deaf ears but she said she'd rather me catch it as a kid than go through it as an adult. To put it in today's medical terms, males past puberty who develop mumps have a fifteen to twenty percent risk of orchitis, a painful inflammation of the testicles. My immune system must have been operating in overdrive because I never caught the mumps and to this day have never had them. I'm not sure if I'm out of the woods or not. Oh yeah, I do still have my tonsils and appendix and gallbladder, all that extra stuff we have but apparently don't need.

That brings me full circle and back on point, after my illnesses, rambling and discussing broken bones. For the record I can brag that I never broke a single bone in my body during my childhood rearing. Possibly I possessed an overactive immune system that refused to give in to all the opportunities. Boys, more so than girls, have a tendency to try almost anything. We'll jump off of anything, no matter how high, just to show we can. We'll climb stuff never designed to be climbed. This goes way beyond simple tree climbing. We'll stick our hands, fingers or almost any other appendages into contraptions or openings, only withdrawing them if receiving a painful shock or reaction.

I once stuck my head through the wrought iron railing bars on our front porch only to find that I couldn't so easily withdraw it. Ears just aren't meant to be contorted in that manner. I was stuck for quite some time, until my daddy rescued me. I never stuck my tongue to a frozen pole but I am responsible for the dare that got others stuck to one.

Calling out someone as a chicken and playing chicken are two entirely different concepts. A chicken as stated earlier is the one who refuses the stupid challenge by not taking the bait or the dare. One can play chicken in a variety of ways. We would ride our bicycles full throttle directly towards one another, seeing who would veer first. Yeah, many of these lead to terrific crashes, most followed by laughter.

Even then the mantra was enforced, never let them see you sweat or cry, no matter how bloody or in pain you might be. Swapping painful licks to each other's shoulder was a form of playing chicken. Who would cry uncle first? We even played chicken from our gym sets, the a-frame slide and swing sets in the back yard. We would remove the swings and transform the a-frame into a single elongated monkey bar. Now let the game begin.

Combatants hanging by their arms, hand over fist, approached the adversary from the opposite end of the a-frame. The objective was to knock your opponent to the ground with your feet and legs, or crush and/or scare them into submission by wrapping your legs around them. Most of these battles ended in one or the other dropping the couple of feet to the ground or just saying I give. Who would have ever thought there was a third option?

In most of our volleys, boy or girl made no never mind. We were equal opportunist, no discrimination among backyard foes. It was my day to take on the girl, a next door neighbor, a few years younger but ready to dethrone the king. We assumed our positions and then made our way towards the middle. After a couple of quick maneuvers, I had Cheryl firmly in the leg lock around her waist. She didn't give. Instead she continued to squirm, determined to break my hold. Undaunted, I tightened my legs, the mighty python (not Monty Python), showing her who ruled this kingdom.

Without warning and no murmur of I give, she dropped towards the ground so suddenly that I had no chance to unlock my legs. Swinging like a pendulum, her weight broke the hold and she landed quite unladylike on her side. She leapt up, screaming in pain and holding her arm. Crying like a wild banshee she ran home, just next door. The ultimate warrior had broken her arm, or rather the fall had. I had to recant our battle royal for her parents and mine. From hence forth proclaimed the new Ruler of the land, the backyard gym set was to be used as designed; no more acrobatic antics and daredevil feats would be allowed. I retired with my crown in tack.

Some years later, now in junior high, I had distanced myself from my tainted pass and reputation as an arm breaker. I had managed not to break any more of my friend's or foe's appendages. Beware you cannot outrun what is meant to be. During gym period, one of those rainy days when we were in the confines of the school gymnasium, and with no specific directives from our teacher, innovation would not be denied. The gym mats made the perfect stage to wrestle and practice our best grappling moves.

We tussled about; taking turns being counted out until boredom overcame us. We invented a new version of wrestling, an accidental discovery of course. I remained on my knees as several classmates circled the mats and made running and dive bombing passes at me. I attempted to take them down, almost King Kong like, fending off the planes without the Empire State. My catlike prowess kept them at bay. I was defending my kingdom once again.

Billy Red Bowie, with a running start, swooped close; too close, similar to that unfortunate plane attempting to gun down Kong clutching the tower at the top of the building. Caught briefly off guard by the first dive bomber, I twirled just in time to grab at Billy Red's ankle as he passed way too closely. This counteraction caught him by surprise and off balance. He soared through the air in a freefall, not crashing carefree onto the gym mat but instead on the hardwood gym floor. You guessed it; he landed in a precarious position, breaking his elbow, it bending in the opposite direction from its original design. I had broken my second arm, neither belonging to me.

For the years that passed, each and every time I crossed paths with Billy Red, no matter the setting or who was around, he'd make a point to call me out as an arm breaker and recant the episode for the listeners. He did this with a sarcastic smile, no real animosity held towards me. I bet if I saw him this very day, the first thing out of his mouth would be, *'how you doing you old arm breaker?'* Then we'd venture down the nostalgic path and replay it as if it were yesterday. I'm not so sure the girl, Cheryl; my first victim would find the sentimental journey quite so entertaining. Possibly I have broken the jinx or maybe I've just lost my touch. I haven't broken anyone's arm in forty six years. Billy Red Bowie would be unimpressed by my record. Once an arm breaker always an arm breaker; plus he relishes telling that story as much as I enjoy listening to his version. I had put my spin on the saying, 'break a leg', I suppose.

'The world breaks everyone, and afterward, some are strong at the broken places.'
- **Ernest Hemingway**

Myths and Madness
'Ain't no boogers out to night, Grandpa killed them all last night.'

No, this is not grammatically correct but that's the way the song went back in the *way back then* time. It was a game we played and we'd repeat the lyrics as we ventured into the darkness, those places where near pitch blackness awaited us. The Boogeyman might exist and in our young impressionable minds it was safer to weigh on the side of reality than just myth. The game was simple. We took turns, many times on a dare, to venture around the house and through the backyard in the dark. You'd chant, *'Ain't no boogers out to night, Grandpa killed them all last night'*, over and over during your solo journey, hopefully to fend off the boogeyman or whatever else might be out there in the outer reaches of your vivid imagination.

It was an adrenalin rush for sure, that fear of being caught, combined with the thrill of escaping what might be lurking. Of course, one or more of your so called friends would slip around the opposite side of the house and ambush you from the shrubbery or some other concealed location, with growls or banshee yells. You knew it was coming but yet that didn't stop your heart from pounding or quench the surprise. You would haul butt and run back to the front yard. It was fun being scared.

A deviation of this would be for the group to make this journey together, hand in hand, chanting, with one hidden as the boogeyman, ready to bounce. The front porch was the safe base and getting there protected you from the pursuing boogeyman. The slowest and last person often was caught by the boogeyman and now had to take his or her place. If everyone made it back safely, the same kid remained the boogeyman.

Once, a bunch of my cousins were visiting from Adams Run, a curve in the road not far from Charleston, South Carolina and near Edisto Beach. Granny Winn hauled us out in the country to Henry and Jenny's to retrieve a bushel or so of corn. It had gotten dark before we headed back home and dark in the country is darker than any were else known to mankind. Everyone was sitting on and around the front porch, the dim porch light drawing moths by the millions.

Henry decided to spin a yarn for us who didn't know any better. He began telling us about the fierce black bear that lived and prowled the area. I can't remember the specific story but his captive audience was mesmerized and hanging on every word, certainly believing it as factual. When finished and the seed firmly planted, the dares began; who would make a circle around the house? Doing so was the equivalent of going into a black hole. Even the side yards were engulfed in darkness so once you left the safety of the front porch you were on your own. Darkness was not our friend. It existed on the outer reaches of our imagination.

One by one, we took the challenge, Claude, Louie, Donnie and me, even Uncle Jerry. Most of us made that trip in record time. Eventually the adults went inside, but we continued with our daunting challenges. Lee, the youngest cousin, a fiery red head with a tempter to match, was the last kid standing. He hadn't taken a turn yet and was catching it from the rest of us. Relentless peer pressure soon doomed him to his fate. Red would take his turn, bear or no bear.

As those who had gone before him, he cautiously eased around the corner, allowing precious time for his eyes to adjust, not anxious to run head on into the black bear,

Henry's version of our worse fear, an unseen boogeyman. We all heard it, the loud growling of the bear from the backyard. It had snuck up on us undetected, and now we feared it had gotten its claws on Cousin Lee. A streak flashed around the corner, reminiscent of the comic book character, The Flash. I don't think I'd ever seen eyes that big on a human being before. Lee was in an uncontrollable frenzy, attempting to recant his encounter but doing more babbling than making sense. The bear was here, in the backyard and had tried to get him. He had all but felt its hot breath on his neck when it growled and attacked from behind. He had been lucky to escape.

Now we all peered left and right into the darkness and began back peddling up the steps. The adults came back outside after hearing the commotion. Lee recapped the encounter. Henry smiled; assuring us it was gone now. Was there an actual bear or not? We could only go on what we had heard and the story Henry had told us. Needless to say, no amount of peer pressuring or daring was going to cause any of us to take that trip around the house again, not even while chanting, 'Ain't no bears out tonight, Henry killed them all last night.' Looking back now, Henry did make a fine black bear.

There were many other so called mythical creatures in my world. The Easter Bunny made his annual trip, leaving my Easter Basket on the front porch. None of us actually saw the rabbit or knew why he brought us the baskets. Who really cared? It contained all sorts of goodies, end of story. The rabbit was our friend, unlike the bear. Easter also meant I had to dress up in funny looking new church clothes. Mama always wore these big hats. Maybe she thought she was the Easter Rabbit.

The Tooth Fairy was another visitor to our world. He worked from no specific schedule or from the calendar. He somehow knew when we had lost a tooth and had placed it under our pillow. He'd sneak into our bedroom, snatch the tooth and leave us a quarter. I guess that was the going rate for a kid's tooth. No one every explained to me what he was doing with all these teeth. I tried many times to stay awake so that I could catch him, but my attempts were always thwarted by his accomplice, the Sandman. Magical dust in my eyes put me out every time for the count. Same goes for The Easter Bunny and Santa, they had the ability to wait us out and still get the job done. Jack Frost always came nipping too but we never identified him; we only saw the results of his night time work.

Cupid was the Mystery Valentine Marauder. He was one of the few that were actually armed and dangerous, packing a bow and arrow, spreading love supposedly. I never ever saw the winged wonder in a diaper. Possibly he nailed me while I was on those monkey bars in the first grade. Something prompted me with the uncontrollable urge to Kiss Sherry Hall. Yep, I think he played a part in it.

All said, the backyard boogeyman black bear is hard to beat as was the look on ole Red's face priceless. We're all long of tooth now. I wonder if Lee, Louie and Claude remember this episode as vividly as I still do. Perhaps the next time I see them, I'll bring it up and find out. Thank you Henry for making this memorable for me; in my mind the bear will always be a reality. I have no evidence to debunk its existence and that's the way it will remain for me. There was a certain madness to those myths in our lives.

> 'You can't stand up to the night until you understand what's hiding in its shadows.'
> **~Charles De Lint**

Don't Peek out the Window, Something Might be Peeking Back

Monsters are real. Well, they were in my day. My name is Tommy and yes, I am a horror movie addict. Today's blood and gore in vivid color can't hold a candle to some of those black and white classics of my childhood. Now, modern day vampires battle Werewolves for supremacy of the planet. I grew up fearing only one vampire and one Wolf Man. Late at night you never ever chanced peeking through the blinds or a curtain, especially if you thought you heard something outside. My worst nightmare; something would be on the other side of that window looking back, nose pressed against it, teeth snarling, big ole red eyes hinting it was meal time, me on the menu.

Count Dracula and the Wolf Man, only once do I ever remember them sharing the billing, and that was in the flick *Abbott and Costello meet Frankenstein*. That one was a humdinger, even for a comedy, having the Frankenstein Monster, the Wolf Man and Count Dracula appearing in the very same film. For good measure the Invisible Man made a vocal cameo at the very end of the spoof, voiced by Vincent Price. Price had previously played the no-see-um in other movies, so acting invisible came quite natural. Obviously I didn't see this flick during its original release in 1948, a few years ahead of my arrival through the birthing canal, but I still caught the reruns on *Shock Theater*, a Saturday afternoon monster matinee on local television. The film was considered to be the swan song for the "Big Three" Universal horror monsters. Still who could forget Boris Karloff as the Frankenstein Monster, Lon Chaney Jr.

as the Wolf Man and Bella Lugosi as Count Dracula?

Universal had about all the great monsters back then, including the Mummy, Jekyll & Hyde and eventually, The Creature from the Black Lagoon. I confess. The first time I watched the *Creature from the Black Lagoon*, I watched it alone and in broad daylight, and I was afraid to go outside afterwards. I didn't even live near a lagoon or a swamp or anything larger than a creek. Two other movies impacted me similarly; the original versions of War of the Worlds and King Kong. Invaders from space were just too real to discount. I wasn't afraid of King Kong but the claymation antics just mesmerized me. I still love to watch any old movie utilizing this technique.

I'm not so taken by today's computer generated creatures. For one thing, they have moves that just aren't consistent with reality on any level. Computer generated anomalies jump too high, run too fast and just leave too much on the plate for my imagination to be utilized. I liked it better when the monsters of my day at least offered a little hope, that chance you might just outrun them or successfully hide. Why is it today that those who hide don't just stay hidden? No, they have to come out of hiding way too soon and then they're history. Just stay in the closet, under the bed or behind something. Venturing out will just get you killed.

If I ever escaped one of my childhood monsters and found the perfect hiding place, I'd not venture out until I knew it was daylight. My Dracula and Wolf Man couldn't get you by the light of day. It wouldn't save you from the Frankenstein Monster but fire could be a deterrent. I don't like what my favorite monsters have become today. Vampires venture out into the light, live somewhat normal lives and can transform into grotesque fiends. Count Dracula used to be almost normal, at least in appearance, fearing the sun, crucifixes, holy water, garlic and those wooden stakes. Part of the suspense was the vampire having to return to his or her coffin before dawn and those attempting to locate their hiding place before darkness fell once again. Dracula didn't possess super human strength but you better never stare into those eyes. And he transformed women into vampires. There was none of this man on man crap. The women were spellbinding, alluring Sirens, quite voluptuous in many cases. I miss my vampires.

The Wolf Man was just as intriguing. Lon could not control the change or change at will. He agonized over the pending change heading his way. Only under the shine of the full moon did his hair go wild and those fangs and claws transform from human ones. It's funny though how no matter what he was wearing just before the full moon; he ended up in the same ole shirt, pants and rope belt. He tended to dress down before the change. The Wolf Man always killed his victims, unlike Dracula who would occasionally transform one of his. You didn't have a band of werewolves running amuck. You only had to deal with one at a time; not hordes of them.

Oh yeah, the monsters never won. You knew in the end that they would be destroyed or at least you'd be left with a cliffhanger, often casting doubt as to whether they really got their creature or not. I was so enthralled by my monsters that I even had models of each. Ah yes, I had the Wolf Man, Count Dracula, The Frankenstein Monster, The Mummy and the Creature from the Black Lagoon on display in my room. Assorted parts came in a box. You followed instructions and assembled the numerous parts with glue to build and then hand paint a perfect specimen, each erected in some sort of related scene from the movies. These were spin-offs of the car and airplane type assemblies. Shameless plug time, I referenced these in my novel, *Dark Thirty*. Pick up your copy today and read the rest of the story.

Similar to the afternoon *Shock Theater* on Saturdays was another local telecast, Friday nights' eleven thirty time slot, *Inferno*. It broadcast reruns of old classics from the dusty vaults. The opening scene depicted a bodiless head floating and wavering about, engulfed in flames. I can still quote the intro precisely from memory; no Googling required I assure you.

'Come in. I've been waiting for you. Venture with me into a world of strangeness, a world where reality slips past you like sand in an hourglass; Inferno, the meeting place of the supernatural and the unknown.' A creepy long winded laugh ensued before going to the opening credits of the featured movie. And yes, I was allowed to stay up and watch them, even if sleeping with the light on was required afterwards. *Inferno* didn't showcase any of the Universal Monsters. I guess there was some sort of copyright or proprietary protection in place. Fridays were reserved for the more bizarre cult type classics.

Boris Karloff even hosted a weekly horror show in his waning days as a movie monster actor. His American anthology series aired on NBC in the early sixties. Karloff had a brief opening monologue, introducing a mix of macabre horror tales and suspense thrillers. These were made for television versions. Karloff had such a distinctive voice, one you could always identify, similar to that of Vincent Price, another one of my favorite actors who played an array of villains in horror films. *House on Haunted Hill, the Fly* and *The Abominable Dr. Phibes* come to mind. Price could be quite theatrical and Shakespearian in many of his roles. Karloff of course played the Frankenstein Monster to Bella Lugosi's bearded Igor in those early classics.

Who could forget the true ringmaster, Rod Serling and the original Twilight Zone on CBS from 1959 until 1964? You want to talk about weekly television features that could traumatize a young impressionable mind; his were landmark breakthroughs. The music, you could be in another room and hear that unmistakable music and know what was coming on the TV. I'd rush to take my place, ringside. Then there was that weekly intro to go along with the music and the scenes on the screen.

There is a fifth dimension, beyond that which is known to man. It is a dimension as vast as space and as timeless as infinity. It is the middle ground between light and shadow, between science and superstition, and it lies between the pit of man's fears and the summit of his knowledge. This is the dimension of imagination. It is an area which we call the Twilight Zone. — Rod Serling

Looking back on the reruns, I am amazed by the star quality that filled the episodes. The series was quite notable for featuring established stars like Joan Blondell, Ann Blyth, Buster Keaton, Burgess Meredith, Ed Wynn and younger actors who would become more famous later like Veronica Cartwright, Bill Bixby, William Shatner, Leonard Nimoy, Robert Duvall, Mariette Hartley, Burt Reynolds, Dennis Hopper, Robert Redford. Serling served as executive producer and head writer; he wrote or co-wrote 92 of the show's 156 episodes. He was also the show's host and narrator. His opening and closing narrations usually summarized the episode's events and explained how and why the main characters had entered the Twilight Zone.

After the Twilight Zone sadly ran its course, Rod eventually emerged again with his new version series, *Night Gallery*. Sort of like Karloff's *Thriller*, it was also an American anthology. It aired on NBC from 1970 to 1973, featuring stories of horror and the macabre. Serling appeared in an art gallery setting and introduced the macabre tales that made up each episode by unveiling paintings that depicted the stories. *Night Gallery* regularly presented adaptations of classic fantasy tales by authors such as H. P. Lovecraft, as well as original works by Serling himself. The series first aired as pilot in 1969. A young Steven Spielberg directed it and Joan Crawford appeared in one of her last acting roles. *Night Gallery* was scary but not nearly as terrifying as the *Twilight Zone*. Serling didn't get to summarize the ending in a closing monologue. The camera would usually just focus on the final scene or image then go black.

Then there was *The Outer Limits*. You want to talk bizarre. Like the original Twilight Zone it began with an unforgettable opening to each episode.

There is nothing wrong with your television set. Do not attempt to adjust the picture. We are controlling transmission. If we wish to make it louder, we will bring up the volume. If we wish to make it softer, we will tune it to a whisper. We will control the horizontal. We will control the vertical. We can roll the image, make it flutter. We can change the focus to a soft blur or sharpen it to crystal clarity. For the next hour, sit quietly and we will control all that you see and hear. We repeat: there is nothing wrong with your television set. You are about to participate in a great adventure. You are about to experience the awe and mystery which reaches from the inner mind to – The Outer Limits.

It always ended the same way, with the same voice saying, *we now return control of your television set to you. Until next week at the same time, when the control voice will take you to – The Outer Limits.*

The original and best version aired in the 1960's. Sure it resurfaced in syndication on Showtime and the Sci Fi channels between 1995 and 2002, but to me it had lost its luster. Sometimes you just can't improve on perfection. Its stories were pure science fiction, unlike those of Serlings. You can still catch episodes of the latter version on the Chiller channel.

Tales from the Crypt tossed its skull into the arena in 1989 on HBO. I remember collecting the comic book series in the 1950's and beyond. Airing on HBO, the episodes didn't have to worry about censorship. That upped the ante. Graphic violence, gore, profanity and nudity now became common practice. My classic black and white versions were gone forever, replaced by the bloodier the better. Slasher crap such as Friday the Thirteenth, Halloween and Nightmare on Elm Street would soon follow. I liked the first couple in each series but then it just got old and predictable. The original Texas Chain Saw Massacre was a classic but too much Leather Face can just gets lost in translation.

I'm still a sucker for Alfred Hitchcock reruns. Birds and Psycho did a number on me. He would sneak in a scene in almost every movie. It was a game to watch for his appearance. Somewhere in the background he'd make a cameo. Hitchcock had a series too. I always tuned into *Alfred Hitchcock Presents*, his weekly show. The opening theme music was off the chart as was his first words each episode as only he could speak them, 'Good Evening.' There are two episodes that I will never forget, *The Jar* and *The Monkey's Paw*.

    Yep, there was a time when I was afraid of things that go bump in the dark. Strange creatures waited underneath my bed for me to dangle an arm or leg. An evil creature could lurk in the shadows just waiting for an opportunity to claim you as its very own. I loved every minute of it and it never deterred me from watching more scary movies. Halloween is my most favorite holiday. Visiting alleged haunted houses and cemeteries was my passion growing up in Abbeville. No I didn't visit them alone. There is such a thing as safety in numbers. Shameless Plug Alert!!! It inspired my fictitious novel, *The Perfect Spook House*, with Abbeville and an old house down the Cedar Springs Road as the backdrop. I'm Tom and I have a horror movie addiction…

Here are a few of my favorite monster movie quotes.
See if you remember any of them.

"Look! It's moving. It's alive. It's alive… It's alive, it's moving, it's alive, it's alive, it's alive,
it's alive, IT'S ALIVE!"
Frankenstein (1931)

"I think we'll start with a reign of terror."
The Invisible Man (1933)

"Let's let our friend here rest in peace…while he can."
The Curse of Frankenstein (1957)

"Help me! Help meeeee!"
The Fly (1958)

"We all go a little mad sometimes."
Psycho (1960) (Norman Bates)

"Love means never having to say you're ugly."
The Abominable Dr. Phibes (1971)

"He-e-e-e-re's Johnnie!"
The Shining (1980)

"They're Heee-re."
Poltergeist (1982)

"I'll go check it out."
First Dead Guy in every slasher flick.

"I've seen enough horror movies to know that any weirdo wearing a mask is never friendly."
Friday the 13th Part VI: Jason Lives (1986) (Elizabeth)

"That cold ain't the weather, that's death approaching."
30 Days of Night (2007)

Smokey Mountain High

1963, and an only grandchild, ten years old, a week in The Great Smokey Mountains with your grand parents, with no parents tagging along, I couldn't dream up a better gig, could you? Bryson City, near the Cherokee Indian Reservation had been their vacation choice, always staying at the same vacation spot with family log cabins backed up against a babbling stream filled with trout. It was called an efficiency because it came equipped with a kitchen.

A huge ominous black bear statue trademarked the Smokey Mountain Lodge on the front lawn. My luck, it came with a pool too. Better still, I caught whiff that Jerry Mathers, the Beaver from *Leave it to Beaver* fame, would be appearing in Frontier Land, a theme park with an authentic fort and western town. I had all the entertainment I needed or so I thought.

Meeting the Beaver turned out to be a bust, a major disappointment. I had envisioned meeting Wally's little brother and instead The Beaver ended up being a foot taller than me, pimple faced and overweight. Dressed as a gunslinger he did perform in a western shoot out as one of the good guys, but still he had not been who I had expected to see. I left Beaver to the Indians.

I still had the pool but unfortunately mama hadn't packed my swim trunks. I suppose she thought you couldn't swim in the mountains. That made my granny extremely happy. I pouted and pitched a fit until the lodge manager rounded me up a pair of trunks, several sizes too large, but beggars can't be choosey. Three minutes in the water and the manager of the lodge told granny not to worry; I could swim like a fish. That still didn't comfort granny. Papa slapped his knee, satisfied I was next of kin to a tadpole.

There's just so much swimming a kid in oversized swim trunks in an undersized pool can do by himself before boredom sets in. One other family had a kid, a cute girl, dark skinned, brown eyed and my age, but she wasn't as fond of the water as me. This didn't prevent my papa from razing me about her. He tried to play match maker and almost convinced me to fall in love with her, but then they checked out and again I found myself surrounded by adults.

We had done the Cherokee Reservation, the Fontana Dam boat ride and had ventured into Smokey Mountain Park in search of wild bears. Too many days remained on the family vacation and boredom again sharpened its claws with me in its vicious grip. It takes a lot to keep me occupied. I spotted a helicopter ride. I'd never ridden in anything that flies. Granny drew her line in the sand when it came to letting me ride in a helicopter. Pouting and fit pitching didn't work. She countered with a nervous spell, her adult version of pouting and pitching a fit. The copter option was off the table.

The lodge employed this old Cherokee Indian caretaker and papa would sit around in the afternoons with him and swap old man stories. I think they tried to one up one another. I couldn't really tell when the truth stretched into fantasy. I don't think either of them cared. It made for good entertainment for them and me. Papa found out that the old Indian was really terrified of cats for some superstitious reason I can not remember. Papa knew how to play the game and milk the moment, so he quickly saw his next venue for attack.

He began by telling the old Indian of how cats could sense when someone didn't like them. He went on and on, citing incidences of this and that. An old black stray resided at the lodge and the Old Indian always gave it wide berth.

Now if the truth be known, papa didn't really care for cats either. He didn't fear them like the Indian, but he had no real use for them. Cats simply didn't contribute and were useless critters, until that night anyway. Sitting around in the large wooden rockers after dark, in the ambiance of the little courtyard's flood lights, he and the Indian began their ritual of swapping tales, country boy versus the reservation, their version of Cowboys and Indians I suppose.

Papa wove this story about how he had seen a cat take a knife and cut this old codger because the cat knew the man hated it. A kitty cat if given the chance and a sharp knife would seek out the one that mistreats or dislikes it, so papa explained. I could tell that the old Indian didn't like where this one was headed but I'll hand it to him, he held his ground. He wasn't going to be outdone by a crusty old paleface.

I wondered if the old Indian had once been a chief or great warrior because to save face, he called my papa on it, all but politely calling him a liar. That played into papa's hands. Papa didn't have many teeth in his mouth but what he had made for an almost jack-a-lantern smile. His counter part had taken the bait. Hooked, he was now reeling in the Indian. I watched and waited, glued to the story playing out; knowing papa had something sneaky up his sleeves.

He summoned the cat calling kitty, kitty, kitty. Apparently cats can't resist some one repeating kitty three times in a smooth and charming good ole country voice. The black cat hurried to Papa's side and began doing what cats do, rubbing along his legs and purring up a storm. I immediately saw fear in the old Indian's eyes just from the cat's arrival. He wanted to leave but stood his ground. This was going to be good.

Papa always carried a pocket knife. He pulled the knife

from his pant's pocket, opened the largest blade and then stuck the knife in the dirt between him and the old Indian, sitting less than four feet away. The Indian's eyes appeared so large that I do believe he could have auditioned for the part of Little Orphan Annie and would have landed it. Just what was papa up to; I hadn't quite figured out this one.

Papa repeated the story about how a cat could sense his enemy and that if given the opportunity it would grab the knife and turn on that person. I could see the brave original American now squirming in his seat. He did not wish to believe what papa spoke as the truth. I waited for him to say paleface spoke with forked tongue but he didn't. He held challenged papa, calling his bluff.

Papa scooped up the cat in his lap and began rubbing the purring feline. I had never seen papa show any affection to a cat. This was almost scary on its own. He began talking to the black cat, asking it if there was anyone here that it disliked. Papa positioned the cat so that it appeared to be eyeing the Indian. I saw the Indian swallow deeply and then lick his lips. He didn't like this one little bit. Papa sure enjoyed milking the moment.

Papa positioned the cat over the top of the knife. The Indian leaned back in his chair to distance himself from the feline. Papa then whispered for the cat to seek out the one that hated him the most. He then grabbed the cat by the tail, allowing it to sway and dangle freely above the knife. The cat made a protesting shrill like scream and immediately clamped its front paws on the knife's handle. Papa assisted by lifting the cat up so that old Tom now swung wildly by its tail, knife still clutched firmly between its clawed paws.

In one fluid motion the Indian tilted backwards in the rocker, flipped over backwards, and high tailed it for the front office. Papa released the cat; it dropped the knife and shot off in the opposite direction. He cackled with delight, slapped his knees. I laughed too, still not fully understanding what I had just witnessed.

Papa explained if you dangle a cat by its tail, instinct kicks in and it closes its front paws on anything within reach. The knife just happened to be conveniently positioned. He made me promise to keep his little secret and not tell granny, so I did until now. It was cruel to snatch that cat up by the tail. It was still just too funny.

I never saw the Indian or the cat the remainder of our stay. That was the best vacation I had ever experienced. It made up for being disappointed about the Beaver. I still wish I could have ridden in that helicopter. Granny actually did the next year. Papa snitched on her. She said it just went up and set right back down, but I never let her live that down, her riding and me not. Mountain memories had been made, another papa episode for the books, Papa and Indians, priceless.

'Great men are rarely isolated mountain peaks;
they are the summits of ranges.'
*- **Thomas W. Higginson***

A Pig's Tale

As families grow, it often becomes tough and expensive to buy everyone a Christmas gift. Some revert to drawing names and buying only one gift, but at least everybody gets one, unless that favorite uncle forgot to bring his. Sometimes families just limit it to buying gifts for the kids, each drawing a kid's name, putting a limit on the dollar value of course to keep it Even Stevens. We have even chosen to forgo the gift swapping and have bought toys for a pre-selected charity such as Toys for Tots.

Some have an Angel Tree, names of specific less fortunate children, their age, gender and clothes sizes listed on each tree ornament. Flat out donations are the way to go, choosing a cause like Ronald McDonald House and allowing everyone who wishes to contribute. These are just a few ways for families to celebrate that time of year; but wait, there are other ways to celebrate and/or tarnish that Christmas cheer. There's our way.

A popular, or maybe not so popular, game played at many Christmas gatherings these days is where everyone brings a gift and then based on the number of gifts which equate to the number of participants, the numbers are written on separate pieces of paper. Then each person draws a number, 1 to 20 let's say for the sake of argument. The number represents your pecking order in the game; the higher number the better your chances in this case. If you're lucky #1, you go first and select any of the 20 wrapped or bagged gifts. Lucky, I don't think so.

Player #1 opens the gift, revealing what has been selected. Excitement over with, the player with #2 on his or her paper goes next. Options are to select any of the remaining 19 gifts or confiscate player one's goody if you like what you see. Player #1 then has to pick another gift, setting up the arrival of player #3 in the game. You get it; take what's behind door number one or what you already see on the stage. This game can be fun if you don't have an overwhelming amount of people playing. Endless is not so joyful, leading to boredom and people seeking out the spiked eggnog. It can also be agonizing to watch your favorite gift change hands, helpless to do anything about it. Sometimes this can lead to not so merry hard feelings.

Enough of the warm and fuzzy fluff, traditions are different in most families and the evolution of the Christmas spirit can often mutate into unimaginable yet intriguing realms; innovation run amuck. Such was that time in my life growing up in L.A., tis the season at my grandparents' mill house down South Main, Lower Abbeville, just a few houses past the train trestle. There were those on the Bowie side of the family that were devious come Christmas time. I should know. It's in my genes too, the gift and curse combo again.

The saying goes that there are often surprises in small packages. Not necessarily. Bigger can hold its own at our gathering and it doesn't always equate to better; been there, done it. In the day before gift bags, everything and I do mean everything, was basically wrapped in a box. There were exceptions; those things that wouldn't fit into a conventional box. But what is a box? It is a mere vessel for containing that special gift, right? Wrong!

Let us begin with Cousin Billy Joe; it's a southern thing having two names attached to your last. Every family has the alpha prankster. Billy Joe indeed wore that crown in ours. I learned from the best and eventually ranked a close second. Presents were never what they seemed. Santa had a nice, a naughty and a nutty list. We learned quickly that if the gift tag stated From: Santa, be on guard and be very afraid. Santa was not necessarily your friend, nor was he bringing what you had asked him to bring you. Santa's helpers were never to be trusted.

Almost guaranteed, what was inside could be anyone's guess and not something that should be opened in the company of others. Most had a subliminal catch. Daddy once got an elephant sized pair of lady's panties and another time, a banana with two pecans strategically arranged in the box; use your imagination for this one. Papa opened his. It contained a rake sized comb. He had not a hair on his head. Once he received one of those wind up sets of chattering teeth. His mouth was toothless. Note the theme and hang on to your britches; it's going to be a wild ride.

Billy Joe set the tone for these types of gag oriented gifts, but others quickly landed on the bandwagon; raising the bar to be expected each Christmas. We gathered in the front room where the silver Christmas tree took center stage. It had one of those multicolor rotating lights shining on it. The front room was one of only four rooms in granny and papa's house, hardly ever used except for Christmas or when they had sleep over company. It doubled as a bedroom, a couch with a hide-away bed.

Mama's ill fated attempt to make fig preserves offered the perfect venue for Christmas glee. The homemade jam was petrified inside the pint jars. Nothing short of a stick of dynamite was going to free it. With the jam and the jars ruined, what else was there to do but to give them as Christmas gifts to friends and family? It made the dreaded fruit cake look like an exquisite delicacy. The fun did not end here. The jars were squirreled away and circulated many Christmas's to come; the jelly that kept on giving, incredibly uneatable.

A favorite gimmick was to wrap up someone's personal possessions; embarrassing items or articles of clothing, often those worn and threadbare vintage pair of underwear. Once Billy Joe received a pair of his with well staged skid marks, an artful masterpiece I must admit. Oh yeah, we definitely got our revenge countless times on the original instigator of gag gifts. Another great trick, sign the *From* by someone else other than Santa, and then you got a two-for, the expression on both their faces being priceless for sure.

Fake doggie do or up chuck in a jewelry box was always a show stopper. Granny was a good target. The electrical corncob made the perfect bathroom accessory. Get an elder to explain the significance of a corncob equipped with a plug in electrical cord if you don't quite get the gag. It was an alternative to the Sears catalog in the good ole days of outhouses. Two holes were for community use with a friend and the one-hole variety ensured privacy. I preferred the latter one. Cousin Jenny and Henry had one for many years, as I recall from those trips to their house in the county. Sorry, the nostalgic road trip is speckled with potholes and numerous forks in the road that tend to get me sidetracked and off course.

A risqué red pair of lady's laced crotch-less lingerie with fake female genitalia always made its rounds each Christmas. Santa did not discriminate. A male or female could be the recipient. I think we all received it at least once. Another gift triggered the rubber snake inside to move when the lid was opened; screaming allowed. Laughing, screaming and turned up noses were common around our Christmas tree of wonders.

One of the best gimmicks was the endless box. Open the first box then numerous ones to follow, each inside the other. Starting with something large enough to hold a bowling ball might end up matchbox sized by the end of the journey and hold nothing very special. I implemented a derivative of this box by wrapping the gag endlessly with an assortment of materials, including tinfoil. I still have vintage soundless Super 8 footage of Billy Joe experiencing my greatest creation while chatting away on the silent screen. I would have given anything for sound back then.

Possibly the greatest gag of all circulated not just at the Bowie gatherings but at the Winn, the Campbells and any others offering an audience each year. The size of the box varied. Sometimes it was from Santa; other times from a person present at the party. The giver had to keep the receiver off their guard. The element of surprise was crucial to the delivery. The reaction was always priceless. How this single object survived from Christmas to Christmas paid credence to the almost shrine like homage and recognition bestowed it. It seemed to get better with age and that in its self was a huge accomplishment.

The infamous pig's tail was a legend among the gag gift world. Where's the pork? We're talking the real deal, right off of old Porky Pig's butt. Billy Joe came up with the idea after his dad slaughtered a pig at his farm. As they say, nothing goes to waste on a pig but the oink. Everything else is edible. I'm still not sure how Billy Joe pried the tail from Mr. Campbell's clutches. I think the old man was a bit of a jokester too. I remember many a trip to their place; where else…out in the country.

The pink tail adorning a red ribbon was always placed on and under pretty paper. You wanted the person to peel back the paper, their fingers being as close to the tail as possible to obtain the best reaction. Ah yes. I have some of those moments captured on Super 8 too. Billy Joe requested the proud owner of the prize to return it to him. Usually that was met with no opposition. He'd simply preserve it by placing it in the freezer and serve it up to someone else the next Christmas.

Those receiving the surprise eventually caught on to his

little devious plan and began keeping the pig tail. Possession is nine tenths of the law, right? A pig in the freezer is worth more than a pig in a poke. Per Google: Pig in a poke refers to a confidence trick originating in the late middle ages when meat was scarce. The scheme entailed the sale of a suckling pig or pup in a poke (bag). The bag would actually contain a cat or dog (not particularly prized as a source of meat), which was sold to the victim in an unopened bag. Now you know the rest of story so would say Paul Harvey.

I might just have to find a pig's tail and rekindle the tradition. There are those today who haven't experienced a real gag gift before. I can almost envision those potential expressions. A pig's tail, hamming it up at a Christmas near you…

"Th-th-th-that's all folks!"

The Constant Gardener

Sometimes destiny chooses one's course or maybe the genes just eventually kick in; either way I had never been much interested in gardening while growing up. Maybe it was just a kid thing or my southern primal instincts had not yet developed. Either way, it wasn't because I wasn't exposed to it at an early age; often forced to do gardening chores, moaning and complaining the entire time. Mama had told me she was the same way growing up; hated it. So maybe the genes were in force from her; the deeper rooted ones hadn't mutated yet. Papa and granny sure believed in having a garden, but one must remember they grew up in times where having one put food on the table; it wasn't just a hobby.

Living in their mill house on South Main, the small yard didn't offer a great spot for having a garden, especially when much of the back yard was taken up by a chicken pen and a pile of coal used for the cast iron stove for heating the house. Chickens weren't raised as a hobby or for pets either. With chicken you had eggs and deep fried delights occasionally. Where we lived on Hunter Street, we had several acres, the back forty so to speak, butting up against the Langley Milliken School yard. This made the perfect spot for papa to plant a garden. He had one of those front tine tillers and soon had cleared off the perfect spot in the far right back corner of our property. There he cultivated his master piece.

On the garden menu: Marion tomatoes, pickling sized cucumbers, yellow crookneck squash, bell, banana and cayenne peppers, okra, speckled butter beans, pinkeye purple hull peas, green snapping beans, onions, radishes, red beets and white potatoes. In late summer, when everything had pretty much been picked over or withered by summer's heat, all was cleared and then turned under to plant greens (a mixture of turnip, mustard, kale and rape), collard plants and sometimes cabbage. There were always green onions available. My mouth is watering thinking about them. I'm ready for black skillet cornbread.

Early mornings and late afternoons the familiar sound of Papa's 1961 Chevy Apache 10 pickup could be heard as it rattled by the house heading to his garden spot. A pre-teenager, I dreaded that sound because he'd surely expect me to help with the planting, watering or picking, no fun at all. Once planted, he'd haul countless buckets of water in the bed of that truck because there was no water source nearby. It would have taken five hundred or more feet of hose pipe to reach it from the nearest spigot. Hose pipe and spigot are southern terms for garden hose and faucet for those readers originating from northern regions. Learn it, breath it, live it and stop trying to change it, if you reside here now. Sorry, a slight derailment rant session; southern privilege.

Planting that perfect garden and in papa and granny's eyes it was just that, consisted of a few simple rules. Once the ground had been tiled numerous times, removing all newly discovered rocks and smoothing out the dirt, then came laying-off the rows. Papa did this with a plum line. He'd stake the starting end of the row and then attach the string to it and roll it out to the opposite end where he'd stake that end too, making sure the string was pulled tight. He'd align his front tine tiller and follow in a straight line just to the right of the string. He'd repeat this process, spacing between rows contingent on the type of crop being planted and how much room they needed to spread out once the plants were full grown. When done, every row was straight as an arrow. People were in awe of his perfect rows. He'd already mapped out which types of seed were to be planted in which rows. His perfected madness came with a method.

Planting by the signs was a critical part of that Good Friday garden event and yes, Good Friday was always the targeted date, unless hampered by rainy or cold weather conditions. Papa planted by the signs. He went strictly by the Farmer's Almanac and moon to guide him in his planting. Top crop and root crop were never ever planted at the same time. Clarification: Potatoes and peanuts were root crops; being that they grow beneath the dirt and you pull dirt up around the growing plants forming mounds for them to produce. Beans, okra, tomato, pepper and so on; anything picked from the plant above ground was top crop. The moon's monthly cycle impacted the success of producing a bountiful crop. Funny, Papa couldn't read so I wondered how he followed the Almanac. I discovered later that one of his overhauled cronies would read it to him or if all else failed; he'd just follow the moon.

Sometimes preparing the soil required heading out into the country and hauling manure. Chicken or *Toby* seemed to be the best. I've shoveled my fair share of both, kicking and screaming the entire time. Digging, planting and fertilizing done; it became a watering and waiting game until those first seed sprigs pushed through the ground and sprouted green life into those straight rows. Weeding and pulling dirt up around the plants was done several times a week.

Granny simply loved digging in the dirt for whatever reason. Give her a hoe and she was a happy camper. I almost said happy hoer but that didn't quite sound right. Papa had made her a special one due to her bad leg. It had an extra long handle so that she didn't have to bend quite as much. I still have the very same hoe, the original long handle in tack, weathered and used, anointed with love and care.

Papa's teachings fell on deaf ears when I was a kid. He'd tell me stuff like choosing Marion tomato plants because maters were the right eating size and had plenty of acid in them. Merit corn was planted because it had the least amount of silk and was easy to shuck from the cob. He preferred planting pinkeye purple hull peas because they were easier to shell and he just liked the taste better. He always planted bush speckled butterbeans but climbing green beans; not sure why. A teepee shaped formation of cane poles were used for the bean runners to climb.

Wire baskets fabricated by him were placed over the tomato plants. He preferred this to staking them. The baskets kept the plants upright. Open on one end, the plants could grow tall and spread their leafy branches. He and granny ate bell and banana peppers, didn't eat cayenne, but it was used to season stuff. Mama and I loved hot peppers. It had to be crookneck yellow squash even though there was a straight neck version. I never knew why he chose one over the other; wish now that I would have asked him.

Gardening held no interest to me. I was over it from the get go; guess having been forced into child labor one too many times had shied me away from it. Let's fast forward to the early 1980's. As a man now in my thirties, I had bought a house with over five acres in the country. Out of nowhere, defying explanation, I decided I wanted to plant my very first garden.

Well, there was but one set of experts to assist me in this major challenge. I told papa and granny what I thought I wanted to do and they beamed with delight. Their only grandson had come to his senses, jumping the mama generation, and was ready to follow down a traditional path. First, we had to pick the spot. Second, I would need my very own tiller. Papa knew where to get the perfect knock-off brand over in Lincolnton, Georgia for a mere $199, not cheap based on my budget back then.

Breaking up that rock infested ground was more than I had bargained for; the more I tilled the more rocks I found. How could one patch of ground have so many? Eventually we de-rocked the landscape as best we could and with papa's guidance we utilized the plum line to make those rows straight. Planting that first one was no easy task, let me tell you, just as hard and tiresome as I remembered. He was one proud papa though and I must admit, my chest was pushed out just a tad too.

That didn't compare to the first time I laid eyes on the plant life first poking through the dirt. Those little green sprouts were my doing, ours actually, but my garden just the same. From that very moment I was hooked. I guess that's the way it is supposed to be. Just like granny and papa, I was destined to dig in the dirt from now on. No one was prouder than papa. Granny was beaming too.

Just because I had sprouts didn't mean I could just sit back and watch the garden grow, so to speak. A vicious battle was wagered, me against the weeds; more tilling and hoeing to fend off the unwanted invaders. Later I learned the meaning of side dressing; spreading fertilizer along the edges of the rows and blending it into the soil. I was becoming quite the seasoned sod buster.

Nothing beats picking that first thing from the garden, realizing that you did this. Over the years my garden just got longer and wider. I tried to grow a little bit of almost everything. I eventually got rid of the bone jolting front tine tiller and bought me a Troy Built Horse. If you could walk, you could plow; the best investment I had ever made, gardening for dummies. Papa never experienced this investment unfortunately, having passed before I bought it.

In those early years he was forever teaching me the ways of gardening, like whipping my okra. No, you didn't do this and scream 'bad okra.' Cutting off the bottom leaves was called whipping it, and by doing so it was supposed to promote okra growth. Guess the plant's energy could focus on the blooms and okra, not the fruitless limbs. Mister Jim Creswell had introduced me to Tommy-toe tomatoes when I was just a kid. These are what many call grape tomatoes; delicious plop'um in your mouth sized ones. I've always had them in my garden.

Some traditions eventually fell by the wayside. I don't use a plum line or necessarily go by the signs when planting mine. My rows can be quite crooked but I call it adding character to my garden. As for the signs, I had to explain to papa numerous times, the signs were right for me to plant when I had the time to do it. He always frowned but gave me a pass, just happy that I was gardening.

Harvesting was another labor intensive chore. Picking, plucking and cutting, filling those woven baskets and then bringing them inside, was part of the ritual. Shelling parties were not uncommon. The women folk took the lead but the guys participated. Everyone had a pan and filled it with butterbeans or peas, shelled until you filled it and then you dumped it in a larger pan and started over again, until all that was left was a trash can full of shelled husks.

They were washed and blanched, bagged and placed in the freezer, always marking the date on the bags. Blanched means cooking them just a tad before freezing them; the color transformation from dark to light would tip you off the blanching was successful. Granny canned green beans, peeled and stewed tomatoes and beets in mason jars utilizing a pressure cooker. Okra could be cut and frozen in freezer bags; same for corn on the cob.

As in hunting, harvesting the garden crop is not for greenhorns. As one story goes, my brother-in-law, Jerry Solomon, was given the opportunity and permission by the garden owner, to pick a mess of turnip salad; and pick he did. He left little for a reoccurring crop, pulling the greens up by the roots, instead of plucking off mature leaves. The gardener was livid to say the least.

Jerry made a grave error while mowing granny's lawn once. She had a nice stand of spring onions in a spot in the backyard. Now these onions had some history to them. Granny had swapped some Thrift from her front yard with another lady for a handful of onion bulbs, the parent onions some fifty years old. The trick to replenishing and having an endless supply of onions is to allow some of them to go to *taunters*, actually allowing the onions to produce more bulbs on the green stems. Don't Google *taunters*; it was a Granny word. You then simply replant the new bulbs. Jerry, mistaking them for wild onions, mowed them to the ground. Granny experienced flashbacks from the time daddy trimmed her huge snowball bush to the ground while it was in full bloom.

My in-laws are fodder for good stories. I once planted

a crop of snow peas. When the pods are plump and ripe for picking, I often shell a few while walking about in the garden and pop the little raw green peas in my mouth; good eating. I shared a few with my sister-in-law, Charlotte while strolling between the rows one afternoon. As we made our way through the garden, I didn't notice that she had plucked a couple of butterbean pods from plants, until I heard a spitting sound from behind. Sadly she was raised on a farm and should have known better. Papa taught me better. I wasn't raised on a farm. Eating raw butterbeans… seriously?

Gardening, you either love doing it or you don't. If you don't, stick to grocery shopping. Granny and Papa loved digging in the dirt. I dig dirt too. I didn't at first but it grew on me. I'm smiling again and it fills pretty doggone good. Miss and love you both granny and papa; bet you are the Lord's best gardeners now. Digging in the dirt is digging in the dirt.

'In my garden, after a rainfall, you can faintly, yes, hear the breaking of new blooms.'
- Truman Capote

The Pusher

Working in quality assurance most of my adult life and in the manufacturing world, one of those sayings I just hated to hear was, "well, that's the way we've always done it." Sorry, as a part of everyday thinking we're supposed to explore ways to continually improve the system, never settling for the same old way. There are always better, quicker or safer ways to get the task done. Use your brains, people. Granny Bowie could have possibly invented this phrase and thinking back, maybe I should have had it printed on her coffee mug or stitched on her lounging gown. No, she would never have been accepted the premise of deviating from the way things were supposed to be.

Granny in her twilight years lived under mama and daddy's roof; mama opting for this arrangement and volunteering as the primary caregiver for her and my daddy, who was bedridden, ravished with Parkinson and Alzheimer's. Here I go with another shameless plug, but read more of these adventures in my memoir about the *Caregiver's Son*. The household, I suspect because of circumstances, had succumb to life governed by routine. Now don't get me wrong, sticking to some sort of schedule is not necessarily bad. Mama had to structure her life around the hand she had been dealt, I get that. Granny, on the other hand, was a piece of work, the ageless puppeteer, manipulating the strings to ensure everything stayed somewhat frozen in her very own time warp. Let's explore this, shall we, a day in the life so to speak.

Granny was into her nineties, still of sound mind, even though that body of hers wasn't up to snuff. Her face was smooth as a baby's behind. She attributed the texture to her frequent use of Oil of Olay. Some would joke and call it Oil of Old Lady. Say what you will but no wrinkles or crow's feet blemished her complexion. Granny was quite set in her ways, her rite of passage after living a long and fruitful life. She had her morning ritual before making the long tedious trip from the opposite end of the hallway to her lift chair in the den.

The breakfast menu was always the same, a bowl of Special K cereal with half of a banana precisely sliced, served with a small glass of orange juice. The bananas were kept refrigerated and wrapped in a cloth to prevent them from ripening and blackening too quickly. I'm still not sure if this was hers or mama's idea. She also had a cup of coffee, creamer and sugar, in a special coffee mug. It had to be the very same mug because she would scrutinize any others, most being too heavy or handles too small, so she would point out.

All meals were served to her on a tray positioned on her lap in that lift chair. She had long ago given up sit down meals at the table, the chairs hurting her back. Granny's wardrobe deviated very little. She sported a gown and robe. Everything else made her itch. She even had a special lap throw, non-itch fabric too. A small box rested by her side. It contained her assortment of personal goodies and gadgets, tissues and whatnots. It was like her little treasure-trove of essentials. Throughout the day she would retrieve the box, appearing to take inventory and rearranging the things inside. She'd even fold and refold tissues. It was her little personal domain so we let her do as she pleased; being trapped in her lift chair world, it tended to occupy her mind and give her something to do besides napping and watching television.

Napping, ouch, it was painful to watch her drift into la-la land and she would always deny ever sleeping when we made sport of her. Same scenario each and every time, she'd slip to her right side, her head tipping so far to the right and downward, a maneuver that would make a contortionist give her a standing ovation. She'd flatly dispute she had nodded off. Wiping drool from the corner of her moth with her tissue didn't prove a thing, not in her mind. She'd spring up like a jack in the box, only to repeat the feat minutes later. A trip to the chiropractor would be in my future if I attempted that move.

Granny had no limitations to what she could eat, providing it wasn't hot or spicy. Her lunch and dinner were served on that very same tray, meals delivered to her like meals on wheels to her lift chair. We were allowed to deviate what was served for lunch and supper. There were no hard fast rules applicable for either except for one very important stipulation. She had to have a piece of cornbread, biscuit or slice of bread with her meal, unless serving her a sandwich and plain potato chips. Food must be corralled to ensure every morsel was consumed. She made happy plates. I think she bought into to those stories that she had to clean her plate because others, elsewhere in the world were starving. Others lived *over yonder*. Possibly she had just been brought up during the hard times when food was scarce. Maybe she appreciated its value and didn't believe in wasting or squandering it.

With the bread item in hand, Granny would move the various food items about, pushing them towards her utensils. This was quite the ritual and all inspiring to watch; if not just a tad comical too. She manipulated that pusher with skill unmatched; don't try this at home. Whatever you did, you better not forget to provide her with a pusher. She would call you down. The pusher had a dual purpose. It could often serve as a *sopper*. You heard me right; I can't make this stuff up. Some items on a plate must be *sopped*. For instance, one *sops* gravy with a biscuit. Butterbean juice must be sopped to savor those little puddles left when the last bean has been consumed. Turnip greens, cabbage and collards leave their marks on the plate. Cornbread served as the sponge to capture every little droplet of wet residue. Her plate was basically clean once she finished her meal; not a crumb left for starving children in some third world county.

Snack time, now this was an entirely different ordeal, one that left little wiggle room. I say that, but she did welcome change, especially if they were homemade goodies such as cake, pie or cookies. But she had her preferred ones and let me tell you, she could be the little hoarder and quite selfish when it came to sharing these. Mama had to make sure the pantry had the following: her Little Debbie's and Cheez-its. Fact, you better not run out of either one.

She could be very protective of those Little Debbie's and often maintained her own stash. Printed on the back of the Cheez-it box, *Get your own box*; Granny must have submitted this slogan as this was her mantra. These cheesy crackers were chasers for Little Debbie. Southerners insist that if you eat something sweet, then you have to follow that up with something salty to get the sweetness out of your mouth. I think it's just an excuse to eat more stuff, I'm just saying. Snacks were served routinely about the same time of the afternoon and night. You couldn't chance messing with her digestive system.

Medication, if you really want to call it that, was served at specific intervals each and every day. This consisted of Tylenol, Advil, and Benadryl; simply amazing that a woman in her nineties was on no prescription drugs. Mentally Granny was sharp as a tack, too sharp most times, but physically she had her limitations. The Tylenol and Advil were rotated out during the day at precise intervals to treat all her aches and pains. Benadryl warded off her itching and allergic reactions to most everything she came in contact with. She had two gowns she could wear and that was her everyday clothing while perched there in her lift chair. Personally I think we could have served her 'make believe' pills, placebos, and she would have never known the difference. What am I thinking? We could have never perfected that and have gotten it past her. She would have probably detected a change in size, color or taste; not the way it had always been.

I love to kid about her habits but Granny was really an angel and we were blessed to have had her around for ninety four years. I think she had a direct line to the Lord, maybe as one of his consultants. She grew up during simple times and it spilled over into her everyday approach to life. She never tried to impress anyone. Proper etiquette eluded her and everyone gave her a pass.

If she burped out loud, we just laughed or ignored it all together. Motoring down the hallway with her walker, one of us trailing her; if she had a case of the walking farts, which wasn't usual; she'd pause and make a joke about it, saying she was playing a little tune. A friend of mine calls this uncontrollable act, crop dusting. If she mispronounced words or put her twist on them; so what, we still knew what she meant to say. *Hoping* someone meant helping them.

The term, *over yonder,* covered everywhere from across the room to another country. It was never down yonder or up yonder, only over yonder.

The Dictionary term for over yonder: The adverb *yonder,* from Old English *geond,* is not exclusively Southern but is more frequently used in the south than in any other region of the United States, and not only by older or uneducated speakers. *Yonder* is not merely a Southern synonym for *there,* which in the South tends to mean "only a few feet from the speaker." *Yonder* carries with it an inherent sense of distance farther than "there" and is used if the person or thing indicated can be seen: *the shed over yonder.* Or it might be nearby but completely out of sight, as in the next room. Lesson over, aren't you glad?

Granny was the ultimate weather worrier and watcher. Mama would often have the television set to the Weather Channel. From Granny's perspective, The Weather Channel didn't know beans about Abbeville's local weather. Only WYFF4, channel 4, out of Greenville, S.C., with weather meteorologist, John Cessarich could accurately predict the weather. John was her man. She trusted no other. No one could hold a candle to him, not in her eyes. He hung the moon. The aches and pains of ole Arthur, as she referred to her arthritis, typically supported John's predicted forecast. If he said it was going to rain, she believed him because Arthur was acting up too. For someone who rarely ventured outside anymore, she believed in knowing what the weather was doing. That's the way it had always been.

Yep, Granny was quite a unique grand old lady. Like Papa, I miss her too. When any of our elders depart this world, a large chunk of our heritage disappears with them. Those wonderful stories are further removed from those

I am recapping and are gone forever. Back in her day life was simple, yes, but hard. I regret now that I didn't record or scribble down more of my grandparent's wondrous tales. Too often we have a tendency to tune them out when they're talking about people and places unfamiliar to us. Bless her heart. She's now somewhere, over yonder, with Papa and both my parents, sporting her well deserved wings, if they don't make her itch like everything else; pushing and sopping whatever is on the Lord's menu. I hope he has that special coffee mug for her or she'll let him know about it. And God, save the grief, and get your own box of Cheez-its.

> *'We need to go back to the way it was 30 years ago,*
> *when everybody had Grandma and Grandpa,*
> *and we were willing to pass moral judgments about*
> *right and wrong.'*
> **- Steven Tyler**

Nothing but Cornbread Crumbs, Fire up another Skillet

As you should fully understand by now, nostalgia is indeed the pleasure and sadness that is caused by remembering something from our past, often wishing that we could experience it once again. Those memories represent a special sentimentality, typically for a happy period or place with personal associations. Reliving those memories can provide comfort and in some cases it might even contribute to a better sense of mental health. If it doesn't, then perhaps you shouldn't dig up those particular old bones. There is no arguing with the fact that nostalgia is obviously triggered by something reminding us of an event or item from our past. This emotion can vary from happiness to sorrow. The term, *feeling nostalgic*, is more commonly used to describe pleasurable emotions of remembering somewhere back when.

For me, it's all good. Tears of sadness and happiness are one and the same. Mine can certainly trigger crying, laughing or a nagging urge to visit people I haven't seen in forever. Remembering those who have left us behind can often be just what the doctor ordered to heal a hurting heart. Putting mine to paper or computer in this case, came easy. Each nostalgic moment lead me to the next one; so much so that it wasn't fair to the reader for me to cram it all in the pages of one enormous book. While I cherish my memories, it doesn't mean everyone else will; at least not beyond the boundaries formed by family and friends. Your feedback and support is important because waiting in the wings is a potential second helping. Just when you thought it was safe to put this behind you, I have volume two just itching to be released.

Regrets, I've had a Few
More nonsense babbling, because I can...

Kindergarten, little girl on the other side of the fence, should have asked her, her name, since I had the obvious tiny tot crush.

First grade, June and the monkey bar's kiss, I should have followed my heart and asked her to be my girlfriend. Kiss'um and leave'um hanging...what did I know about heart following?

First grade, I should have confessed to being the participating kisser on the monkey bars, so every boy wouldn't have gotten their hands paddled. Scratch that one... Kiss and don't tell seemed to have worked to my favor.

First grade, I should have not slid so many times down that sliding board and worn the seat out of my shorts... scratch that one too, it was too much fun and worth the razing I got.

Fourth grade, Julie, Little Mountain Picnic, should have asked her to be my girlfriend since I had asked her to accompany me as sort of my date.

Fifth grade crush, Doris never knew...stupidity continued its ugly trend, way too may childhood crushes never seeing the light of day...admiring from afar, my mantra.

Sixth grade, coronet, should have practiced and taken joining the band more seriously, especially since my parents bought me the instrument.

High school, I should have never picked on Doug, assuming the role of a bully.

Football, basketball, track, I should have stuck with

them instead of dropping out. It might have built character, laid the foundation for me being more of a team player. Puking and hurting didn't seem such a great trade off when I could be out having fun and getting into mischief. Sticking with track and high jumping in eighth grade would have definitely defused the obvious vengeful punishment I received in history class at the hands of Coach Lurch. He really wanted me to be his star high jumper but I didn't want to do all that gut retching running.

Art class, ninth and ten grades, I should have asked Karen and/or Jane out; they obviously seemed to like me. I couldn't decide which one to ask so I never asked out either one of them. I should have taken the classes more seriously too, since deep down, I loved the artful concept. Reckless abandonment, new mantra...

Junior prom, one and done, should have asked Janie on date after the prom; what a dufus...not one to follow up on anything, especially when it came to girls...maybe deep down I feared rejection if I actually asked and didn't get a *yes* reply.

Junior year, Carlyle, after sharing rides with her at Anderson fair, I should have asked her out too, much too introverted to do hardly any asking back then. So many crushes, so many missed opportunities...break out the tissues and boo-hoo a river.

Junior year, I allowed peer pressure to turn me against one of my very best friends. Sorry about that, Mike. Batman lives forever. Adam West ruled.

Senior year, I should have never taken that chew of tobacco from Speed Hall...gladly one and done on that experience. Gut retching puking cam into play once again, no running required.

Senior year, English class, I should have challenged Mrs. Simmons over the 'F' she gave me for my chess player short story. I didn't misspell the words or screw up the dialogue; I just depicted my main character as a southerner. She didn't get it, thought I couldn't spell or properly structure a sentence, and I didn't step up and explain it. Crushing blow back then for an aspiring young writer…and I shouldn't have been so tough on Mrs. Marshall in College Algebra/Trig class, focused less on my hard headiness and wild nature animal sounds and more on working the assignments and passing. Class clown, yet another mantra…

I should have probably taken my senior year more seriously, not so much laying out and being a causeless rebel. Fun won out hands down over educational opportunities. I couldn't help myself, wild and crazy guy, so claimed Steve Martin.

After graduating I should have completed that enlistment gig, army promising to make sure you and your buddy were stationed at same location. I chickened out. My buddy, Speedy, ended up being stationed in Hawaii, bummer.

Another fork in the road after graduating, should have postponed marital bliss and instead followed my ambitious dream, and ventured to Atlanta to take commercial art classes. It might have been the game changer, might not have been, will never know for sure…even passed up drafting class at Tech. Marriage was over in a couple of years, length it would have taken me to have completed the college stint.

Should have chosen a less reckless and rebellious path, could have saved mama and daddy from much added stress. Selfishness and self centered, sometimes you just can't help who you are. Wild hairs and oats in need of sowing too often take on a life of their own. 'Born for fun, loyal to none', new mantra, had a tee shirt from Ocean City to prove it.

Having had no children...especially a boy, someone who could have carried on the family name...well I broke the only child run, didn't I?

I should have found a better way to deal with family illnesses, deaths, and crisis, strived to be more understanding, caring and supportive. It's that changing who you really are thing again; not as easy as critics paint it to be.

I should have somehow learned to be more compassionate and serious but instead constructed a protective wall of sarcastic wit to fend off the evil spirits. Making jokes and light of everything has always been a deceptive safety net. A fool only successfully fools himself. The raging battle for balance continues, not one easily won or overcome unfortunately. I *yam* who I *yam;* tough to transform an ole dog with bad tricks.

Fear not, all is not gloom and doom. This is no pity party by any stretch. I'm thankful to be here, lucky to have survived a life pot holed and trenched deeply with countless obstacles to completely derail me. Maybe it's purposefully so or just plain luck that I'm still here. I have managed to do a few good things along the way but I'll forgo that list, might sound too much like horn tooting. Maybe I'm just mellowing or finding I'm too old to keep pace. Possibly with age comes a smidgen of wisdom. The time ahead will prove or disprove it I reckon. The past is the past and there is no mulligan. I'd probably *whomp* it any way.

Before I completely become derailed and off the deep end,
if I haven't already done so, sit back and
enjoy the bonus round,
Part II, another nostalgic segment in my life that I call,
Fostering Four and a Much More.

Part II

Fostering Four and Much More

Fostering Four and Much More

Destiny isn't a choice. The chosen are picked for a reason I suppose. I have certainly had my life derailed more times than I can count; much of it my own fault I must confess. Having one's life derailed can be quite traumatic for both bad and good reasons. You think you're heading in one direction and then…bam…that unexpected path is blocked by a fallen tree and you have to make a detour. Hauling that tree out of the road isn't always a viable option; even though the highway ahead would have been less treacherous if you would have tried to move it out of the way. How does it go, the path less traveled or something like that? Stumbling and falling forward, one must trudge along the best one can, avoiding all other obstacles that leap in your way.

In my early life I was never one for long term visions. I typically lived for the moment. The future was always too far to fathom. Plus, if you actually take the time to plan something, there are more chances that something will keep you from reaching your goal. That's why I've never put much effort in the whole goal setting process. Planning can just lead to disappointment or set you up for failure. Take it as it comes and the good stuff is a bonus. The bad stuff is just life, bad breaks, something never meant to be.

That's why I shy away from making New Year's resolutions. Most are doomed for failure because those making them set the bar too high. Keep it simple I say. But then there's that destiny thing out there just lurking to take charge of your life. It can be a sneaky bastard, able to conceal itself much too conveniently; and then at the last second, it's on top of you. You often never see it coming and it rarely ever gives you a fighting chance. By the way, I hate surprises too. Spontaneity doesn't allow you any time to prepare. Sounds like something a planner would do, doesn't' it?

I never envisioned being a caregiver. I never thought about my parents dying. I never ever thought I would see my entire blood line vanish before my very eyes in eleven short months, but it all played out the way it was supposed to, at least according to Mister Destiny. He never consulted me; asked me how I felt about it, or if I was ready for the repercussions. Destiny can be quite heartless and often ruthless. They say there are lessons to be learned in every tragedy or there is always a silver lining if you deep dive to find it.

You know, sometimes you're just not up to all that soul searching crap. When it's fresh in your mind and the pain is consuming you, being rational can be just plain irrational. Yeah, stepping into the shoes of the caregiver was a rough time in my life. Watching my mama die three months after assuming her role was tougher. You have to play the hand you're dealt. I was never a card player for a reason I suppose.

Mama was taken from me just three months before daddy would be snatched away too. I watched both of them die in their bedroom, holding mama in my arms as she took her very last breath, telling me 'I love you sweetie' before she left the pain behind. I held daddy's hand in that very same room as he struggled to breath, aspiration taking him before the emergency folks could arrive. An only child became an orphan so to speak in a blink of any eye. I never envisioned this, not by a long shot, parentless just like that…destiny? Granny, mama's mama, our last patient in the caregiver arena, passed eight months after daddy, eleven months after her only child. I've chronicled this in the Caregiver's Son, Outside the Window Looking In so I'll not be excavating any new dirt piles this go round. I've wallowed enough in that pit.

Old Man Destiny struck much earlier in my life. Thinking back now, possibly it was his way of introducing me to the precursor course for care giving. I had never really thought about it until now, but perhaps I had indeed ventured down this path, even though the tagline caregiver wasn't really associated to the particular event in my life. There are all sorts of caring and numerous ways to give it. I didn't choose this one either. It picked me. Funny how you end up doing things you never envisioned. I should have been at the back of the line when it came to this one; least qualified for the position, no training or life experiences to remotely be considered. That's why they call it on the job training, hands on; just roll up your sleeves and do it.

Jumping from a sizzling frying pan and into the flaming embers isn't my style. Sure, my life has been a reckless one and I've been burned my fair share of times by irresponsible decision making. Boy, I never saw this one coming. I should have. The inevitable train wreck should have been obvious, even to a blind man like me. Lessons, those pesky lessons are relentless.

Like Yesterdays' Garbage

Looking back, I don't really remember how my day was going that particular day. I don't even recall the day of the week or actual time it happened. It just did. My life was fairly normal or normal on my personal scale of normalness. Life is never perfect. Imperfection can be a way of life; such was mine. I'm not complaining. Mine is what I made of it, good, bad or ugly. For the sake of argument, let's say I was nearing that forty-ish milestone in my life and in the middle of a rocky second marriage. Things happen, not by design; I'm no planner remember. Married twice and no children of my own, not by choice; it just played out that way. I had never planned to not have children any more than I had planned to have them. That card playing thing again; never was dealt the kid hand.

As you get older you think about certain things. You see your family and friends with children and wonder, why not me. Throughout my marriages, I had thrown caution to the wind, so if it was meant to be, there was nothing preventing the blessed event. In my first marriage I took that embarrassing step to check me out; to make sure I wasn't the cause of the stork not knocking at our door. A nurse handing you a cup in the doctor's office and pointing you to a vacant room isn't the best experience, let me be the first to say.

First thoughts, I can't possibly fill this thing up. A cold drab clinic surrounding does not offer up the best environment for one to conjure up what it takes to donate sperm for testing. It might be funny in the movies but in real life it loses its humor. You hear every footfall outside in the hallway and take note of every shadow passing by underneath the doorway. Oh yeah, and they provided no copies of Playboy. Dumping your pocket full of change loudly onto to a tile floor in the middle of the naughty little act doesn't help the cause. After the labor of love, I managed to make a deposit. Final results, low counts but nothing to worry about. Still, we remained childless.

During marriage number two, same scenario, same results, no children resulted, sort of. My wife eventually ended up having a hysterectomy so there would end any quest for children. Mister Destiny reared his ugly head just to bring home his point. During the lab work after the surgery the doctor discovered a human fetus. I had finally made a baby but just like that it was gone. Neither of us had an inkling that she was pregnant. The doctor was shocked too, saying it should have been nearly medically impossible, giving her various ailments; but yet, there is was.

There's something so wrong about a doctor telling you news like this. By the way, congratulations and then yanking the rug out from underneath your feet. It was there but now it's gone and there will be no second chances. It just wasn't meant to be for me to be a parent. The only child buck stops here. I had blown my chance at carrying on the family name; something that would haunt me forever. As you grow older you ponder what if.

Happy or not so happy endings have beginnings. We received the phone call. My wife's four grandsons had been placed in foster care. Anytime children are removed from the household and taken away from their parents, the children are the ones who suffer. That is unless they are being removed from an abusive and dangerous situation. In this case, that was debatable, depending on your interpretation of the situation. No, neither parent would purposely harm their four boys. They loved their children, but there is something sadly wrong when the parents place the importance of their lives ahead of the pecking order of the kids. I'm childless and I even know better.

I had witnessed firsthand over the years how these four boys were rarely put first, and it saddened me to see them not being given the chance to live a normal life. Normal is relevant when abnormal is prevalent. I could only imagine who might have reported these two adults to child services, probably more to do with the living environment than anything. I stand firm that none of these boys had been physically or sexually abused but sometimes abuse is as simple as not being provided the best lifestyle. Adults don't always make the best teachers or parents; just an inexperienced outsider's observation.

The plot thickened. The mom had previously deserted the household, seeking some sort of life outside the family circle. We were aware of that and had been trying to help out the dad. Perhaps the burden of raising four boys had taken its toll; maybe she sought a life loss, reclaiming a period in time she had been denied. Who knows what makes people do what they do. I'm the perfect example as I've made my fair share of lousy decisions, so I'm not casting any stones per say.

When children are involved, I guess I'm not as tolerable of the adults not taking their responsibilities seriously. If there is one thing I hate to hear passing through the lips of adults; *we can't have anything because of these kids. They tear up everything.* Give me a break. They're kids. You're the adults. Do the math. It doesn't add up on any level. Look in the mirror the next time you have the guts to make an idiotic statement like that.

Shocking revelation, the son-in-law had taken the kids to social services. No one had reported him. The kids hadn't been taken from him. He delivered them on their door steps voluntarily. Some things you just don't get. This ranked as one beyond explanation. Why would he do this when family members were available to assist? Four boys tossed away like yesterday's garbage, handed over to strangers, not family. Unthinkable, unimaginable, preposterous, insane, irrational…just plain wrong…what could he have been possibly thinking?

I'm childless, not a parent, but, I 'm sorry; I just didn't get it. This was beyond understanding. It's tough not to judge people in these circumstances and I'm guilty as charged. What he did with his children was not my business, right? Neither parent was blood kin to me so why should I care. I cared because the children mattered. Those four boys didn't deserve this fate, not at the hands of their father. I choke on that word father. A real father doesn't pull crap like this.

Sad but true, they were at least in safe hands now. The newscast and headlines are filled with far worse tragic outcomes. I'm looking for that silver lining again, and it's tough. So what now? The boys were where-abouts unknown, MIA, with a fate to be determined. I was still trying to understand it but it defied my ability to process the data and make any logical sense out of it.

Their grandmother, my wife was quite frantic and perturbed by what had happened. How do you just hand over your kids to social services? It turned my stomach inside out just thinking about it and what those boys must be thinking. How had he explained his actions to them? Had he even attempted to justify it? The oldest was ten; the youngest five. I can't begin to imagine what they were feeling or thinking. Tossed away, neither parent willing to do what parents are supposed to do; what children expect them to do.

It's easy for me to stand atop my soap box and say this and that. What really gives me the right to question parenting? After all, I'm not a parent. I'm certainly not a psychologist. I can only base my feelings and comments on having been a kid raised in what I deemed a fairly normal household. I came first. My parents had made sure of that whether I agreed with them or not.

Have no doubt; my mama and daddy always had my best interest in their hearts, rest their souls. I never went to bed hungry or worried about what tomorrow might bring. I lived the life of a boy; not perfect but what did I know about perfection back then. Granted, they both worked the night shift for much of my adolescent time on the planet, but they made sure I was cared for by my grandparents and my black mama. Love was there at every turn. I was indeed blessed.

So what were we going to do about this? My wife thought it would be simple. We'd just go get them and bring them to our house; where they should have been brought in the first place. She received no argument from me. Family should be there for family. Even I got that part, especially when children were involved. Dealing with death would be a greater foe for me, but that was years away at this time. My caregiver life wouldn't come into play in time to help me through this one.

Learning to care for abandoned children is much different than learning to care for ailing adults. At least with children time is on your side. The sick march to another drummer, any day can be their last. The caregiver has no immunity from the grim reaper when he comes knocking. That journey lay ahead for me and was unknown territory in the present snapshot of my life. Discarded like yesterday's trash, unforgivable…

Times wasting; let's go get them. How hard could that really be?

Possession is Nine Tenths

Foster me this, almost sounds like some child's riddle, doesn't it? Nothing is as easy as it appears. I always thought family trumped the need for social services. Stick-um up. Hand over all your possessions. If you can identify the stolen merchandise as yours, aren't you supposed to be able to reclaim it? Granted, the children hadn't exactly been stolen; well, if you discount their innocence. Taken, dumped, handed over, discarded, call it what you want; they were in the possession of strangers, a place children shouldn't be.

Don't take me wrong. As already mentioned there are circumstances that warrant removing children from unsafe situations and I applaud social services for doing the needful, but they had not been contacted in this case. What am I really saying? A parent had handed them over. That's sort of like the criminal waving his rights and admitting to the crime, isn't it? Read me my rights and book me. Otis on Andy Griffith used a key to lock his drunken ass in the cell. No, I can't draw this comparison. It is simply the wrong thing to do for any parent.

I was thinking all the time I'd never want to be a social worker. It's got to be one of those thankless jobs. You're damned if you do or don't; just depends on what side of the fence you're on when they intervene. Necessary evil does have its place and it's for the good of the children. Okay, time to reclaim the grand boys. Keep them until their parents could work out their differences or whatever was going on with them.

One thing agreed, those boys being away from what their parents had to offer them, was not necessarily a bad thing right now. Children deserve normalcy in their lives.

If turmoil exists between the parents, it just naturally filters down to the children. Again, I am thankful and blessed I never had to endure this in my life. I'd like to think I would have made a good dad. Destiny chooses, fairly or not. Dwelling on the past doesn't change it. I'm that live in the present sort of guy anyway, right? The future is just another day. So now what?

Claim check, she's the grandmother. Where do we go to pick them up? We hadn't seen this one coming either. Once in the custody of social services it wasn't as simple as showing up and saying we'd take them home with us. Law would not allow them to simply place the boys in protective custody with us. That was downright insulting.

My wife was the blood grandmother, even though her daughter was missing in action. It didn't make sense to me that social services would prefer keeping them rather than allow family to take care of them. What sort of screwed up law and system was this? How was this taking into consideration the boys' best interest? I was dumbfounded. This wasn't even up for debate, contest over. Blood was thinner than water apparently.

So what could be done to rectify this wrong? Were the boys going to sit idle in foster care until their parents came to their senses and were granted custody? Both parents had basically deserted them; one leaving the home and the other leaving them in the hands of strangers. I wasn't sure they even deserved having them back. It was easy for me to take this stance given the circumstances. One thing was perfectly clear in my mind; the boys didn't deserve this fate.

Priorities were just too screwed up for my taste. The social worker assigned to the case put it bluntly. In order for us to remove them from their current foster care situation and place them in our care we would have to become certified foster parents. Let me get this straight. A grandmother had to become a trained foster care person to be able to take home her very own grandchildren. Try to wrap your brain around that screwy premise.

A goal had been established and you know how I hate goals. How does one become a foster parent? I for one had no parenting experience on my resume. At least my wife did, with two daughters of her own, her oldest being the wayward one caught up in this mess. Her daughter was an adult, and I use that term loosely. She was responsible for her actions or lack of, a deserter in the parenting scenario.

The son-in-law; never mind, I don't even want to go there. What is done is done and the past is just that. How were we going to fix this mess? This was all about those four boys, plain and simple. I was in, so how did we go about becoming certified foster parents? Was there a foster parenting college? Would I be disqualified because I wasn't a parent? I was too laid back for so much drama. DSS, the Department of Social Services would explain the path to us.

Four boys lay in limbo in the company of strangers. There is often irony in tragedy. They were probably being feed better and exposed to a much more stable life style. Sadly, as kids we expect for that stability and reassurance to come from our parents. Take it where you can get it, I suppose; especially when grownups struggle to act their age or be responsible. Me, being childless, take my opinions for what they are worth.

I was certainly the furthest thing from a parenting expert. My experience was merely based from the world on the other side of the fence; being a child raised right. Being raised right and doing what is right are two different things. I certainly knew the difference, but often chose the devil's way just because it seemed the fun and more risky thing to do. I had my share of skeletons for sure, but, that has nothing to do with knowing what's right for kids. My sorted past had nothing to do with the present; another story, another time.

    I spin it like this. Parents brought us into this world regardless to whether it was planned or by accident. Once here, we are theirs and their responsibility. They own us because we can't defend for ourselves. It's up to them to mold us, shape us, and help us become adults. The train wreck occurs when the adults leap from the engine and stray waywardly down the tracks, allowing the runaway locomotive and trailing cars to derail and crash with the kids onboard. Dazed and confused, the kids are battling perils and consequences by the seats of their britches. It takes a lot to overcome the mounting odds.

    For now, the boys still had a fighting chance, if they received the proper support, guidance and love to get them through it. It appeared that this temporarily rested on our shoulders, ready or not. This would be virgin territory for me. I was not a father and would never ever attempt to replace theirs, no matter what I thought about him. You never turn kids against their parents; it's just that simple, an unwritten law so to speak. Right now though, it was time for me to hunker down and become a responsible adult. Was I up for this; to be determined? My first test, graduate from foster parenting college, and then we'd take it one day at a time.

    A grandmother's anguish can be unsettling to endure for those of us watching it unfold. You love your children or should, regardless of their faults. That's Parenting 101. Watching as grandkids are tossed away so easily isn't typically in the envisioned plans. You tend to question where did you go wrong; often blaming yourself. Right or wrong, kids as adults make their choices. I, the one with no children, have no tolerance for those who mistreat children. I don't blame the parents' upbringing. I hold them totally responsible for their actions when it comes to how they raise their children.

I look at it this way. If you believe you were mistreated, wronged or just plain had a terrible childhood; then this is your chance to rectify it by doing what is right for your children. Don't punish your kids for your ill fated life. Please don't blame your parents on your bad choices. Remember, you're the adults with brains and morals, right? The kids belong to you and nobody else. What happens is in your hands and on your conscious. It begins and stops with you. Play the hand dealt to the best of your ability. If you continue to have losing hands, allow those around you to chip in.

It was time for me to understand just what I was about to sign up for, hoping it wasn't more than I could handle. Obviously we were doing this for all the right reasons, but if successful, the world as I knew it was about to be shattered. I was treading into much deeper water than I had ever been. It would be like going from zero to sixty in record time on the parenting scale. I wasn't sure if I was cut out for this challenge.

Refusing to take this on was not a defendable option; not if I wanted to live with a clear conscious. Could I really do it? I was about to find out. DSS awaited, ready to define the path moving forward. Four children's immediate futures rested on that unpredictable outcome. Would I make the cut, one with no experience at this sort of thing? What did I really have to offer in parental guidance? Any optimism I had was being devoured by pessimistic dread.

Meeting with the powers to be, the asphalt soon met the roadway. The basic requirements for becoming foster parents were spelled out loud and clear. First we had to be twenty one years of age. There was no argument with that qualification. We must be financially stable. That one seemed to be applicable. Here's the kicker. We must be responsible, mature adults. I don't think they were implying age here. If I drew comparison to the adults who had just relinquished their responsibilities then I could justifiably so say yes to this one. Everything is relative, I'm just saying. Either way, I was going to give myself a pass on this one.

I am a responsible adult? I was asked my opinion and I gave it. Nobody is perfect. We had to complete a thorough application and had to be willing to share information regarding our background and lifestyle. There was a limit how willing I was prepared to go. Fluffing it up is always the better option so we did whatever necessary to put us in the running. Dig up those skeletons if need be. Boy, did I really want this?

Provide relative and non-relative references. Are you kidding me? We could choose so acing this part should be a cinch. Show proof of marriage or divorce. We were still married and legal. Now came that defining moment, giving them permission to dig in the dirt by allowing a home study that included visits with all household members. This should be easy enough with me, my wife, a dog and a cat.

Staff would have to conduct a criminal background check of all family members. I get that part. Placing children in the care of serial murderers, sex offenders or other felons would not be a desirable home environment. Caution, don't trust the cat. If we cleared all these hurtles we'd attend free training to learn about issues of abused and neglected children. Abuse and neglect are relative terms. They can be physical, sexual, mental or any combination of any of them. Like those famous info commercials; but wait, there's more, if you sign up now…

Additional foster care requirements included having adequate sleeping space. In this case we'd be adding four more to our present family of two. We had three bedrooms on the main floor and we had our master in the basement. We could accommodate the extras. No more than six children would be allowed at any given time and that included any children already members of the household. We didn't have to count the dog and cat, even though we considered them family members. They were sort of our children.

We MUST agree to a nonphysical discipline policy. There would be no making the kids go out in the yard and pick their switch from the bush or any spankings or belt threats. My parenting skills flushed down the toilet quickly because that had been how I had been raised. Spare the rod, spoil the child. You must occasionally beat your children to let them know how much you love them. I reckon the premise was not to take them out of one abusive situation and place them in another, especially when foster parents weren't real parents. My question then was *how do we* get them to mind if this is taken away as an option. I'd figure it out, I guess, just like all this other parenting stuff I would be learning.

I didn't realize that becoming a foster parent was almost like becoming a lifeguard. CPR and First Aid Certification would be required. Ironically, I had this one covered. I had been a volunteer fireman at the rural community fire department a stones toss from our house. I had been trained already. We'd have to allow fire, health and safety inspections of our home. We'd even have to develop an emergency contingency plan for fires, including a posted diagram clearly indicating exit points. Raising children should come with some sort of handbook or manual; foster parenting for dummies.

The local Health Department would have to test household members for TB, Tuberculosis. This was not a common disease so I thought it odd to be tested for it. I didn't even know anyone who had ever had TB. I would think there were more serious diseases to be feared than TB. Oh yeah, and the dog and cat had to be vaccinated. They had been. There were no rabid animals living within the confines of the house. My wife had been scratched and clawed too many times by the cat and had shown no signs of rabid behavior; none that I cared to bring up in front of DSS.

We would also attend training (PRIDE) to learn more about the children available through DFPS and to assess our strengths in parenting children. I sure hoped I did have some of those strengths worth noting. The classes would boost our knowledge and confidence to meet the challenge of taking children into our home and to be sure we were ready to follow through on the commitment. Well, I indeed needed some boosting on all levels. I attempted to muster up the commitment but wondered if I shouldn't be committed instead for taking on this challenge. So what was left? Once we had been knighted as full-fledged foster parents, we'd be required to attend twenty hours or more of training each year to maintain our credentials.

Trying to play the concerned part, I asked about the PRIDE training and was told that Child Protective Services recognizes that 16 hours of pre-service training for foster parents is insufficient. CPS requires potential foster parents to attend Parent Resource Information Development Education as part of the family's required pre-service training. PRIDE covers topics such as child attachment, loss and grief, discipline and behavior intervention, effects of abuse and neglect, sexual abuse, working with the child welfare system, and the effects of fostering and adopting on the family.

Complexity is not supposed to be easy, right? We had kept the grand boys many times for extended stays at our house. We and they had survived. To get them back why did we have to undergo this rigorous process? Explanation, we were signing up for the foster care program and other children might come into play. Whoa Nelly. I hadn't considered that aspect. We could be caring for strangers, kids belonging to other people. I had only considered this as a ploy to retrieve the grand boys from protective custody.

I quickly did my math. If we pulled this off flawlessly we'd have four kids in the house and the maximum allowed was six. Surely DSS wouldn't place one or two more in our care while we still had the four. That would be insane. It might actually lead to insanity on my part. This had changed the game. Maybe I was getting in over my head but I dared not desert the ship at this point. We actually had no guarantees from DSS that by undergoing this process it would for sure place the boys in our custody. Without doing it though, there would be no chance of getting them back.

Confounding Fathers

Okay, so what I had I really signed up for? I knew why we had selfishly chosen this, but, the method to the madness was still in murky waters. Our goals and the primary purpose for foster care were sort of similar. We wanted to get the kids away from strangers. We were apparently intent on taking extreme measures and do it at all cost. The primary purpose of existing in the system differed slightly; to provide a safe temporary placement for children who cannot remain safely in the home of their parents. The children are placed in the custody of the Department of Social Services by court order. Well this was a bit of an anomaly because the court hadn't removed the kids. Good ole dad had forfeited them, handed them over on a tarnished silver platter.

The goal of foster care was to implement a plan for permanency for the boys. If the boys could not be returned home to the parents, another permanent planned living arrangement would be made. Permanency plans, with priority from the most to the least permanent by federal law are first and foremost, reunification with parents. This was a double edged sword in many cases. In ours, it was tough to see them going back into what waited for them right now; their mom not there and their dad apparently not willing to be tasked as the sole provider. It was an ugly situation at best and it confounded me to fathom what was best for them, at least until the parents cleaned up their act. Sadly, deciding their fate did not rest in our hands; at least deciding if and when they could or would go back.

Adoption by a relative or non-relative could be an alternative. I hadn't even considered this one. Granted, no one wanted to envision them being adopted and especially not out to strangers. That defeated the path we were currently pursuing. Did that mean that I would one day be faced with making the decision to adopt them? I must confess, I wasn't sure where I stood on this at the time; talk about the ultimate sacrifice and commitment. The easier approach was just to push this one to bottom of the pile and cross that bridge if I ever had to go there. Raising four boys to adulthood had not entered the equation, not in my brain. Wow, it took my breath away.

Then there was guardianship or custody with a relative or no-relative. I wasn't exactly sure how that was different from foster care or adoption. It implied something a tad more permanent. It sounded like ownership; something you could walk away from if it didn't work. Adoption left no wiggle room. You bought it, you owned it. Here I go sounding cynical again but this was indeed my first rodeo. I had never been a parent so starting off right out of the chute with four was just a bit scary for a potential daddy figure. Presently there were too many unknowns, unanswered questions and the apprehension of totally deviating from my existing lifestyle. Was I really ready to give up me for this? It sounds terrible me thinking like this but it did scare the crap out of me. I was nearly forty years old so what could I possibly bring to the table. Those boys deserved better.

I did the only thing I knew to do; I consulted my parents. Perhaps they could lend some guidance to their wayward only child. Knowing my folks and their opinions of my existing marital existence, this might not have been the wisest of choices. My options were few. I had really nothing to lose by asking. Predictable, mama's heart went out to those four boys. She loved them as if they were her very own great grandchildren, what little time she had been around them. Daddy looked at things a little more practical; didn't become openly entangled in the heartstrings. I should have figured I would receive two diverse opinions and entirely different advice. Maybe I would go with majority rule. Maybe I would just go with my own gut instincts. Flip a coin; something not easily done when children's lives are at stack. I was facing the largest decision in my life and four other lives hinged on what I did or didn't do.

Plowing the furrow, question number one; should I become a foster parent to get those boys out of the hands of strangers? This was a no brainier. Both believed this was the right thing to do and actually supported me on that decision while pointing out the responsibilities involved of course. They certainly weren't telling me something I didn't already know. They never questioned that I wouldn't make a good father figure. They had once seen me in action with a previous girl friend that had a two year old daughter. I had adored the little girl and she had clung to me. In the long run, now looking back, I see how I had basically sabotaged that relationship, possibly because I wasn't ready or mature enough to take on the fatherly role long term. That twist of fate had landed me with my current wife and in the middle of this mess. Mess was a harsh word. Mess was what the four boys were in, not me.

My parents and grandparents had been dumbfounded by the abrupt breakup after having dated my former girlfriend for nearly a year, bringing her and her child around all the time. They had gotten warm and cozy with the situation; apparently more so than me. I had hurt her and her daughter by bowing out. To this day I regret what I did and how and why I did it. They certainly hadn't deserved it. Possibly I was fearful of falling in love and taking on the commitment; especially after suffering one failed marriage. I lived my life quite recklessly back then so possibly the wild demons possessing me steered me to sow a few more ill fated seeds before settling down. Maybe I just wasn't prepared to settle down in a family lifestyle. Was I ready now?

When asked should I consider adoption if ever faced with it; my parents sounded off entirely differently. Quick to the draw, this was a bad decision from their perspective. Mama looked at it from a practical and logical standpoint, taking a page out of daddy's book. My marriage wasn't on stable footing at the time and if I adopted them and things fell apart, I would be responsible for child support, custody battles, not to mention potential alimony. That ownership is nine tenths of the law thing came back into play. Mama and I usually butt heads on most issues but this time she put up a compelling argument, one that in my heart I knew was right. Still…

Playing the what if game, what if after some period of time the parents didn't work out their differences and the court decided it was in the best interest of the children to not return custody to either of them. There were no guarantees that the four boys would remain in our foster care. They could move them to another foster home or worse, split them up or put them up for adoption. They could be divvied out to different families in this process too.

Too much to digest for now; we hadn't even passed the certification process yet. Eat the elephant in small bites and chew carefully. My life was becoming way too complicated. Sadly I had always put me first. Maybe divine intervention had been the guiding source to make sure I had never been a biological father for this very reason. I wasn't cut out for it or maybe this was a test to see if I was. My brain hurt thinking about it. This was a huge responsibility. Was I as responsible as I professed to social services?

I thanked mama and daddy for hearing me out and

offering their advice. I knew they would stand behind me no matter what I decided, even if it turned out not being the decision they had hoped I'd make. We all agreed that something had to be done for those four boys. It rested on my shoulders to act and support the decision. A fostering I would go and hopefully the powers to be would not deny me the opportunity to at least give it a descent shot. Obviously I wasn't blood kin but in my way, I loved all four of them. After all, they called me Papa Tom. It hurt me to see what they were currently going through and confounded me that their parents just didn't get it. Talk about wanting to make a couple of adults go out into the yard and pick a switch, they deserved a reckoning moment for sure. There I go becoming judge and jury again, not my place, I get it, sort of.

Dang it, kids' lives are at stake here. Grow up and do the right thing for just this once. Am I telling them that or me? You can't change people who are not willing to change. I should know. I've fought conforming much of my life, stubborn and pigged headedness being inherited from mama. One difference, for all my flaws I never did anything that would have impacted a kid's welfare. If you didn't count me skipping out on that ex-girlfriend and her daughter, but even then I would have never done anything hurtful to the child. She was young enough to forget about me and that brief time I drifted through her life. At least that's my story and my way of dealing with it, sorry an excuse as it is. I have this knack for putting myself down. I think it's easier to deal with me on that level than have greater expectations or live to higher standards. It makes falling down a shorter distance to the ground. Here I come, ready or not.

Tour of Duty

Ages five, seven, nine and ten, we officially began our first tour of duty as foster parents. Actually in this case it was in title only. These four belonged to us so it wasn't exactly like we were breaking in a new routine. They knew where they stood with us. The difference, this time we were all they had for some extended stay. I knew this as well, but still I looked at the world through a new set of glasses, realizing I had taken a huge step, possibly more for me than them. The learning curve would become steeper, now having full responsibility 24/7. This was no mere snapshot in time, a weekend with us. This was the real deal. From this moment forward I was now responsible for four children's lives literally. I had never had this kind of responsibility. Time to test the water, and it wouldn't be just sticking my toe in; it would be a canon ball instead.

First things first, decide sleeping arrangements. We had opted to relocate our bedroom upstairs to be closer to the boys in case of any sort of emergency. That meant we'd place two each in the remaining bedrooms. The oldest were paired in one and the two youngest in the other. That seemed too easy. Next on the list would be a grocery run. With four additional mouths to feed, this would be a major adjustment. One of the perks of being foster parents is that you do receive a monetary supplement to assist with feeding and clothing those in your care. Every little bit helps. Raising four growing boys wouldn't be cheap but that was the least of my worries. Getting them past the stigma of having been basically abandoned, ensuring they knew they were welcome and loved was of utmost importance.

The oldest of the grand boys was a big boned lad, much

taller and larger than the other three. At an early age he had been nicknamed Moose. I'm not sure if that was a name he appreciated. I didn't call him that. I remembered back to those days when I had been called Toothpick. I was scrawny and lanky and it fit, but I can't say I liked being called anything stick related. Sometimes nick names aren't that funny or appreciated. I always addressed him by his given name, Dale.

Because of the slight age difference in him and the next one in line, I had spent more time with Dale before the others had come along. No, I'm not saying he was my favorite but he was the first so called grand in my life. I was there in the hospital when he had been born. The parents hadn't known whether they would be having a boy or a girl. Dale's dad had run out of the delivery room into the waiting room and announced it was a hard tail, his reference to having a brand new son; one proud papa he was. I'm gritting my teeth and trying real hard to not go there. Us having them right here is ironically a blessing for the kids, regardless to the circumstances that landed them on our doorstep.

Second in the pecking order was Andy, upper front teeth missing, but still he had a contagious smile. He was sort of the clown of the four, always up to something, a seasoned instigator. He and I would have been best friends as kids, because we were carved from the same piece of wood. I could see a lot of me in him; the joker, the kidder, the one skirting along the edges of the rules with mischief always stashed away in the back pocket. I'd keep one eye open if and when things went out of kilter, figuring he'd most likely have his hands in it. A good instigator rarely ever gets caught with the goods. It takes one to know one.

Keeping that in mind, he'd have a tough time pulling one over on the old master of the game.

Scott, second from the youngest had always been the toughest one for me to read and I don't mean that in a bad way. He had tendency to keep to himself. You'd often see him skipping along and singing, almost as if he was surviving in another dimension. Maybe this was his safety net. Again I must confess, I shared similar traits when just a tike myself. Playing by myself, tapping in on my vivid imagination was a magical escape for me. He often expressed this wondrous stare, as if he was doing some major processing when interacting. Again, none of these are bad traits. We all have our ways. I'm sure I was a mystery to many and probably still am.

Then there was Greg, the five year old. The imaginary world was truly his domain. His transformation went beyond mere expressions. He actually became the character and acted out his fantasies. Again, I could relate. Role playing various cowboys or other television heroes were a common theme back in my day; just like playing soldier. Greg was a hoot though. He took his roles seriously. The man of steel, Superman, had to be one of his favorites. I was lucky. I didn't have to poke and prod to learn their traits. I already knew most of them. I was a kid at heart my self, rough housing and tumbling about with them was an escape for me too. The 24/7 stint could be a game changer though. Time would tell. What was important was that we at least had them back for now in familiar territory.

Introducing structure and balance in their lives was a critical part of the transformation process. We had a picnic style table in the kitchen used for all meals. It was important that we gathered as family at feeding time. Thinking back now, we resembled a smaller version of the closing credits of a Duck Dynasty episode. What I noticed however and something I guess I had never picked up on in the past was their veracious eating habits. It didn't really matter what sort of food was placed before them, they consumed it as if it might be their last meal. Second and third helpings weren't uncommon in the early going. While it was rewarding to see them enjoying any food; it saddened me to watch this unfold. An underlying untold story obviously existed. I decided not to go there. Digging up skeletons wasn't useful in this situation. This was a time to heal, a time to build on it and move forward. I was the one being taught valuable lessons so it seemed.

I had a huge vegetable garden and the boys, especially the oldest two, tended to shadow me, so I would assign them various gardening choirs. I thought back on how I so hated being recruited by my papa to help with the garden. This was different. They embraced it. They asked questions, wanted to learn and were up for any task. Being there seemed to be beneficial. Obviously they craved attention. Maybe I did too. It seemed to be therapeutic for all of us. Who would have figured? It's inspiring how something so simple can mean so much. Unlike my papa with me, I tried to make more of a game of it than toil and trouble. I had those boys clearing rocks from the soil, and there was an endless supply, seeing who could toss them the furthest into the bordering field. Somehow we even made pulling weeds fun.

Harvesting was a bit trickier. The learning curve was large. Knowing when to pull and pick various veggies is a science within itself. They were willing and I was able. Trial and error in harvesting can be painful so I tried to make sure they didn't do any without me. You can't reattach immature cucumbers or squash or bean pods minus the beans inside. Patience isn't one of my best virtues but I tried hard not to make them feel bad if they did get over zealous. I didn't infringe on any child labor laws and require them to do any hoeing or plowing, not that they wouldn't have loved to have gotten their hands on my Troy Horse. Overall, it went well. I called it bonding with Papa Tom. Plus it was a way to get them to eat their vegetables, saying look what you picked today.

Over time, their appetites transformed, requiring less food intake and some were showing signs of pickiness, a child's rite of passage. It was a pleasant change; the boys no longer thinking any meal might be their last meal of the day. It's always a challenge, strategically blending healthy food and allowing snacks. We always tried to have that special time of the day designed as snack time for their favorites. In the early goings, it hadn't been as hard as I had expected; except that there was little down time and very few private moments. I became the fifth kid in many ways, playing in the yard, shooting basket ball and passing on to them the games I used to play as a kid. Simon Says, chase, hide and go seek, were throw backs I know, but they were affective and inexpensive entertainment tools. I even made an adventure of hauling the trash away in the truck, rotating that duty among the four, selecting a different sidekick to ride shotgun with me.

Soon things were falling in place. It was beginning to have a warm and cozy feel to it. Normalcy, who would have ever thought it? Maybe mama had been right; I might be cut out for this after all. The boys certainly enjoyed me bringing them by to see them. They loved it too. She could spoil a rock. They never stood a chance. The fruit doesn't fall far from the tree. I enjoyed buying them stuff too, treating them to things they had never experienced. Keeping the reins on me was a full time job.

Now was life perfect; no, not by a long shot. I had my moments when I just needed alone time and kids, any kids, can push your button and cause you to snap at them. One thing though, and not because we had agreed to a nonphysical discipline policy, I never was pushed to the point that I ever raised a hand to any of them. Sure, disciplinary action was occasionally required but it was administrated in ways like taking away privileges. Thank goodness this was before the dreaded timeout era, even though I guess making one of them to go their room is a form of timeout.

I must state for the record; they were well mannered kids for the most part. Not once did I ever utter those stupid words, "we can't have anything because of them." They were not destructive under our roof and their world wasn't cluttered with clothing or stuff all over the place. They quickly learned to pick up after themselves; everything had its place. We didn't have to do battle with them. I think it brought order and calm to their lives and they liked it. No, I'll be the first to admit; I didn't have all the answers and I stumbled about my fair share of the time during the learning process. You make mistakes and try to learn from those mistakes. Sometimes you just color outside the lines and hope it works.

Whatever we were doing, it must be working because the visits from DSS seemed to go well. They identified no flaws in our system. The kids were happy, content and well adjusted and so were we. We passed on all counts. We had even hired a tutor for Dale during the summer. He was in jeopardy of not moving on to the next grade, because he had incurred some difficulties during the last school year. He was big for his age and we were not going to see him stay back a grade. It wouldn't have been healthy for him. I offer a warm debt of gratitude to Mrs. Pat for her time spent with him. It was well worth the time and money; plus she and Dale really bonded. He would not miss that grade because of her nurturing and his hard work. It was a winning situation for all of us. I don't think I have crossed paths with her since that she didn't mention the experience as one she will always cherish. Doing right had its rewards. I'm smiling thinking about this one.

Let's Take This Show on the Road

Family bonding extends beyond the confines of the home and perimeters of one's imagination. Kids need to have an opportunity to be kids and do kid stuff. I grew up in a very fortunate household, with parents who loved to travel. For that reason I'm blessed to have visited most of the United States and both bordering countries by the age of fifteen. Between the ages of five and fifteen we did a couple of Griswold two week trips to California by car; once when I was five and the second time when I was fifteen. On those trips I experienced the wonders of Mount Rushmore, the Teton Mountains, Yellowstone Park, Grand Canyon, Mount Zion Park, the Bad Lands, the Painted Hills, the Black Hills, Salt Lake City, Vegas, L.A., San Diego, Tijuana, Dodge City, Boot hill, the Houston Astrodome, and the Texas desert. As a mere teenager I had visited Disneyland twice on the west coast.

Other trips included going to Detroit and Canada, seeing the wondrous Niagara Falls and my very first professional baseball game in Detroit Stadium, a double header between the Tigers and Angels, splitting the twin bill one to nothing each game. Daytona Beach was a second home for two weeks in July for the big race most years. Daddy loved his races, those featuring the likes of Richard Petty, Buddy Baker, the Allison's, Cale Yarborough, Fireball Roberts and his favorite Coo Coo Marlin. Weekend excursions to the Great Smokey Mountains were not uncommon. Camping was a big part of growing up too with weekend stints down at Elijah Clark State Park on the Georgia side of Clark's Hill Lake, now called Lake Thurman. There we'd crappie fish or put out bottles for catfish. Yes, I have been blessed.

Not to belabor my point, to make it clearly as possible, I wanted these boys to experiences, some of that. No, we'd not be doing a coast to coast two week journey but there were plenty of places much closer and within driving distance to make for a magical and unforgettable experience. What kid doesn't like to visit the zoo? My first had been the Atlanta Zoo, where Uncle Willie, a real silver backed gorilla resided; my first time to ever see a live one. I loved the monkey house and the building housing all the big cats, lions, tigers and Cheetahs. While on that second California trip we had visited the San Diego Zoo. Now that one was breathtaking.

Well, we did have a zoo close by, the Columbia South Carolina Zoo. For kids that had never been to a zoo before this should be awe inspiring. We picked a Saturday and loaded up the van and soon our little traveling circus was on the road, a mere one and half hour trip ahead, if you didn't count all the bathroom stops along the way. It's tough to time stops for four boys and a female. Like my mama always told me when we made a stop; go whether you have to or not. It's worth the try to get everyone on the same pee schedule. Oh yeah, there would be plenty of those questions about when we were going to arrive at our final destination. I loved zoos and animals so I could hardly wait either. I might have been worse than the boys, anticipating our arrival. We eventually made it and toured the wonderful wild kingdom. I can only hope it was as memorable for them as it was for me.

Following the traditional mountain trips introduced to me by my parents, we planned a day trip to the North Carolina Cherokee Reservation. This would be the first time for any of them to see real Indians. I took the old route, the one via back roads of American, with hairpin curves, steep ravines, mountain streams and waterfalls, and those dreaded signs, *Watch out for Falling Rocks*. And watch they did. There were endless souvenir shops bursting at the seams with authentic Indian stuff, most made in China or Taiwan. I didn't realize so many real Cherokee Indians had moved to those countries. While it was basically a tourist trap for adults, it was a must see at least one time for kids.

The Cherokee drama, *Unto These Hills*, had not depicted the trail of tears ending overseas. Even the Cherokee Nation's wisest chiefs apparently knew how to turn a buck. An Indian Chief in full head dress could be found on almost every corner, the boys giving them wide birth, fearful of being scalped I assumed. Regardless, each of the boys was allowed at least one souvenir to commemorate the trip. A visit wouldn't be complete without seeing live black bears or the dancing chickens. I for one just felt every kid should get to do this. I was certainly having my fair share of wonderful flashbacks thanks to them.

Carowinds, a 398-acre amusement park, located adjacent to Interstate 77 on the border between North and South Carolina, in Charlotte and Fort Mill, was another favorite spot from my youth; that and Six Flags over Georgia. We ventured there, and the boys were introduced to a larger than life carnival atmosphere. You had to pick and choose rides that they were old enough and big enough to ride, and those they were not afraid of riding. The log flume they loved and it was the least crowded near the park's closing time. We'd ride it and zip right back through the empty line and ride it again and again. We were quite water logged by the time the attendant told us it would be our last time, the park was closing. These boys definitely brought the kid out of me. I was number five, the elder of the group and resident dare devil.

Some excursions were simplistic by comparison. As

mentioned, carrying off the trash was made to seem like an adventure. Often I would take a couple of them into town where we'd visit the Shaved Hawaiian Ice stand for a special frozen treat. I'd swear them to secrecy, not to tell the others. Next time I would take the other two and we'd play the same game. I'm sure all were the wiser. It is tough concealing red and purple lips or orange tongues. I dare say any of them would probably remember these times like I still do.

Fostering so far had not been a burden. Sure, it wasn't a piece of cake, but I made the best of it, my life impacted and transformed into something I had never dreamt of. If you never have had kids, the uncertainty of such a situation cannot be predicted. It was never perfect but I don't think it was supposed to be. Still, they were being offered what I think must have had to been one of the happier times in their lives. Granted I'm sure they would have rather been with their parents and experiencing this with them. For now they were stuck with Papa Tom. I am recapping this fostering story through my eyes only and it isn't meant to slight the opinions or experiences of others.

I deer hunted so part of the preparation for deer season was looking for signs in the woods, determining a spot to place my deer stands. The boys and I would all trek into the woods below the house, making it a southern safari. There I would point out tracks, dear scrapes, trails and other signs to them. I'd take them to my honey holes where I had slain deer. There I would relive the experience vividly and watch them as they envisioned the scenes replayed in their minds, their eyes expressing the enjoyment. We'd experience a man's afternoon of bonding in the wilderness. None were of age to actually take them into the woods for the real deal. Besides, my latter stand or climbing stand would only accommodate one person. Later when I did slay a small deer, I dragged it to the clearing and then recruited their help to drag it the remainder of the way. I still have photos of them standing proudly beside the prize in the back of my truck.

More DSS visits confirmed we were still on the right track. Eventually there were also supervised parental visits. We'd usually make ourselves scarce for those, DSS rules, not ours, to give the parents' quality time with their children without any distractions. DSS monitored these for specific reasons, seeing how the interactions unfolded; my assumption so it could be weighed in on future evaluations to help determine the path leading back to the boys returning to their rightful place. After all, the ultimate goal or at least one of the main ones is to formulate a viable return, part of the permanency plans. It was part of the process.

The kids came first and would not be placed knowingly back into an undesirable situation. I stand firm. The boys' parents loved them, to that there was no doubt. Loving them and caring for them in a totally unselfish and loving manner are entirely different. Sometimes your *want to* and *can do* don't always work out as envisioned. It was up to them to work out their differences and rate the kids on their personal priority list. Pretty simple, our job was to be there for the boys until.

Help me, My Clothes are Shrinking

Greg, the baby of the bunch, could be the master of disguise. He'd disappear down the hallway and return as Clark Kent and reappear as the man of steel. There must be a phone booth hidden away somewhere because Superman was now in the building. He sported a cape with a large S inscribed in black marker. This made him bullet proof to the world. Able to leap the couch in a single bound or stop a speeding cat, his powers offered up the perfect protection. With just the slightest encouragement Superman would entertain us with his feats of strength. We'd applaud his demonstrations. Although he had the ability to accessorize, we bought him Superman pajamas. A super hero should have proper attire.

Something terribly wrong occurred. Greg was quite distraught. His super hero outfit was not fitting him properly. His favorite clothes were shrinking and he was blaming us. Obviously at this age he was sprouting like a weed but we could not convince him of that fact. Nope, his clothes were shrinking and we had to make it stop. How could Superman fight crime if he couldn't dress the part? Clark Kent could not step in, not without divulging his secret identity. I told him it must be kryptonite that Lex Luther, super villain and archenemy of Superman, must have something to do with this. He bought it, eventually allowing his super hero to fade into obscurity. Other clothes were shrinking as well. A shopping spree was in order to refurbish his wardrobe. Those favorites had to be tossed along with his superman identity.

Peewee's Playhouse was a big hit on television at the time. He was also a member of our household. Greg could mimic his laugh with perfection. The shrinking clothing fit the persona and his characterization of Peewee. Peewee wore trademark high waters and short long sleeve shirts. He had a birthday coming up and I had found the perfect birthday gifts. J.C. Penny in Greenwood was carrying a Peewee Herman line of clothing, a mock up of his suit. They even carried a Peewee Herman ventriloquist doll, very similar to my childhood ventriloquist version, Howdy Doody. Penny's had one of those great sales going on at the time, these particular items marked down as much as 80%. Te price was so good I bought one doll for him, one for me. I still have mine and for a time I had it in its original box. Greg was in heaven, now a full-fledged Peewee Herman clone. Even though his mouth moved when the dummy's mouth did, we never let on and instead praised him for his feat of illusion. The Peewee high water pants and shortened long sleeves were supposed to have that shrunken fit so it worked to perfection.

Greg had a serious persona. Often he demanded to be called Sam, not Greg. Sam was his alter ego, the strong and defiant one. This one yearned to be with his parents. In reality, that's where he should be. While Greg could escape into a make believe world, Sam understood the real world. Sam's place was not with us. Greg filled the room with laughter. Sam pulled at your heart strings. He was mature and knew what he wanted, his mama and daddy; nothing personal, just fact. We just went with the flow when Sam emerged. Eventually Greg would return when ready, and if he didn't, we understood that too. I was learning to adapt as was Sam and Greg.

Not to be fooled, there were other characters looming in that imagination and one in particular would incorporate the services of the other three boys. Enter the era of the Teenage Mutant Ninja Turtles, four of them, the numbers were perfect. Each of the boys took on a half shelled persona, aligning themselves with one of the turtles. Raphael suited Greg to a tee. Raphael was the turtle team's bad boy. The dark red masked hero was physically strong, fitting Greg's aka Superman character. The turtle with a Brooklyn accent was aggressive by nature, and seldom hesitated to throw the first punch, his personality alternating between fierce and sarcastic.

Leonardo, the oldest of the four turtles had to be Dale. Leo was the tactician, courageous leader and devoted student of martial arts, and wore a blue mask. Dale was the eldest in real life so it only seemed fitting. He was devoted to his brothers, the non turtle variety too. When I think of courage, I picture him doing what he must, forfeiting some of his summer outside of school to embrace the tutoring. I think he embraced the one on one experience with Mrs. Pat and appreciated us for making sure he would not be left a grade behind. Dale was indeed Leo in all respects.

Michelangelo perfectly matched Andy, even though the others fought over this identity, each waning to be the surfer dude talking character. Mikey was easy-going, a fun-loving jokester, and free-spirited; the wearer of the orange mask. The pizza lover of the clan had a creative side. Last by not least was Scott, Donatello, the scientist, the inventor, the engineer and technological genius. Donnie matched up well with Scott the quiet one and the least violent of the turtles and grand boys.

Cries of cowabunga were not uncommon throughout the house and in the backyard. A lingo consumed the four fostering our world with terms like bummer, dude, bogus, radical, far-out, tubuloso and bodacious accenting their dialogue. It was nothing but fun times I assure you, never a dull moment with those tasked at defending good and fighting the evil doers, the imaginary Shredder and his Foot Soldiers.

I guess I could have been cast as Splinter, the humanoid rat and the sensei, the adopted father of the four Ninja Turtles. We had no one to fill the shoes of April O'Neal or Casey Jones, two more among the assortment of many characters rolled out on the cartoon series. If you think about it, living in an imaginary place, one where the turtles defended their turf, seemed quite appropriate for the world the boys now resided. While living in our home in no way resembled the sewers where the turtles lived, it was still symbolic of abandonment, mutated misfits shunned by the world and now surviving on their terms. Possibly Shredder and the Foot Soldiers represented the fear of uncertainty in their fragile lives. The turtles' masks offered the boys a sense of antonymous protection from those who might be intent on harming them. The masks would not shrink like clothing; offering stability and a bulletproof existence.

One's imagination can be a powerful tool, a defender of evil and an escape from physical and mental anguish. No, the boys had not been physically harmed but mentally they had been battered and bruised. There is something shamefully wrong when children at any age are subjected to parental abuse on any level, whether it might be brutally physical or something just as harmful as neglect and abandonment. Their young lives are molded at an early age and once the image has been shaped, it isn't always easily reshaped.

I'm no expert, just making comments stemming from my observations. Love can cure a lot of hurt, even when the ones hurting don't realize the extent of their pain. We were mere Band-Aids in life's journey filled with spills and skinned knees. We couldn't fix everything that was broken and we certainly couldn't shield them from what might lay ahead. We could only believe in hope and those who would eventually take back the reins.

No Greg, your clothes aren't shrinking. You're growing. Superman's cape is a powerful security blanket but even that magical 'S' can't fend off father time. Evil always lurks in the shadows, tugging at your life strings, pulling you back into a dark pit where all can seem to be lost. There is truth in that light at the end of the tunnel. Allow those who love you to love you and reality will be the most powerful tool you'll have going forward. The youngest tend to struggle the most when life crumbles about them. They're too young to defend for themselves but ironically understand right from wrong. No doubt, regardless of one's home environment, being tossed into foster care had to be a traumatic experience for all of us. Adapt and survive.

Clinging to the way it had always been, even something as symbolic as clothing, nurtured hope in a young boy's mind. Not that Greg hated being with us, but Greg yearned to be with his parents. That's where he belonged for better or worse. That's where all of them belonged. We could only serve as the bridge across life's deep raven, a pathway hopefully leading back to a happy home awaiting them. Kids deserve to be with their parents but only if their parents deserve having them there.

An Amazon among Men

Obviously we thought we had our hands full with the four grand boys. Selfishly we had signed up for foster care duty with purpose. DSS did not follow our lead unfortunately or share our motives. Remembering back now, we were instructed that we could have up to six children in our household. Currently we were two shy of that number; a quantity we had gotten quite cozy with. Our present situation offered more than enough responsibility for us to handle. We were contacted by the social worker assigned to us. A girl was in need of foster care for the weekend. Guilt ridden, how could we decline? Surely we could manage one more for just three days. The boys had not been a big deal and they were well into an adjusted routine. The main issue ahead would be sleeping arrangements. We'd adjust and make do. How difficult could this be, right?

The social worker delivered a twelve year old girl to our doorway; a tall drink of water, nearly as tall as me and I'm six, two. She was easily around six feet in height, Amazon in stature for anyone twelve years old. Let's just call her Jane-doe for the sake of argument. She took a liking to the boys right off as they did her. Soon they were out and about playing. She could be the sister they never had or possibly playact the roll of the turtles' reporter friend, April O'Neal. I'd let them decide. My role remained the same regardless to whether we had four or five or a girl in the mix. The boys soon had her referring to me as Papa Tom. That was fine with me. I just went with the flow. I treated her like one of the boys. Whatever I did with them, she was welcomed to join in like one big happy family.

The DDS worker hadn't given us too much background

on her so we'd have to fish that hole on our own. She'd answer what was asked. We were careful not to dig too deeply and stirrup any bad memories. What we had learned is that she had been moved about quite a bit in her short time in foster care, for explanations unclear to us. Oh well, she seemed to be adjusting, as were we. Even I had managed to take on one more, going well beyond the boundaries of my perceived capabilities.

The three days passed uneventfully and she was returned back to foster care destination unknown. We didn't ask and they didn't tell. After she had departed, the boys didn't seem quite so taken by her as I had originally thought; even though none of them gave me much to hang my hat on, leaving me to suspect she was a girl, what did I really expect. Undaunted I marched onward.

As it approached the weekend we were again contacted by DSS, requesting that Jane-doe return to our custody again for the weekend. Old hats at this, we accepted our dooly sworn responsibilities as just another day in the neighborhood. The social worker arrived, Jane-doe in tow, and requested some alone time with my wife before I arrived home from work. Later my wife shared with me what the social worker had shared with her, the specifics of what had landed Jane-doe in foster care.

Sometimes not knowing is much better than knowing the rest of the story, *Paul Harvey*. Shocker, every male in her immediate family had sexually molested her. Because of this, Jane-doe gravitated to all males, especially the leaders of the household. I was in full panic mode. She was here again. How was I going to deal with something like this? Before I had just treated her like any other kid, boy or girl. With this new knowledge I was gun shy to even be around her. I was the one who needed therapy now.

I was clueless at what to do, how to react to or interact with someone who I now knew had been sexually molested. I had never knowingly been around anyone who had ever been assaulted by perverts, worthless family members at that. It sickened me to my stomach and enraged me simultaneously that family members could have done something so horrific to kin, an innocent girl at that. You read about this sort of thing or see it on the news; never ever thinking about coming in contact with it.

Just being this close to it made me a basket case. The foster parent was nearing a meltdown. So how was I going to face her and handle the new information? It made me nervous that the boys were being exposed to this too. I had to do some serious thinking and soul searching, and I wasn't sure any amount of either was going to help. No training had prepared me for this moment. So what did I do? I made every attempt to avoid her and that wasn't easy when someone is in your care 24/7 for three days. Doing so meant I had to sort of neglect the boys too.

One bad decision just leads to the next. What was I supposed to do? If I spent any time with her it might be perceived wrongly by her. I couldn't get it out of my head and just treat her like I had been treating her. My goal was to survive the weekend with minimal contact, especially any one on one interaction. By the final day I had done just that; staying busy or finding reasons to run errands, anything that would remove me from the equation and situation. I was indeed a basket case, acting too much out of the normal, doing the worst possible thing for the girl and me.

I continued to justify my behavior; rationalizing that I would not put myself in a compromising position, rather than spend quality time with her to show her that all males weren't monsters. All the time I just couldn't visualize kinfolk doing the unthinkable to a little girl. It struck me like a bolt of lightning. She didn't have the body of a twelve year old. She had the mind of a twelve year old in the image of a sixteen year old. She couldn't help that those bastards had taken the liberty to help themselves.

After she had been picked back up by the social worker, my wife told me that Jane-doe had come to her, distraught and confused about the way I had been treating her all weekend. I took a defensive posture, stating I had not touched her or done anything to her. This wasn't an accusation, on the contrary. Jane-doe was upset because she said I was mean and wouldn't have anything to do with her. She thought I no longer liked her. Ultimately by taking the approach I had taken, I had done more damage. She thought I hated her. Lessons don't come easy, even for foster parents. I was supposed to have helped her overcome the abuses she had endured, no matter what kind they had been. I had flunked royally.

There was much more to fostering than meets the eye. I hadn't even skimmed the surface. I had found a comfort zone with the boys and their reason for being here. I had been ill prepared for far worse scenarios. I vowed then that I would learn from this experience and I'd do better next time; make things right with Jane-doe. She never returned and we never knew whatever happened to her. Such is the life of a foster parent; we have no rights in the matter. I regretted that her last impression of me was that of one who didn't care. I had squandered that last weekend with the twelve year old Amazon Princess.

I should have made her feel welcomed and loved and instead I had withdrawn, fearful of giving her the wrong impression because of how others had abused her. I should have just been me, like the first weekend visit. It hadn't been her fault she had been molested. She came to us as a twelve year old in need of love and parental guidance, I had given her neither. I almost felt as if I had assaulted her by ignoring her. Maybe I had been fooling myself; I wasn't really cut out for this, not when faced with the real horror stories. How can people be so cruel? I hadn't seen everything yet by a long shot but I just didn't know it yet. There was a lot I didn't know about this fostering thing and to what extent adults could harm children.

Tail of the Why Monkey

Art Linkletter hosted a television show back in the 1950's, *Kids Say the Darndest Things*, and that for sure holds true to this very day. Many an awkward moment has been instigated by a kid's innocence and ill timed inquisitiveness. With no parenting experience I was often unprepared for questions launched from the mouths of babes while fostering the best I could muster. Luckily I'm a pretty good improviser. I can typically react on the fly, especially if witty or sarcastic responses can buy me some time. Foot in mouth disease runs a close second. Children don't always grasp the significance of my sarcasm, taking the responses for face value and way too seriously. I don't get why they can't stick to my script. My voice is deep and loud so that doesn't help. It can be quite intimidating and sound like I'm royally pissed off when I'm not. My technique obviously requires some honing when dealing with the boys or any other foster kids for that fact.

Humor has been a powerful tool in my defensive arsenal; however, making light of serious situations can land me in not so flattering consequences. Obviously none of these defense mechanisms helped me while trying to deal with the abused twelve year old girl. None came in to play. I was a floundering beached whale from the first earth shattering second. The boys were different. I could handle situations concerning my kind, the male species, even the miniature version. Fortunately for me, none of the real tough questions were being asked. The boys seemed content in their surroundings and environment. Stability had offered them comfort I suppose. They were being fed and clothed well and exposed to a better lifestyle than they had been accustomed, so they were cozy and comfy as was I.

That being said, there is always one in every bunch. Inquiring minds require answers. Andy's favorite question was why this and that. With every response echoed another why. He seemed to have an endless supply of whys. I get it. You ask questions to learn, but there can be a tipping point when bombarded by one why after another. It's okay to toss in a what, a when or a how sometimes just to break the cycle. After a while, I think he did it just to pester me. You can only play Papa Tom for so long. He will eventually win. Take that to the bank.

I had to break him and it wasn't as simple as telling him to stop asking why so much. I had already played that card. Papa Tom was one devious foster parent. The wheels were turning inside my scheming brain. The boys enjoyed bedtime stories and I could spin a good'un on the fly. All good stories should teach a lesson or have a moral, or maybe just scare the crap out of you. I decided to take the low road and go for something scary and to the point. A boy named Andy would be the central character, my protagonist of course. I usually tried to incorporate them in my tales. They loved it.

I began spinning the yarn, the *Tale (Tail) of the Why Monkey*. The title alone had set the hook. I had them wide eyed and mesmerized, spellbound and ready to hear the story; just where I wanted them. Deem the lights, its story time; this is the Tail (Tale) of the Why Monkey.

Tale of the Why Monkey

"Andy, it's time to get ready for bed, sweetie."

"But mama, why do I got to go now, it's not even dark yet?"

"It's time for all four year olds to be in slumber land so hop to it young man."

"Why is daddy not here yet?"

"He had to work late sweetie. He should be home soon."

"Why he have to work late, mama?"

"Sometimes he just has to. Now go wash your face and hands, brush your teeth and tinkle. I'll be in there in a few minutes to tuck you in."

Andy finally did as mama had asked and waited impatiently clutching Patch, a one eyed ruffled parrot, his bed buddy. He stared at the bedroom door wondering why he always had to go to bed first. "It's not fare Patch. Grown-ups get to stay up and watch TV and do all kind of fun stuff. Why can't Andy and Patch?"

"All righty young man, sleep tight and don't let the bed bugs bite."

"Mama, why would the bed bugs bite me and Patch if we sleep real tight?"

Mama smiled, kissed Andy on the cheek and Patch on the head and switched off the light. She left the door cracked after clicking on the Papa Smurf night light.

Andrew arrived home thirty minutes later and greeted his wife, Sandra with a kiss and a hug. "Guess the little munchkin is bedded down and in dream world?"

"Only after we played the why game as usual."

"That's my boy. He can wear out a why for sure. Think I'll go take a peak at him before I unwind."

Andrew eased open the door, the hallway light creeping

across little Andy's face. Three eyes stared back at him. "I see you and old Patch are still wide awake."

"Daddy, why you have to go to work? Why you not here with me and Patch so you can tell us a bedtime story?"

"I'm here now boys so guess we'll just have to make it right. Did you mind your mama today?"

"Yes sir. We minded so good that mama gave us Oreos and milk. It was Patch's idea to have Oreos. He likes to lick the inside."

"Patch is pretty sharp."

"Daddy, why do we have to go to bed before it be dark?"

Andrew thought for a second how he could break Andy from why-ing them to death. Tired and not quite up to it tonight, a remedy evolved in the form of a bedtime story. "How about I tell you that quick story and then you and Patch promise to go to sleepy town, alright?"

"Me and Patch like bed time stories almost as much as Oreos."

"All right then as all stories start, once upon a time in a land far, far away, a little boy prince ruled a special kingdom of tropical exotic parrots. His head honcho parrot wore a big red patch on his eye. "

"Why it not be black like Patch's?"

"Quite now or I won't finish the story. The prince summoned head honcho and asked him why the rest of the parrots were sad and not talking. The parrot said they were afraid the evil Why Monkey had been threatening to put a curse on the young prince for asking why all the time. He was the meanest of all bullies."

"But daddy, why him not like the little prince? Why did him have to be a bully?"

"The Why Monkey was a bully because bullies are only bullies when they can scare others. He didn't like anyone using the Why word because it belonged to him. He warned the little prince to never utter the Why word again or bad things would happen. The prince laughed and asked why he should listen to a silly little brown ring-tail monkey. His bullying wasn't working on the prince so the Why Monkey warned him one last time, chanting a curse, saying the next time he asked why, a tail would appear on the little prince's hinny. Each and every time, he spoke the word why, the tail would grow longer."

"Why was that monkey such a mean bully? Did the little prince grow a tail like the monkey, daddy?"

Smiling, Andrew said, "Bullies are really cowards but it makes them feel powerful when they can be others do what they want them to do. The prince wasn't buying it and he defied the monkey, and said the W word over and over before going to sleep that night. The next morning he awoke and had a long tail just like the Why Monkey had warned. The parrots flew away, now too frightened to stay in the kingdom. The little prince looked in the mirror, felt his newly grown tail and asked why this had happened to him. His tail immediately grew another foot and curled over his shoulder."

"How did him make the tail go away, daddy?"

"We'll save the rest of the story until tomorrow. It's late and your mamma's going to have mine, yours and Patch's hides if you don't go to sleep. Love you and don't let the bed bugs bite, sport. Good night."

"Good night daddy, sleep tight too. I wish we could get rid of all the bed bugs."

Some time passed midnight Andy woke. Thirsty, he stumbled awkwardly to the bathroom sink, filled his Spider Man glass and drank half of it. The running water made his bladder ache so he pulled down his PJ's to heed nature's call. Standing in front of the potty, he finished his business and reached to pull up his pants when it snagged on something.

He reached behind and touched what felt like a six inch nub. He whispered, why did he have a bump on his fanny? Too sleepy to understand, he made his way back to bed, felt around for Patch but couldn't find him. The Z's won and Patch-less he fell into a deep slumber.

Hearing voices, he pried the sleep from his eyes and looked around his room, now splattered with morning sunshine. Whispers persisted. He eased to the side of his bed and saw huddled in the corner on the far side of his room, his toys, all of his toys.

"Look, he's awake!" yelled Baby Kermit.

"Be careful, he could be dangerous," warned the California Raisins.

"He's not our Andy. He's evil and will suck out our brains," whispered Fraggle.

Alf pushed ET toward the bed. "You go over there and check things out."

Inspector Gadget and Gizmo slipped under the bed and climbed up the head board to have a better vantage point. "He's got one! He's definitely got one!" yelled Gadget.

"Why you toys talking and pointing at me? Why you look so scared?" asked Andy.

"There she grows! He's got the curse! He soon won't be our boy at all," screamed Gadget.

Perched high on the Teenage Mutant Ninja Turtle lamp, Patch now shouted a warning, "You must stop Andy, my shipmate. You must stop, I repeat, you must stop now!"

"Why you up there, Patch? Why you not in bed with me like always?"

"Because you're becoming Not-Andy, I repeat, Not-Andy."

"You heard Patch. He's almost not our Andy. We must hide," mumbled a Smurf.

"Me still Andy and you my friends."

"No, you are becoming an evil Why Monkey, a mean

bully and you will make us all followers of the Why Monkey World," explained the lead Raisin. "Look at your tail!"

Andy felt where his fanny used to be and sure enough there was this long furry curly tail protruding through his pajama bottoms. "Why I have a tail, Patch?"

"Do not say the W word. I repeat, do not say the W word. Every time you do, the monkey tail grows longer. It grows longer. Soon it stops and you become a full fledged Why Monkey, I repeat, a Why Monkey. You will be mean to us, a big bad bully; yes a big bad bully."

"Andy don't want to be a monkey. Don't say I am a bully. I want mama and daddy."

"Kid, the parents can't help you now. They can't even see you because you've crossed over into me Tarzan, you Cheetah world, monkey boy," warned Alf.

"He's right, soon you'll look just like a monkey, craving bananas and climbing trees. You'll grunt but won't be able to talk. We'll be cursed to serve you because you were our boy and you will make us do things, bad things, scary things," explained Inspector Gadget.

Andy tried to respond but strange monkey sounds emitted from deep in his throat. He hungrily eyed the Chiquita banana squeaky toy on his play bench that belonged to his dog Snoopy. He suddenly felt like swinging on something. His lips kept puckering and he was much too fidgety. He was mad, angry at all his toys. He poked out his chest and snarled like a big bad bully.

Patch shouted, "Andy has left the building, I repeat; Andy has left the building, hail to the Why Monkey, hail to the Why Monkey."

The Why Monkey grabbed the bed sheet and tossed it into the air, chanting monkey talk. Suspended then floating down like a parachute, the sheet engulfed the Why Monkey. He fought the smothering fabric as it pinned him to the bed,

screaming wild and making crazy monkey sounds."
As if by magic, the sheet lifted. "Mamma and Daddy are here, Sport. Why are you screaming? Were you playing or just having a morning-mare?"
"No daddy, don't daddy, don't say the W word! You'll grow a tail too. Mamma won't play with you no more because you'll be a bully. You'll make monkey talk and be real mean."
"You'll be okay, Sport. Go back to sleep. You were just dreaming."
"I'm not a monkey, daddy?"
"You're not a monkey."
"I'm not a bully, daddy?"
"You're not a bully, sport. Sleep tight."
"I won't let the bed bugs bite me or Patch." And with that Andy quickly drifted back off to sleep, snuggling patch.
"Andrew, tell me you didn't tell him that stupid Why Monkey story last night, the one your dad told you."
Andrew broke eye contact with Sandra and smiled then whispered, "To quote Patch, it works, I repeat, it always works."

Spell bounded, mesmerized, morale delivered, the whys were less frequent from this day forward.
Mission accomplished, winner, this round, Papa Tom.

Boys will be Boys Because They Are

Part of growing up is experiencing those awareness cycles. Boys love to hate girls even though they don't really hate them. Boys are traditionally exhibitionists. Boys like to show off. I was once a boy so I can concur. Problem, I had not been on this side of the boy fence, looking through adult eyes and contemplating how to handle strictly boy situations when faced with them head on. I lacked the parenting gene so my approach was not always the appropriate approach; certainly nothing by the book. Rules, you had to know parenting rules and I didn't.

While being a foster parent did come with general guidelines, it lacked that how to manual. *Foster Parenting for Dummies* would have been a helpful reference book. It would probably be difficult to cover how to handle every possible situation in a playbook though. Like a real parent, I did the best I could as awkward as it could often seem. Climbing out on the very end of that tree limb, hearing the cracking sound, paints a precarious outcome. Once out there on that limb you have to make split second decisions and you don't always have a chance to second guess; been there, done it, and one has to live with the consequences.

Two incidences jump out at me as I treaded water in the fostering pond. Incident number one, Grandma of the household had discovered that someone was trashing her catalogs and newspaper flyers, Sections were being cut out and removed. We narrowed down the suspects, excluding us, the cat and the dog as guilty participants. Still not tipping our hand, it required the gumshoe approach, a little covert private eye investigating. It wasn't difficult to uncover the evidence, but we still had no prime suspect among the four in the eventual line-up. I opted not to go for the sting operation. I regret that oversight now. My way was the direct approach. We were leaning towards one of the final four, only because of the room and side of the bed the evidence had been discovered. I chalked up the content squirreling to growing boys having inquisitive minds and infatuations. I was once a boy after all, I get it. The greater concern was that of destroying personal property. As Barney Fife would say, 'Nip it, nip it, nip it.'

The boys were gathered and shown the evidence; watchful of any changes in facial expressions or nervous fidgeting. Each was cool as a refrigerated cucumber. We explained that no one was going to be punished, but cutting out photographs of ladies in their undergarments from catalogs and newspaper flyers was not permissible; mainly because it was viewed as destroying personal property. The guilty party held his ground, apparently still not believing us about that punishment part, or maybe just too embarrassed to lay claim to the incident.

Having only circumstantial evidence we tried another approach, one based on where we uncovered the clippings. We called out Scott but he didn't confess as being the guilty party, forever the silent loner. In an unexpected turn of events Dale spoke up saying he had done it, offering no further explanation. We accepted his guilty plea and moved on, but not before we turned this into one of those lessons learned sermons. This was more of the grandparent approach and not that of the foster parent.

To this day, over twenty years later, I still wonder. I had my suspicions back then who might have been our guilty boy, but I let it go. There was really no point of making a big deal out of it. We had done the necessary thing, explaining the actions and ramifications of those actions, and it never happened again. I honestly think we got it all wrong. My gut tells me brotherly love intervened that day. Here's the way I believe it played out. Dale stepped forward and claimed he had cut the clippings and stashed them away to protect his brother. After all, he was Leonardo, the oldest of the four turtles and the tactician and courageous leader. It just felt like something he would do and if that is the case, I commend him for his actions. The evidence said otherwise because it had not been found in his room or under his bed. Four boys, whether they might be in the care of grandparents or foster care, must stick up for one another. Blood is truly thicker than water when it comes down to it. The Red Badge of Courage goes to Dale; at least that's my assessment of the situation.

We boys at some point in our lives do begin taking notice of the opposite sex. It's not planned. It just happens. Sneaking picks at stashed away Playboy books or just ogling the ladies dressed in panties and bras in the Sears catalog, it's just part of growing up. There's nothing wrong or perverted about it. Boys will be boys; been there and done it too. Girls are yucky and nice; like biting into a green plum. You can't help it because it is there in front of you, tempting you the entire time.

Lessons don't always come with a structured lesson plan. The childless one had learned a valuable one that day during the clippings inquisition. Just let it run its course next time and in the end, it will work itself out for the best. Curiosity is an act of nature, a tool in the steep learning process. Once satisfied, we move onto the next thing. Sears taught plenty of valuable lessons. For all the boys, thank you Richard Sears and Alvah C. Roebuck for the corporation you named Sears, Roebuck and Co. that you established in 1893. You certainly developed a page turner for many impressionable minds.

Event number two was a boy's scenario that came out of nowhere. We had been fostering for months so I'm not exactly sure what triggered the sudden change. Kids march to their own drummer and innovation can be good or bad, dependent on the outcome of their actions. Having four boys under our roof was much easier than the mix match of genders. It certainly made room assignments a piece of cake. Clothing all boys is much easier than accessorizing for girls; one man's opinion, I confess. I digress, recalling the issues with our Amazon placement, but then again, that experience was probably an anomaly and certainly no fault of hers. I had absolutely no parenting skills as I have claimed more times than I can count thus far, but boys just seemed easier for me to manage than girls. This had formed my fostering template so I really had nothing else to go on.

Bath time was assigned in twos. I'm not sure why or how this arrangement had been made. Maybe it was to conserve water or something, save time, who knows? I had stayed out of it, my wife having basically established the routine, herding them like cattle or sometimes more like cats, to the tub once the bath water had been drawn. Grandmothers are better suited for these chores. It offered me a little downtime in front of the television while the final touches were being put on bedtime.

My role was more the tuck them in and tell them bedtime stories. I liked this arrangement and had comfortably fallen into the nightly ritual. Most of the time the two younger ones were paired together as was the elder two. I didn't choose the pecking order. Maybe the younger ones needed to be in bed earlier; might have just been grandmother's draft picks. Again, I had no dog in this hunt. Baths were more adventurous playtime opportunities from the way it sounded down the end of the hallway. I'd just crank up the TV volume and tune out the activities until time for me to do my part of the ritual and tuck them in.

One particular night we heard the pitter patter of feet approaching the den, accented by squeals and laughter. The two oldest boys shot through the den, then the kitchen, and looped back through the dining room and living room buck naked. I could hear noted comedian Ray Stevens shouting, *don't look Ethel*; we had juvenile streakers among us. I just rolled my eyes and shook my head; boys just being boys. I returned to my television watching, drama over with, so I assumed.

Their bare butts quickly made another lap. Obviously they were enjoying their new found freedom just a tad too much. Liberated of their clothing or just feeling their oats as amateurish exhibitionists, their freestyle laps were not slowing down, even with grandma insisting they needed to go put on their pajamas. It was time for Papa Tom to intervene. On the next pass through I shot a similar warning in their direction, but apparently the game was on in their minds. Even my booming voice made no impact on their over zealous antics.

Here's where lack of parenting experience eludes me. Still sitting in my television watching chair I told them, just what were their friends at school going to think if they heard they were running through the house naked as jaybirds? How did that go you ask; not too good. Naked they remained. I warned them if they persisted I'd have no choice but to go find my camera and snap a picture to show their friends. Finding my camera wasn't the right thing to do, but I figured it was worth the bluff for those in the buff. Dared me they did. Watch what you wish for; never dare ole Papa Tom. I headed down the hallway to the bedroom to search for my camera as they backtracked through the living room, still not willing to dress for bed. These two were having way too much fun. Worse still, they were now disobeying two adults. Fun time was over. Their antics had worn out its welcome. Time to get dressed for bed, streaking was officially a done deal.

I somehow located my ancient Kodak Instamatic, not even sure if it had a cartridge of film inside or not. It didn't really matter as I figured just the mere threat would put the fear in them; and if not, a flash would serve the purpose in my blackmail threat. A bluff should be as good as the real thing. They'd run one way and then the other. Now it had turned into a combination game of chase and hide and go seek. I hadn't signed up for this game, and it was obviously messing up my TV time, but I played it out. Points had to be made. Lessons had to be learned. Nakedness needed to be covered.

As they cut the corner and through the kitchen on their next lap, I headed them off at the pass. I held the camera up and pressed the button, pretending to snap a photo and indeed the flash caught their attention. Soon after that, they located their PJs. Mission accomplished; game over, win goes to the innovative Papa Tom once again. I held that threat over their head and they never pulled that stunt again. My bluff had been successful. I found out much later that there had been film in the camera when we used it to take pictures for some other family event. I had forgotten about the streaking episode. Upon having it processed we discovered that we actually had evidence of their little naked romp as an insurance policy in that single photo. In the end, all of us had a good laugh about it. That's what families do. Fumbling and stumbling ahead, Papa Tom was learning too.

I remembered those embarrassing photos my parents had taken of me at various ages, sprawled out on the bed, buck naked for the world to see, or sitting in my grandparents' kitchen sink during bath time. All were innocent enough but some folks today would label it child porn. It was family memories when I was growing up. I still have those photos of my naked little scrawny butt, dated on the back to recognize me as one year old. Heck, even spankings are almost illegal now and society wonders why kids are the way they are. They rule the roost with no fear of being punished. I thought it was bad when I was a kid to get spanked or have to go pick my switch, but now looking back I see it was teaching me to be good, or at least the difference in right and wrong. DSS rules, we couldn't beat our foster kids, even if they were grandkids. We played by the rules; we just didn't let the boys know that we couldn't spank them. There's nothing wrong with keeping the upper hand right?

The Legend of Lizard Man

There was a fifth grandson in the mix, their cousin; belonging to my wife's other daughter. He often visited. Foster parenting rules were null and void where he was concerned. Brandon was in the eight year old age bracket. I'm going to get off track a tad but I think it's worth including him in my nostalgic memories. For the record, let me say that terrorizing children is not a recommended practice. That being said, I am quite masterful at doing my part. The Why Monkey story proved to be quite affective, right? The boys truly loved me making up stories and sometimes I even made a stab at poetry.

Along about the time we were fostering, newspapers were covering a developing story in Bishopville, South Carolina, near Darlington and Florence. A creature had been sighted and was wreaking havoc along the dark roads near swampland. Locals began calling it the Lizard Man, mainly based on the eye witness accounts. It was large, green with a long tail, red eyes and clawed hands; a southern version of Big Foot. Captivated by the story, I wrote a silly poem; or at least my sad attempt at poetry. Kids loved it and I would vary the poem using my friends' children within its content. I even drew my version of the Lizard Man at the top of the page.

I can't recall what prompted me to zero in on Brandon, but I'm guessing he had done something to warrant me doing it. Ole Papa Tom doesn't usually do something without just cause. He had obviously pulled some sort of stunt worthy of drawing my attention. It was the season to be jolly and a letter ended up as one of his stocking stuffer, one from the good ole Lizard Man. Disclaimer, I am not a poet. Trust me. I know it. It didn't really matter. Kids didn't know it. Scaring *the you know what* out of little Brandon was the objective. What can I say? Chalk up another win for good ole Papa Tom.

To: Brandon
From: Lizard Man
Subject: A Lizard Man Christmas

*Santa is said to know
Who's Naughty or nice.
For those who are naughty
Let me give you this advice.*

*Don't look for any presents
Underneath the Christmas tree.
Keep your sneakers on your feet
And make preparation to flee.*

*Only one creature will be heard
Stirring in your house that night.
It has a mouth full of yellow teeth
Making a meal of you in one bite.*

*He wears no familiar read suit
But has two very red glowing eyes.
There's no eight tiny flying reindeer
But when he runs he can still fly.*

*From the corner of his big old mouth
There rests no black smoking pipe.
Instead there's a glimmer of chrome
Leftovers from his last fender bite.*

*He has two very large green feet
That can make tracks in any snow.
And once you have seen them
To Grandma's house you will go.*

*You may use your jingle bells
To wishfully keep him away.
But it'll be one scary silent night
If Lizard Man decides he'll stay.*

*Leaving a treat of milk and cookies
Will hardly to do the trick.
He has his eyes on juicy you
Because sweets make him sick.*

*Don't scream for your mama
Once he has you in his sight.
It'll take boxer Mike Tyson
To help you win this fight.*

*Dressed in scales of green
From ugly head to toes.
He'll take you by a hand
And try to get you to go.*

*Unless you prefer a life
Of a fugitive on the run.
Refuse his slimy invitation
And shoot him with a gun.*

If all else you tried has failed
And you've done all you can
Have a Merry Swampy Christmas
With the legendary Lizardman.

Brandon still remembers. He reminded me on Face Book not so long ago. It warmed my heart that he had, twenty some odd years later. Okay, wiping the tears and now returning you to **Fostering Four**, after a little side bar.

Four Equals Three

Our fostering journey was ending. DSS and the court had decided to grant custody back to the mother of the four boys. We had given them the best life we could for over seven months. One should never become comfortable or attached to a situation. These seven months had taught me valuable lessons that I will forever cherish. Going from zero to four is a huge transition and is not something I'd suggest for anyone to take on. Speaking for myself only, I did and I have absolutely no regrets. I don't know if my foster parenting techniques will have a lasting impact on their lives but it certainly will on mine. I've always been selfish with my life and life's choices, but for once I put others ahead of me. I for one would like to believe that I impacted theirs positively during that snapshot in what I hope is a long and fruitful life ahead for all of them; a life with purpose and one filled with love.

There will be a definite emptiness in the household, a void where four entirely unique personalities once romped and played and made every day an interesting one. Through their eyes and lives I became a kid again. I visited the zoo and journeyed to the mountains and experienced both from a child's perspective. A rush of memories was awakened from my childhood and similar trips with my folks. I'm not saying this was a piece of cake, far from it, but all in all, it wasn't a tough pill to swallow; not as I had anticipated it would be. One thing for sure, I never knew what challenges the next day might bring, but I met them head on and we got through them together. I had thought that taking on this would be the toughest thing I had ever done, but I missed that one by a long shot. Letting them go was the tougher row to hoe.

There is a silver lining of sorts. Forfeiting the fostering life just opened the door to a new beginning. The boys were still family so they wouldn't just vanish into obscurity as is the case for other foster children. For that I am thankful. I could still be Papa Tom if they'd let me. I could kick dirt around and do some serious critiquing about their lives before joining us and what they might be walking back into, but I won't. Children should be with their parents, but only if their parents are willing to be parents and put them ahead of everything else. The jury was still out but you're innocent until proven guilty; that is the American way. Hopefully the boys, having experienced life from the other side could be the teachers. No, I'm not saying life with us was perfect, that would not be a truthful statement. Mistakes were made and I learned from those mistakes I made. We evolved and learned together.

I once thought Social Services was a hurtful organization, yanking kids from their parents and placing them in the hands of strangers; not any more. Let me clarify that perception. I think certain circumstances warrant removing children from a harmful environment. If they are being abused, not fed or clothed or just being badly neglected, they should be moved to safe ground. In this case there was no physical abuse or intentional neglect, but the mental anguish was there whether the boys realized it or not. If that's the only life you have lived then you don't know there is a different one out there. I had first thought that the father turning them over to social services was the most horrific act I could imagine, but now I view it as a blessing in disguise. While the act still mortifies me, the end result worked out for the boys and for me personally. I lived a life I would have otherwise not have lived, so thank you boys for being the perfect mentors to Papa Tom.

Life was almost too boring afterwards. There were no

more afternoons of my apprentices assisting me in the garden. The sounds of *cawobunga dude* didn't echo down the hallway; no masked turtles battled the evil Foot Soldiers. Meal times were no longer a feeding frenzy. The ritual of tucking in and imaginative bedtime stories had vanished from the schedule. Normalcy seemed quite complacent by comparison. The absence of children's laughter haunted my memories. The childless parent was again childless.

Who would have ever thought a hectic pace and nosy existence would be so sorely missed. Ripping, romping, wrestling and tussling, running and hiding and just plain horsing around can't be achieved by your lonesome. Those trips to haul off the trash were just trips to haul off the trash. There were no side excursions to the Hawaiian Ice Shack. How would I ever have an excuse to go to the zoo? I couldn't wait until their next visit, as grandkids and not as foster kids.

The phone call came sometime after midnight in the wee hours of a week day. The social worker informed us that she had three children in need of placement. I had forgotten we were still registered foster parents and just because the boys were no longer with us, our responsibilities hadn't expired. What could we say but bring them on. The social worker accompanied by two deputies soon showed up at our back door, each carrying a child, the oldest being just over three. Like stepping stones, the youngest was a girl, one year old, the next a boy of two and the third an older brother. The social worker gave us a brief description of their circumstances and would follow up with more details later.

The oldest of the tots was two years younger than the youngest of the four boys that we had cared for in our inaugural stint as foster parents. These were the faces of strangers as were we to them. This obviously put a new spin on things. Diapers, oh man. The little girl was soon smiling and laughing, but the boys weren't so sure about this arrangement. I wasn't either. The two year old boy's appearance was the most disturbing. He had what appeared to be large sores or burns on both arms in different stages of healing. The oldest had a black eye but kids are prone to accidents, right? Beds were prepared for the boys and a pallet on the floor for the girl. None of them were ready to give in to sleep and it was nearing 3 AM. My normal wake-up call was but three and half hours away. After some coaching all were tucked in and had gone beddy-bye. Sometime before daylight the screams broke the silence.

Rushing into the bedroom we found the two year old there still in bed and sound asleep, but the three year old had vanished. I followed the sounds of the sniffling sobs and located him under the bed in a fetal position. It wasn't easy to convince him to come out, even with the lights now on. He must have suffered a horrible nightmare to send him squiring underneath the bed. Eventually I got him out but he didn't openly warm up to any coddling from wither of us. I thought about the Amazon girl and what she had been exposed to and couldn't begin to fathom what these children had encountered.

My gut told me this wasn't going to be the case history I would want to hear. These were babies. Who could mistreat mere babies? It had been a short night thus far and a long day waiting ahead. I called in sick, figuring missing a work day was justified given the circumstances and uncertainty. I should have realized that earning my foster caring wings had been way too easy. This was what it was really all about, removing children from dangerous situations. I just didn't know the extent of the dangers and situation yet.

Accessorizing with Spaghetti

With little sleep, it was time to see what the day would hold for us and our three newbie foster kids. To keep it simple I'll just use their ages as names when referencing them. Three had survived the night, or what little bit was left of it, with no more nightmares. Two was bouncing off the walls, testing out the new surroundings and my fortitude and patience. One was precious but needy of motherly attention. From the get go, I realized this wasn't going to be as easy as fostering the four boys. It was going to be much, much more. I felt as if I was trying to herd cats. Keeping a watchful eye on them and attempting to prepare breakfast was nearly impossible. We were ill equipped for whipping up breakfast for children this age so the quick route was taken, scrambled eggs and buttered toast.

What transpired next was heart rendering to say the least. I had already witnessed the grand boys upon arriving, displaying overzealous attitudes when eating. Scott had even been dubbed Hog-Pig by his brothers because of his veracious appetite and hoarding of food in the early going. Nothing could have prepared me for what was happening with this new batch; at least not the two boys. They scooped eggs up double fisted, cramming them into their mouths; all the while glancing about wildly, arms wrapped around their plates, protecting their food from encroachers. I wondered when they had been fed last and if they wondered if they'd be fed again today. All but licking their plates clean, they were served a second helping. Devouring it while protecting their rations, the scene played out once again.

Most children can be finicky and choosey when it comes to what's on the menu and their plates; not these.

I believe they would have snapped up anything placed on their plates. The milk glass bottomed out numerous times. Number one greeted ever spoon full, never once turning her head away. It was a near tearful experience to endure. The more I watched, the more I dreaded hearing their case from the social worker. Nothing good was going to be reported based what I was watching right now. Only the tip of the iceberg was exposed. There was much more ugliness beneath the surface; you could take that to the bank. Against better judgment, they were allowed to gorge themselves. Taking away food until they had gotten their fill just seemed wrong. Over time, this would work itself out, once they realized more meals would be served during the day.

First on the agenda, I needed to make that grocery run. We were ill prepared to serve up the necessary vittles to provide proper nourishment for children three and under. Store bought diapers were on the list. What did I know about buying diapers; about as much as I did about changing them? It almost seemed sinful leaving my wife alone with the new arrivals but it had to be done. After all, tomorrow I had to go to work so maybe this would be a test run. Obviously I was not the best choice to stay here alone with them. I definitely lacked parenting skills for children this young. Selfishly I welcomed the escape, and may have lingered a bit longer than I should have. I decided to allow that to remain my little secret. There would be no reward in gloating.

I did make one side trip to my parents' house. In their attic they still had my childhood high chair and rocking horse. I figured both might come in handy for this brood. Possibly I needed some motherly encouragement. Instead I got the opposite, mama just asking me what I had gotten myself into. Hanging out with her wasn't going to build up my self esteem or boost my morale, so I retrieved the items I had come for and made a hasty exit stage right. Upon returning to my house I entered what can only be described as a war zone. I glanced about, looking for the safety of a foxhole. Belaboring my return had led to the children apocalypse. Maybe another promised feeding time would bring calm to the stormy turbulent waters around me. I think offering my wife a sarcastic life ring was way too late and would not be quite as humorous from her perspective.

Groceries un-bagged and put away, it was time for round two in the feeding arena. Keeping it simple, canned spaghetti was on slate. Hindsight, I should have opted for *Spaghetti-o's* instead of the string pasta. Number one, the girl was placed in my highchair, after cleaning it up of course. It was still sturdy and fully functional. Two and three were positioned at the table. I almost wanted to count ready, set and go before placing the bowl in front of them. Plastic utensils were provided but for the life of me I'm not sure why. What followed was a classical Kodak moment.

Their faces, especially the face of and head of number two, were a mass of pasta and sauce. Strings of spaghetti were hanging from his earlobes and lodged in his hair. He had virtually accessorized with the Italian apparel. His face…I'm not sure I have the words to describe the smeared catastrophic figure that had once been a two year old boy. His eating utensils, both hands, were evidence that his two fisted approach had once again been utilized. Laughing was a welcome relief. Cleaning up the carnage was a chore.

Chaos ensued. Have you ever tried to coral a two and three year old, dripping of pasta, before they reach the den or living room and the furniture waiting there without the sufficient stain guard to ward off the attack? Compound that with a screaming one year old now ready to be removed from the confinement of a highchair and the highchair not cooperating. The mechanism allowing the tray to slide away from her had locked in place and wouldn't budge, nor could she be removed. Perhaps we should have applied a bit of WD-40 before assuming all was mechanically functional. I felt totally outnumbered three to one, even with one safely locked in place in the chair. It was becoming all about me apparently, me against them, my previous fostering experience feeling completely worthless. Papa Tom didn't feel so daddy like with this new brood of tiny tikes.

Smaller, quicker and persistent, the boys were worthy adversaries. Yelling for them to stop only sent them into a screaming frenzy, fearful of what we might do if we caught them. Sadly, I couldn't blame them for that. Something told me they had just cause in this reaction. Fostering had taken an ugly twist. Mama saying I told you so echoed in my brain. *America's Funniest Home Videos* had nothing on us right now. This might have won us the grand prize if we would have had the opportunity to film it. You really do have to find something to laugh about when you're in survival mode. Laughter is supposed to be the best medicine, right? I'm usually the joker in the deck but right now the joke felt as if it was on me, the cards not stacked in my favor or I should say ours. I wasn't the lone ranger now matter how I liked to spin it.

Fostering Hatred

The social worker graced our presence later that afternoon to bring us up to date on why these kids had been removed from their home. Tired and worn out, I almost reverted to sarcasm and said something like did the parents run away from home, but I bit my tongue. While humor is an easy escape, better senses prevailed. My gut told me she wasn't going to paint a pretty picture this time. I could just feel it. Luckily we had wrestled the kids into submission and they were currently napping, so she had our undivided attention whether we wanted to offer it or not. Her tale began as a slow burn, informing us that this hadn't been the first time the children had been placed in foster care. There had been numerous other times, it only getting worse as the next child was born into the world. I had that queasiness in the pit of my stomach. Nope, I wasn't going to digest this well.

She started with the good news first. At least the little girl had not been sexually or physically abused. She had suffered her fair share of neglect but mostly in the form of not being fed well or diapers being changed regularly. Her raw and badly chaffed bottom had been a testimonial to the latter. The social worker had no explanation for why the girl had basically been spared except that the other two had received the brunt of any vented frustrations. I thought about how we had chased them down earlier, now regretting my actions. I felt almost soiled, as if I probably seemed to be an attacker to them. I took a deep breath, exhaling like a deflating balloon. I rubbed my hands through my hair and shook my head, not wishing to give into to my imagination, dreading where this most likely was heading. I remembered the revelations of the sexual assaults by every male family member on the twelve year old girl. How could anything be any worse than that?

The mother had a live-in boyfriend. He had been the father of the girl but not the two boys' daddy. Now it was becoming clear; that's why the little girl had not been harmed. This live-in dud was apparently a drug user, a drunk and extremely jealous. It was the perfect recipe for disastrous results she added. I took another long breath, thankful the four boys had not been exposed to anything like this; not that we ever saw any signs of at least. Just spit it out I wanted to say, but then again I wasn't sure I wanted to hear it. The two year old was in the middle of what many call the terrible twos stage. In the blink of an eye he can be into almost anything. I had witnessed firsthand to that earlier when attempting to stay one step ahead of his antics. I get this but tell me the rest. She asked if we had noticed those marks on his arms. Of course we had, figuring this rascal was prone to getting into most anything.

Without warning she got to her point. They were cigarette burns. I repeated what she said…cigarette burns? It hit me square between the eyes. The bastard had used this two year for a human ashtray. Instinctively I wanted to get my hands on him. Who can do this to a two year old? Who can do this to any child? Both of his arms were dotted with these marks in various stages of healing, some fairly fresh. Apparently pissed by the antics of the rambunctious boy, this unworthy excuse for a human being had punished the boy by burning him with a lit cigarette over and over. I was fuming. There was no punishment harsh enough for someone who would do something like this. And where was the mother? Why hadn't she put a stop to it? My brain was in overload mode. You read about this; you see it on the news, but I had never been this close to it before. I was about to explode and was sick to my stomach. This lower than life son of a…had been arrested thankfully.

How does a child get over something like this? Sadly, with nothing to compare this to, the boy probably thinks it's a normal part of his life. Still, a mother knows better. She's supposed to protect her children. In a way this made her almost more evil than the guy who was doing it, if that is possible. I had only known these children for less than a day and what I now knew about their situation was tough to digest or handle emotionally. Oddly the two year old didn't appear to be in any pain that I could tell, but maybe his tolerance and threshold for abuse had made him almost immune and oblivious to the punishment. That saddened me, just thinking about the possibility. I took another long deep breath, preparing myself for the rest of what she had to tell us.

Number three, the oldest, was just more of the same. I now knew how he had gotten his black eye and it had nothing to do with an accident. He had been used as a punching bag. There were other bruises on his fragile body to support the viciousness of the attacks. It explained the nightmares and his attempt to escape them by crawling underneath the bed. This felt more like one of those nightmarish movies, not any part of my life. Even someone like me, with no children, cannot fathom how an adult can do such horrible things and live with themselves afterwards. I could envision this scum being locked in a room with a vigilante force doing the exact thing to him or worse. Sign me up; I'd be the first in line. I don't smoke but I'd light up a huge cigar for the occasion and gladly use him as an ashtray.

Beyond the initial shock, I couldn't fathom DSS ever placing these children back in the custody of the mother. I choked on the word…mother. If ever a parent didn't deserve children, this was that time. The children would certainly be better off in foster care or being put up for adoption. What was I saying? Was I really up for this fostering gig? There was so much emotional baggage, theirs and now mine. I tried to put all this crap on the back burner, but it was like trying to push a rope; my brain just couldn't shake free what I had just learned. I was shell shocked.

Dale, Andy, Scott and Greg had been the lucky ones. Far worse evil lurks in this world. First the twelve year old being sexually abused and now this; I clinched my fists. I wanted to hurt these adults, make them pay for their sins. Somehow I refrained from screaming it from the top of my lungs. I held it in and in ways that made it even more unbearable. Me…without children, seeing how some people blessed with children abuse their privileges; I could just puke.

How does one move forward after learning something like this? I wasn't naïve. I understood the ramifications and possibilities I could be facing when signing up to provide foster care. Hearing about it via the orientation process is one thing; experiencing it first hand is an eye opener and almost too much of a reality check. I was just having a tough time shaking it. Mere babies being treated in this manner was beyond comprehension. I didn't know these despicable human beings but yet hated them with a passion. I'm not a violent person by nature, but in this case I could easily and without guilt make an exception to deliver do justice to those deserving no mercy. I sound like a monster but the true monsters did this, not me. Think of me as the one hammering the stake in Dracula's chest or firing a silver bullet at the Wolfman. Evil needs to be eliminated.

Okay, calm down I tried to tell myself. What's at hand is doing what is right for these kids. I can't rectify the wrong doing, and I can't go beat them within an inch of their lives. Heck I don't even know who they are. For that I am thankful. If I ever passed them on the street I would probably be the one behind bars. I can't even begin to imagine how I would have reacted if this had happened to my children or grandchildren. There's a blessing in not having children just from this standpoint alone. Then there are those who should have never birthed them. Crossing the fostering line had changed everything.

The social worker wrapped up her visit, saying to let her know if we needed any additional assistance in caring for the three. We'd make do, but how can you really undo this sort of damage? Answer, you can't. You can only show them that there is a better life outside the nightmare they were in. It was time to roll up my sleeves and put their nightmare behind me. I wasn't sure I could. Black eyes and burn marks would make that virtually impossible. The emotional scars incurred by these children could only run much deeper. I faced the toughest challenge of my life and wasn't sure I was cut out to do what was required.

Screams from Very Dark Places

We had somehow gotten through day one after digesting the abusive scenario the kids had been exposed to in their so called mother's home. The children had been fed, bathed and bedded. Staring into their eyes and wondering what they might be thinking still haunted my thoughts. My heart ached for them. It had been a grueling day for one not accustomed to the dark side of parenting. Well, parenting was not the appropriate term. Eventually I was able to shut down the brain and give into sleep. Hopefully the others would rest peacefully, having grown more accustomed to their surroundings and having not been abused here.

Banshee like blood curdling screams made me set straight up in bed. Shaking the cobwebs I wasn't sure if I had just awoken from a bad dream. Blinking and getting my bearings I realized the screams were still continuing. We leapt from the bed, sprinted across the hallway, following the frightful walling. Flipping on the overhead light I first spotted the two year old boy, standing in the bed awake this time, backed against the head board. He was looking about wild eyed but he wasn't the source of the crying. The three year old was in his hiding place under the bed. I crawled about on the floor, reaching under there in an attempt to drag him out. He resisted and just withdrew into a ball. The two year old began shaking his head, no, as if expecting us to take our frustrations out on both of them. In their minds they were under attack. We were making no headway in convincing them otherwise. Neither of them responded to tones of reassurance.

I surmised in that instance that adults were perceived to be evil enemies who inflicted pain and punishment.

They had done nothing but have nightmares. Why should they be punished for that? The looks on their faces painted a much different picture. My tug of war adventure with the one getting a foothold underneath the bed for now was a losing proposition. His wails continued to upset his brother on the bed. He was now clambering for higher ground avoiding my wife like the plague. I'd move to the other side of the bed only to have him crawl to the opposite side. These tactics weren't working. It was going to take a combined effort to get him out. Kicking and screaming eventually we were able to pull him from his safe haven.

We realized he had wet himself. A change of clothing was needed. I'm not sure how but eventually we were able to restore calm and order to the situation. I had first thought the older one had wet himself while under the bed, but we realized he had wet the bed before climbing underneath. Now the bed had to be stripped. The clock indicated it was nearing 4 AM. We were a good thirty minutes into the ordeal. The night was about gone and I couldn't miss another day's work.

Once the linen had been changed and we had gotten the kids settled back down and drifted off to sleep, I tried to catch a few minutes of shut eye, but it was futile at best. The digital display on the radio clock told me it was time to rise and shine. I switched off the alarm long before it alarmed. I completed my work time ritual and regrettably had to desert my post and allow my wife to hold down the fort alone. Work became my escape, but I couldn't block out the horrors, no matter I hard I tried.

While the daytime antics caring for three children this age reached epic proportions, my wife, worn and frazzled, had hung in there until I had gotten home. Unlike with the four grand boys, I wasn't met with open arms. Only the little girl mustered a smile and then only after I squatted down and talked to her while she was sitting there in the little wheeled walker. The ritual was eventually repeated, feeding them, bathing them and lulling them to sleep. I crossed my fingers and held my breath that tonight would be uneventful. Everyone in the house badly needed a good night's sleep. I'm a light sleeper. That is a curse I live with. Compound that with I'm a night owl and have a difficult time just shutting down the brain at night. It equates to me requiring quality sleep when I finally do give into it.

From somewhere in the darkest recesses of my mind I vaguely heard the screams. She yanked and tugged on me until I finally woke up and heard the urgency in the child's pleading voice. I had been sleeping much too deeply for me. A replay of the two prior nights ensued. The three year old had wet the bed and had scurried back underneath, hiding from the darkness or whatever terrifying beast he thought lurked topside. It was three something by the time we restored order and got the two boys back to some semblance of nocturnal napping.

I stumbled into the bathroom and propped on the sink counter. I looked at the man in the mirror. The wear and tear of the past three nights was etched deeply in the face looking back at me. Unlike the children, I had endured no beatings or burnings. This was no pity party, just a mere observation. I sighed and ambled back to the bed, but not before popping a couple of Tylenols for another throbbing headache. I shook my head. Even in this state I had never considered taking it out on the children. I couldn't understand why anyone would have doing something so heinous.

The theme played out a forth night. Suddenly two distinct patterns dawned on us. First, the panic attacks always happened during the night, never during the daytime naps. Secondly, the exodus to the underworld only occurred after he had wet the bed. The dark part I could understand. Darkness is not a kid's friend. If you're awake, you can often see those monsters lurking in the shadows, moving about the room, just ready to pounce. Oddly, most kids feared what might be under their bed. He didn't. Under the bed was safer than being under the covers. I got it. The monster attacked from above, so the only escape was going where the monster couldn't get him or better still, reach him. I remembered the difficulty I had experienced trying to remove him.

Possibly being in the dark prompted him to wet the bed or just maybe the darkness played no role in at all. Perhaps he was a deep sleeper and his bladder urges didn't awake him until it was too late. When mother dearest or hells' prodigy that lived with her discovered the accident, a beating ensued. He escaped the onslaught by going under the bed. Now I envisioned the scenario. The warmth from the pee woke him up. Instinctively he began screaming; expecting a brutal attack and the same instinct drove him under the bed. It was a programmed reaction. That left the two year old to receive the fury of the attack. Man, this was wrong on so many levels. A plan evolved hat hopefully would rectify the problem.

First, a night light was placed on his side of the bed. Next, a curfew was put on liquid consumption. Then we made sure the last thing he did was tinkle before bedtime. Lastly we woke him a couple of hours after bedtime, escorted him to the bathroom and prompted him to pee again. I'm not sure if cutting off his water consumption earlier, or adding the use of the night light, or maybe just maybe a combination of everything, but miraculously the night time episodes ceased. By not wetting the bed, there was no fear of punishment. Eventually we were all having a restful night. Over the next few days, the back eye faded. All but a few minor burn scars remained on the two year olds' arms. At least the obvious reminders diminished for all of us. We had made it through nearly a week but having three children these ages in the household and meeting the challenges to maintain balance was wearing on us. Possibly we were too old for this line of duty.

Terrible Two's for a Reason

Kids and monkeys mutated from the same genes. It's true. Evolution is alive and well I assure you. Before you go all Bible-Belt on me, allow me to explain. We now had three children in the household under our ever vigilant watch. The one year old girl was easy to contain. Just place her in that low rider highchair on wheels and let her have at it. The tiny leg motorized contraption restricted her reach even though she was now a self made bumper car. The only thing to keep you on your toes was when she flung a toy or food from her mounted tray. They should market these things all the way up to age six. Heck there should be an adult version for those declining years, replacing walkers and wheelchairs.

Then we had the oldest, the three year-old and night time bed spelunker. We had worked through his screaming and hiding issues for the most part, having discovered somewhat of a deterrent. Still, close supervision was required. He was quite agile and fleet of foot. He could quickly find something to get into that you'd prefer he didn't. Most of his was innocent curiosity seeking expeditions. He was still feeling out the lay of the land and would have questions as he explored the vast new universe. It was easier to provide various toy distractions to occupy his inquisitive nature. Still, close supervision was advised. I was at work, a day shift away, so I was of little help in these matters during the primetime hours.

Then there was the two year old; the one who had been used as a human ashtray. The world was at his fingertips. If curiosity indeed killed the cat, this little boy had surely strung out most of his nine lives. Heck, I think he was on borrowed cat life time if truth be known. I'm not just insinuating this because of him having survived all the abusive punishment from that spineless bastard who had lived in his home. That alone was worthy of some sort of metal. I wondered what sort of tike he would be now if he hadn't gone through all the pain and punishment. Obviously it had impacted who he was; how could it not have? I better get off this subject. It only gets me worked up and wanting to inflict bodily harm to those responsible.

I've heard of the term, 'the terrible twos', but not having had any kids or having really been around others who do for any extended periods of time, I figured it was just an old wife's tale. How terrible could a two year old really be? Adults rule the land, not kids; or at least they did when I was growing up. In my day, even thinking about being terrible came with a price; one that you'd dare repeat more than once after you finally grasp the process. That was then and this is now. We had sworn to use no capital punishment on any of the foster children under our watch and thus far we had not broken that promise. In my day a good spanking went a long way in developing my thought processing. It forced me to consider the consequences before I acted on what I thought might be a good idea. That didn't mean I didn't make my fair share of bad decisions. Stumbling and falling is part of the learning process; often a painful one.

Let me set the record straight though. While we interpreted our little spankings as beatings, they were not abusive. No one ever spanked me until I bled. I wasn't black and blue afterwards, but they were attention getters; meant to make you think better next time. Whippings were restricted to the hinny and legs. We received no blows to our upper torso or heads. My parents would have never used me for an ashtray or socked me in the face. Actually my mama would cry while she was spanking me; or so she told me after I got older. I was too young to remember and I have no witnesses to support her story. I think daddy let her do most of the dirty work if punishment was required. I reckon I am blessed. I don't have any childhood memories marred with frequent whippings and I was a daredevil. Maybe the mind just has a way of blocking out this sort of thing. I do recall having to pick a switch a time or two, and I have some recollection of stinging legs. No, I was far from perfect. The punishment always fit the crime.

It didn't take us long to figure out that the two year old almost required 24/7 parental policing. I'm convinced he was some sort of hybrid. Mutation had taken on a cruel twist. Being small was not a handicap. Secondly, it was obvious to me that we couldn't childproof the entire house. Just staying a step ahead of him while keeping at least one eye on the other two was almost an impossible feat. This being said, there was no justification for the punishment that had been inflicted on him. We soon discovered that anything breakable had to be removed and stored away. Do you realize just how much breakable stuff there is in a house? Some items you think can't be broken, can. Closets and kitchen cabinets were favorite targets. This kid was always in search of something editable and not because he hadn't been fed well. Can you visualize tapeworm with an attitude?

He definitely possessed the monkey gene. Maybe all two year old tikes do. All he needed was a Spider Man costume to complete the image. He climbed where no kid had been before. We'd find him at the top of places and had no clue how he had gotten there. When caught, he would just have this evil smirk on his face. If ever a child deserved a spanking, this one did, but we held firm to the fostering rules and refrained from giving him one. That made it tough to break him of the habit. Saying No certainly wasn't working. As soon as we'd pluck him off one plateau, he'd be scampering up another or disappearing down the hallway. Without hesitation we'd be in hot pursuit. You would have thought by the time I got home in the afternoons he'd be worn down, but instead, he'd catch that second adrenaline rush. We made sure we curbed his sugar intake. We needed it worse than him.

He didn't possess much of a vocabulary. His communication skills were limited to short spurts of gibberish, animated jesters and odd little facial expressions. I chalk this up to no one spending any quality time with him. The three year was timid and shy but did talk a little. His brother was anything but. His eyes were filled with dares; the dares aimed at us. Sometimes it world become a stare down completion. He'd stand there, his hands on or almost on an object he shouldn't be touching. We'd point a finger at him and shake our head saying no. His eyes locked on ours, would ooze defiance. The kid was good at it, I must admit.

We'd shake our head no, just to make the point understood. He'd ease his hand closer, looking for our reaction. You could visualize the wheels turning in that little head. It was a standoff. Obviously he enjoyed the game. Bad visions came to mind; ones where the adults didn't bluff. A chill went down my spine. I saw the culprit snatching him up violently and imbedding that hot cigarette tip into his arms. Even scarier, I could visualize this kid not shedding a tear and instead, starring down his attacker. I cringed, thinking through this ordeal. I didn't like playing this game. There were no real winners.

I wondered how long it took for a kid to outgrow the

terrible two persona. The thought flashed through my head. We were three shy of the maximum allowed children. Surely the social worker wouldn't consider sending more our way. Having three foster children ages three and under was more than a handful, one that had accelerated my aging process. A week had seemed like a month. Not too fret, we were still providing them with the good life, hands down better than what they had experienced. Sustaining day in and day out had been the challenge. There were no breaks in the routine. It was full throttle and our gears were wearing. We're the adults and they're the kids, right; but they had us outnumbered. It seemed a much larger spread than three to two. Would there be a light at the end of the tunnel? I wasn't seeing it if it was there.

Three Too Many

Half way into week number two, the rigors of caring for three tiny tots was taking its toll. The ability to continue recharging the batteries was dwindling. Zombies don't make good foster parents. Yes, I had signed up for this voluntarily. I had not been forced or threatened. I had made the decision for all the right reasons. Well, maybe not all the right reasons because selfishly the motive behind the madness had been to get the four boys into our custody. That part of the plan had worked flawlessly. We should have probably deserted our posts after they had been shuffled back to their mother. I hadn't really given it much thought one way or the other. Managing the four boys hadn't been that difficult, so why would I have thought any other scenario would be. The truth is not necessarily in sheer numbers. I wasn't ready to toss in the towel just yet. Maybe there was a way to make this thing work.

Two in diapers and the third with sporadic bed wetting tendencies, it was a steep and slippery slope to climb. Even though my nine to ten hour reprieve at work offered me some escape, it was waiting for me when I arrived home, my wife more than ready to tag out. Hitting the floor running, I did what I could to keep things on track, but the tires were becoming harder and harder to keep on the rims. I kept trying to remind myself that these children didn't ask for this. They were faultless and innocent. At least here with us there were no beatings and burnings. I was the one burning out and being beaten down. Sarcasm isn't an appropriate escape, but I was in a weakened state, brain cells fried. Every man has his breaking point and I was certainly near my brink. We pushed onward, trying our best to pull this off.

By the end of the second week we were all but screaming uncle. It had taken only fourteen days to break us. I was running on empty; all my reserves depleted. Me, caring for them, wasn't in their best interest. We needed a change in plans, a life preserver if we were going to keep our heads above water. It was time to circle the wagons with the social worker and lay all our cards on the table. I was taught never come the table with problems if you don't have some solutions. We had ours, but we weren't sure if it would fly once presented to those calling the shots. We had nothing to lose by pleading our case. Honesty is supposed to be the best policy, right? We were prepared to be brutally honest.

The assigned social worker arrived for her scheduled visit. After going through the customary formalities, she commended us, quite pleased with our efforts in the fostering arena. With much regret, it was time, true confessions were in order. We couldn't keep all three children. It wasn't fair to them. We played down the unfairness for us. We proposed keeping just one, maybe two but not all three. What were we saying? We certainly wouldn't have spit the four boys up, but they were all older and didn't require 24/7 intervention. We were open to keeping the girl and maybe the oldest boy if we had a choice in the matter. Just defining our terms sounded all wrong; as if we were tossing the one who had been abused the worst to the side. Let's face it, he was a handful; the other two were manageable. Shameful, splitting up brothers and sisters should never be done if you really think about it.

Proposing this scenario hadn't come easy. We had given it considerable thought. It came down to doing what we thought we were capable of doing and what best worked for the children in our care. The social worker advised us she would run this by her superior and let us know. I was really sorry about not being able to complete our obligations but fact is fact. We couldn't do it. It was not sustainable over the long haul. A man has to know his limitations, or so said Clint Eastwood as Dirty Harry. My limits had been clearly defined and fully understood. All we could do now was wait.

We received our answer very quickly. The powers to be weren't willing to split them up. I totally understood and fully agreed that this was the right choice. Just like that, they were moved to other foster parents, hopefully someone younger and more capable than us. The social worker had but one request; that we would not drop out of the foster care program. Foster parents were in short supply. She would make sure the system never put us in this situation again. What could we do? We would remain with the program. We owed her and it that much.

Oddly, after the children had been removed, I felt almost ashamed for having done this. I knew it had been the most logical thing to do, but still, a part of me missed them. One of the toughest challenges of being a foster parent is to become too attached to those you are fostering. I had fallen into that trap. It's odd, the emotional stance one must take when crossing over into the fostering world. You have to be caring of the kids in your care but on the flip side you must be thick skinned, avoid getting too emotionally involved in the formalities of the situation. It's tough to balance the two. I hoped that where ever the three landed that they would be in good hands. As foster parents we can't keep tabs on them unfortunately. We had forfeited that privilege when they were removed from our custody.

I shifted my world into the neutral position once again. The fostering roller coast obviously wasn't for everyone. I was questioning whether it was right for me, even with the commitment promised to the social worker, that we would remain a part of the system. I was having regrets for having made that promise. Maybe I was childless for a reason. Possibly I couldn't handle the emotional baggage that comes with caring for kids, even when they weren't mine. The fact that they weren't mine and I allowed myself to get too involved and attached was probably a foster parent red flag. It was foster taboo.

I had a tough time viewing it as a job, one with no pay, but with high levels of stress. I had never been the type to volunteer for anything. I had certainly set the goals high by picking this one as my first tour of duty on the volunteer circuit. No, I had to shake these feelings. I had enjoyed doing it, even with the three little ones; but everything has its limitations and I had definitely reached mine attempting to care for these. Life requires balance and I was just a tad off kilter right now. I'd regroup and be ready next time.

Training Day Blues

We had hit a lull in the fostering care rotation. Hopefully I could interpret that as a good sign; not for me but for the children. If parents do their jobs then the system has no reason to intervene. Maybe the parents were getting it. Having more foster parents in the wings than children to fill the slots is the perfect recipe, right? I had a year under the belt; how time does fly. Fences had mended with the parents of the four grand boys and relationships while still fragile, had shifted more towards the normal realm. We were seeing them fairly regularly, even though we were still being held partially responsible for the stint they had spent in foster care. Funny, we certainly had not been the ones who had deserted them or turned them over to social services. Guilt is a tough thing to stare down in a mirror, I'm just saying. Lessons learned. Do right by your kids and be thankful you have them. I had witnessed the ugly side of parenting, remembering the child sized ashtray.

DSS contacted us saying in order to maintain our foster parenting status we'd have to undergo recertification. I thought once we had been anointed it was a lifetime achievement. I dreaded going through more training. Maybe I had my out. She advised that there were numerous options for maintaining certification. Remembering the agreement, I reluctantly listened to the options for retaining our two year license. A commitment is a commitment I suppose. There were in house training seminars and all sorts of traditional training programs to obtain 28 hours of training over a two year period. If I had any desire in continuing I'd have to bite the bullet and do something. Sitting through some of the classes earned more hours, but then she tossed out another possibility that fell into my wheelhouse.

There were certain movies that could be viewed for credit hours. These weren't necessarily documentaries; some were real Hollywood produced flicks. I was a movie buff but it came with a hitch. I'd be required to do somewhat of a book report on behalf of the household. You had to prove you had actually viewed the movie and learned something from it. Nothing comes easy. There was always a rest of the story so said Paul Harvey. Still, we could reduce the amount of classroom hours by going this route. I was in. Sign me up for movie critic. I figured if Ebert and Siskel could do it, so could I. Roger Ebert and Gene Siskel were the movie critic duo of the time. They had a syndicated program reviewing the weekly releases. I didn't have a show or a reputation.

Looking through the library of possibilities I selected one titled *I know my first name is Steven*. The brief description on the VCR case spelled out a plot involving the kidnapping of a boy and his ordeal. I had never heard of it so that made it even better as a first time viewer. Paying close attention to detail while munching on popcorn can be a challenge Thank goodness for pause and rewind. I went into this with a light hearted approach but walked away with anything but. Maybe it was because I had already tasted the fruit of being a foster parent, and just possibly because of my experiences I now had a new appreciation of being a parent. Regardless, I could relate to the pain the family had incurred; especially realizing the ordeal had been based on fact, an actual event. Those based on real stories depictions usually ambush the emotions. It gets you in the soft spot and unleashes the tear ducts. I'm a sucker for this sort of thing.

The real life depiction revolved around the kidnapping of seven year old Steven Gregory Stayner, December 4th, 1972. Convicted rapist Kenneth Parnell had enlisted the help of an accomplice named Ervin Edward Murphy to pass out gospel tracts to boys walking home from school that day. He spotted Steven and claimed to be a church representative seeking donations. He asked him if his mother would be willing to donate any items to the church. Steven acknowledged that she would. Murphy then asked Steven where he lived and if he would be willing to take him there. Steven took the bait. Parnell then arrived in a white Buick pretending to be working with Murphy on the church project. Steven climbed inside and just like that the abduction ensued. Lesson one, kids are naturally too trustworthy and naïve.

Steven was taken to Parnell's cabin where he began molesting the boy. He convinced Steven that his parents couldn't afford him any longer because they had too many children and they had granted him legal custody. Keeping Steven's middle name, Parnell began calling him Dennis Gregory Parnell. Ironically, Parnell's cabin was located only several hundred feet from Steven's maternal grandfather's residence in a nearby county. Parnell portrayed Steven as his son as they moved about from one place to the next. I couldn't help but think of the twelve year old girl who had been molested by every male family member. Kids are at the mercy of deranged adults. I still say that this should be a death sentence conviction. To me it has to top out as one of the worst crimes, destroying one's innocence.

Most of these abductions end in one of two ways; the children never being found or their bodies being found. There is seldom a happy ending. The parents never ever knowing what happened is probably worse than finding out their child was murdered. The irony in Steven's case is that as he grew older he wasn't being held as a prisoner in Parnell's residence. He allowed Steven to begin drinking at a young age and to come and go virtually as he pleased. For whatever reason, Steven stayed. As sad as it was, this had become his way of life. It's an oddity why people remain in abusive relationships. Again I think back to the girl. She apparently thought it was natural for all men to treat her that way. When I didn't and shied away from her after finding out what others had done to her, she thought I didn't like her. Young minds can so easily be distorted. My homework was impacting me more than I could have ever imagined. Valuable lessons were being learned.

Steven's tragedy didn't end in death as so many do. He had reached the age of fourteen when Parnell decided he needed a younger victim to abuse. Five-year-old Timmy White was kidnapped. Steven impacted by the little boys stress and pain decided enough was enough, and while Parnell was at work, he took Timmy and they escaped. Can you wrap your mind around this? Both boys were free and alive; unheard of in most abduction cases. Steven intended on just returning Timmy White to his parents, but after being unable to locate the boy's home address, he decided to take him to the police station and have him go inside and ask for help. Miracles do work in mysterious ways. Instead, the police spotted the two boys and took them into custody. Steven identified Timmy White and then revealed his own true identity and story. Justice served, Kenneth Parnell was located and arrested.

Parnell was tried and convicted of the kidnapping Steven and Timmy in two separate trials. He was sentenced to seven years but was paroled after serving five years. The child rapist was not charged with the numerous sexual assaults on Steven and other boys. Their excuse was because most of them occurred outside the jurisdiction of the county or were outside the statue of limitations. County prosecutors decided not to prosecute Parnell for the sexual assaults that hadn't occurred in their jurisdiction. The prosecutors' believed that they were protecting Steven Stayner. Back then rape and molestation victims were perceived as damaged goods. Stupidly they seemed to think that they were respecting Steven's parents' reluctance to discuss Parnell's crimes because of the stigma of male sexual abuse. Because of these perceptions, a monster was allowed back on the streets. . I'll say it again. The punishment does not fit the crime.

Steven had been kidnapped at age seven and had lost seven years of his life, his childhood to a lowlife that pretended to be his father, while he had his way with the boy over and over. I'm a non parent but if he had been my child, I would most likely have been the one behind bars. I might have posted his bail just to have him free where I could deliver justice. Of course, while I wouldn't sugar coat my opinions in my synopsis of the film, I would edit out these details. I'm not sure I would come across as a role model for fostering if I threatened to snuff out a serial child molester. That thought had previously crossed my mind when I had seen the two year old and the burns on his arms after realizing it had been no accident. Steven had a tough time adjusting to regular family life after his had been stolen away from him. He died in 1989, at the age of twenty four, in a motorcycle accident while driving home from work.

One more film was viewed for credit titled *Do you know the Muffin Man*. Just the title rippled chills down my spin. This was one about a woman named Kendra Dollison who is shocked when she learns that a child who attends her son's preschool has been making allegations about teachers molesting the children there. Letters are sent out to all the parents by the police stating that indeed the employees are under investigation. Her son eventually admits he too has been molested while undergoing therapy. You leave your kids in the care of others, pay for that care and never expect anything like this to happen. My thoughts, how do you ever explain this to the children when you took them there and left them to the wolves?

Foster care falls into this category with one exception; the parents don't get to choose who has their kids. It makes one wonder how thorough the screening process is for foster parents. Could a pedophile sign up for foster duty and fly under the radar undetected. If they had no documented history of child abuse, they certainly could. I can't even begin to imagine a situation where children were taken away from their parents and then dumped in the devil's playground. If anything, these films instilled in me the importance of being a foster parent. I could make a difference in these children's lives, even for a short period. Giving them love and showing them what life can be is what it's all about. Fostering is a journey and a feel good experience if done as designed. Just maybe I would try it for a tad longer.

The Little Red Headed Stranger

We were open for business but had gone for quite a while with no children in our care. This wasn't necessarily a bad thing if you think about it. We existed for the sole purpose of being available if abused or neglected children were in need of temporarily placement. Either none were being mistreated or reported as being so, or there were more foster parents than children requiring care. Maybe we had been placed on a black list after our fiasco with the three little ones. If so, DSS shouldn't have been persistent about us remaining certified. One thing for sure, rust was gathering on the fostering gears. With practice comes perfection and I for one was out of practice. When you fall off that bicycle you're supposed to hop back on it and try again. I was instead falling back into a comfortable routine.

There were five grand boys in our family, the four we had kept and one more with my wife's other daughter. Spending time with them were just mere snapshots in time compared to the rigors of daily foster care. My mind would occasionally drift to that of the twelve year-old Amazon or the three we had cared for, for only a couple of weeks. I guess it wasn't uncommon to wonder what had become of them; if they were still in foster care or if they had been returned to family. Given the circumstances, in both of these cases, I couldn't help but lean towards hoping they hadn't been returned to their parents. They each had already survived enough physical, sexual and mental abuse to last for a lifetime. Where was the mom when every male in the family had assaulted her daughter? Where had the mom been when the boys had been burned and battened?

No, sometimes the system is a better alternative.

Out of the blue we received one of those phone calls. DSS had a three year girl in need of care and asked if we were up to it. Saying no really wasn't an option. She was on her way. I tried to prepare my game face, time to roll up the sleeves once more, slip on the big boy foster britches. History had painted me as better with boys than girls. Unfortunately, a foster parent couldn't be gender specific. You had to take them as they came and as already experienced, all came with a set of emotional baggage. It was up to us to adapt and make it work. My record of dealing wasn't exactly blemish free. The fear of the unknown consumed me. Just what had this poor child been exposed to in her three short years in this world?

The doorbell chimed her arrival. Judgment day was here. Luckily for us this was not another trifecta. Standing on the opposite side of the sliding glass doors was our same case worker. The little girl clung to her bosom, arms wrapped around her neck. She tilted her head and glanced at us as I slid open the door. After entering and having a seat on the sofa, she pried the girl from her death grip and eased her onto the couch next to her. I can only imagine what this little girl must be thinking.

She was a little doll with flowing red hair and mesmerizing large blue yes. She seemed too fragile for a three year old though. Her legs were almost stick-like in appearance extending from underneath her dress. Dark circles were visible under her eyes. Her skin was the color of milk. The social worker introduced her as Brittany. She sheepishly buried her face in the woman's side when we spoke up and welcomed her. I cringed, wondering who had done what to her. Thankfully it hadn't been any worse than mere neglect; no burn marks, black eyes or sexual molestation.

Completing the formalities, the social worker passed Brittany to my wife and departed. Here we were, alone, on Foster Island with the newest castaway. I looked into those blue eyes, wondering what she must be thinking, surrounded by strangers. She was bathed by my wife while I prepared something to eat. Unlike those before her, she didn't possess a ravenous appetite. She actually ate almost reluctantly, making you feel as if you were force feeding her. She sure needed a little meat on her bones. She was fed until she refused to eat any more. Brittany ate like a bird. Figuring her out would come with challenges it appeared.

Our fostering arrangement was going to be a bit different this time. We were both working. I had the more flexible of the two schedules. I'd be tasked with taking her to daycare on my way to work. We picked what I hoped to be a reliable one that wasn't too far out of my way. The child seat was strapped in the backseat and her strapped safely inside. We were off for our first road trip together, less than a ten minute drive. This was a new frontier; me, a three year old girl, a car seat, headed to daycare.

I struck up a one way conversation with Brittany, glancing in the rearview mirror for any signs of a reaction. There were none. She just eyed me with those baby blues and then sheepishly took in the scenery. Soon we arrived. I dropped her off with her bag of support stuff, biding her a fond farewell as I existed. She followed me with those eyes but basically had no reaction. It didn't appear that she was going to miss me. I was sort of disappointed, but what did I really expect; we had only had her for a couple of days. Egos can be fragile.

The workday passed agonizingly slow. It was an odd feeling, being anxious about picking her up. Was this how fathers acted on the first day of daycare for their daughters? Could I be experiencing a parental moment? Come on, it had only been a couple of days with the red haired stranger; how could that be remotely possible? I did feel just a tad guilty. It seemed unjust leaving her with strangers all day after she had just only recently met us as strangers. Passing her around had to be confusing. I wondered what she might be thinking. Did she miss her mother? How could she not, even given whatever circumstances she had been exposed to while there. Possibly I was just over thinking the situation. Still, I remained antsy, on edge and contemplating how the after work reunion would go when the stranger returned to take her to the new house. Fostering was definitely getting no easier.

I shared my feelings with a few close friends at work. All were very supportive, offering words of encouragement and commending me on doing this. I wasn't seeking any recognition. I didn't need a pat on the back because this wasn't my first rodeo in the fostering arena. I don't know; this just felt different. Maybe there was something safe and cozy about just being responsible for only one child. It was definitely comforting to know she had not been physically or sexually abused like this girl placed in our custody. Those baby blues haunted my thoughts. Just what must she be thinking about her current situation, about me, about us? Why was I allowing this to get to me this time? I didn't have an answer. I just knew that my work day couldn't end soon enough to suit me. These were indeed odd emotions bombarding my system.

Finally the hands on my watch indicated it was time

to go pick up the little blue eyed, red headed munchkin. The apprehension overwhelmed me. Could it just be the daycare thing? I'd never dealt with a daycare facility before and now I had dropped off a girl that I was responsible for, to strangers. Had they treated her special or was she just another snotty nose kid in the system? These were new thoughts for me, thinking about a child's welfare, even after having been a foster parent for awhile. Why was I so consumed by these thoughts? It suddenly clicked. I suffered from reasonable doubt. It was that awful Muffin Man movie I had watched about those evil daycare workers abusing the children. Apparently in the recesses of my brain I had stereotyped daycare centers and didn't trust any of them.

I pulled into the parking lot among a sea of real parents retrieving their children. I sat briefly behind the wheel for no apparent reason that I can come up with, before venturing inside. The owner of the business recognized me and held up her finger before stepping into another room, indicating that she would be right back. She returned with Brittany in tow. She released her and blue eyes ran to me. I wasn't sure how to take it. The worse fears flowed through my head; had someone done something to her? Before I could ponder further she was prompting me to pick her up. She smiled and placed her fragile arms around my neck. All was forgotten. I melted. Something magical happened to me that very moment. I wasn't ready to admit to anything but it had happened just the same.

I chatted with the non responding little girl in the backseat on the ride home. She listened and focused on the refection of my eyes in the mirror, never uttering a word. After we arrived, I unbuckled her from her car seat and helped her out the door. She reached for my hand and we walked to the back deck. I picked her up and carried her up the steps before setting her back down. An odd feeling came over me, but I attempted to shake it off. Something was definitely happening. It was one of those defining moment occurrences, but still I struggled to wrap my mind around it. The remainder of the afternoon was filled with the regular ritual, allowing her some play time, feeding her, bathing her and putting her to bed; nothing out of the normal. The next morning we repeated the ride, the drop off and later that afternoon the pick-up. I was falling into a pleasant routine.

Helicopter Tommy

A couple of weeks had passed and Brittany was fitting right in, even though her vocabulary was quite limited. I fell head over heels for the little gal, no longer a red headed stranger, and had begun buying her dolls and toys, exceeding any foster care repayable budget. It didn't matter; I was going to do what I wanted to do. My wife enjoyed dressing her up. It was so much easier caring for one. Luckily she didn't come with any obvious emotional baggage. She was simply precious.

I was in unfamiliar territory, gushing over a child. She was quite possessive too, clinging to her new foster dad. From what we had found out from the social worker, her mom had been a single mom; no dad per say was in the picture. I guess I was the first real male figure in her life. Poor dear, she had nothing to compare me to. My job was perfectly clear; to spoil her rotten. I embraced my role seriously. It felt simply marvelous. I had found the perfect foster fit, so it seemed.

We had planned a little vacation getaway, a long weekend in the Great Smokey Mountains. We received permission to take Brittany on our little family excursion. No one knew if she had ever been to the mountains or not. Instinct told me she probably hadn't. With Pigeon Forge in our sights we were on our way. It wasn't a particular busy time of the year, early spring and school still in session, so we hadn't made any hotel reservations in advance, figuring it shouldn't be an issue. You wouldn't want to do this during the summer or in the midst of fall when the leaves were changing or your chances would be slim to none and prices would be quadrupled for a room. We were hitting it at just the right time, the closest thing to an off season. We easily found a nice affordable place, two double beds with a small kitchen; what they called a room with efficiencies.

Soon it was time to take in the sights and sounds of the mountain tourist trap. As a kid I never perceived Pigeon Forge or Gatlinburg as such. It is funny how my perception changed when the money being spent came out of my pockets. Those authentic Indian replicas made in Taiwan didn't appear quite so desirable. Every souvenir shop was just the mirror image of the last one for the most part; having seen one, you had indeed seen them all. You can't tell a kid that though. It's lost in translation. We had allowed the grand boys to pick mementos of mountains, so why should this trip be any different. It is easier to sway a three year old girl than four gung-ho boys. Still, I couldn't help myself, taking her to those same spots my folks had taken me. That's why they call it a family tradition I suppose.

It didn't take long to realize that totting a three year old can get old after awhile. We opted for push strollers when available in places like some of the outlet malls. Brittany was the picture of patience. She never whined, begged or complained. Those mesmerizing blue eyes simply took in her surroundings like a sponge as we meandered about leisurely. Whether in a stroller, me carrying her or her walking between us holding our hands, the scene was surreal, one resembling a Normal Rockwell family moment. If it would have been me, I would have been tugging at my parents, pointing at this and that and trying to hurry them along. A zillion things would have already caught my eye. Patience was not one of my virtues, still isn't. Not Brittany, she went with the flow, seemingly just happy to be here with us. It had a nice feel.

Back in the car and riding along, I spotted one of those small amusement parks, most rides designed for small children. Brittany saw it too but never uttered a word, just stared in amazement. Adults usually avoid these places like the plague, even ignoring the pleas from the kids to go there. Not me, I wheeled into a parking place, my inner kid tugging at me, beckoning me to stop. I listened and figured it was a perfect venue for her. It wasn't crowed and most of the rides were indeed for tiny tots. Not knowing much about her, I wasn't even sure if she would enjoy this or ride anything. It was dice roll at best but we were on vacation and certified tourist, why not?

I looked over the rides trying to decide how to break the ice and test the water with my little red headed gal. I wasn't sure if she had every ridden any rides or even would. A miniature train encircled the pint sized amusement park. Perfect. I asked her if she wanted to ride it. She just smiled back at me but didn't make a grunt. I couldn't allow her to ride alone so I purchased two tickets. We climbed on board, opting for the caboose. To any passerby I must have looked like an oversized frog crammed into that train car.

We were all aboard and ready to burn up the tracks. Actually we were the only two passengers other that the engineer. He was larger than me and looked equally out of place anchoring the opposite end of the train. Clanking the bell and tooting a horn, the Peach Blossom Special was on its way. I felt like belting out, "I hear that train a coming, coming around the bend, I ain't seen no sunshine since I don't know when…" I can't carry a tune so I quickly dismissed that thought. Each time we passed my wife I waved and soon Brittany was waving too. Oddly, she never laughed or giggled as one would expect, but the expression of delight and wonderment on her face was priceless.

    A little girl was living a dream, or so that's the way I'd like to think of it. We picked a couple of more not so risqué rides, ones that I could shoe horn myself into and had a grand old time. It was almost as if we had rented the amusement park just for us. Sometimes things work out for a reason. I wasn't sure who was enjoying the adventure more, her or me. I'll call it a tie. Part of the fostering creed is to make the children feel welcome, loved and part of the family. All the boxes had been checked. I was certainly beaming along with her. Another one of those special moments had stabbed me directly in the heart. She certainly brought out the best in me. Boy I had missed a lot by never having been a daddy. I had to regain my composure; getting too mushy on the tiny merry-go-round is inappropriate. There's happy and then there's happy. I was suffering from a double doss.

    Upon completing our quest to ride the simpler of those offered; those I could actually fit in, we opted to call it a day and find somewhere to eat. The sounds of whirlybirds filled the air. Touring helicopters are common. For twenty bucks per person you can be whisked about seeing the landscape from a bird's eye view. Those sounds awoke memories of another trip to the Smokey Mountains. I was just a pre-teenager and joined my grandparents and an uncle and aunt on their annual trek to Bryson City near the Cherokee Indian Reservation. I had hungered to ride a similar touring helicopter but granny wouldn't consent to this, while papa thought it was okay. He'd even ride with me. Granny won that argument. There would be no liftoff. What goes up, can crash back to the ground had been her argument. I was furious and disappointed. I did lobby this into a trip to Frontier Land, an old Wild West replica town.

The next year, without me along with them, papa snitched on granny once they returned from their mountain vacation. She had sat in a helicopter and it lifted off the ground just to demonstrate to her the safety and the feel. She didn't take the tour but a least she rode in a helicopter, something she never allowed me to do. Boy how I held that over her head for a long time thereafter. It's funny, as an adult, I've still never ridden in a helicopter. I'm not sure why not, now that I come to think of it. Perhaps I should add that to my *to do list*. It wouldn't be the same without granny present. She's gone and I'm nearly sixty one. Boy has it been that long since that mountain trip with them. It's funny how it still stands out in my mind. Nostalgia is a sneaky little critter.

As another copter passed overhead I pointed to the skies and said, "See the helicopter Brittany." She was leaning over from her car seat and peering where I had pointed. I'm not sure why I pointed it out to her but I did. I suppose they are not everyday common sights back home. Possibly she had never seen one. Maybe I was just making conversation with blue eyes in the backseat that rarely spoke a word. As we made our way down the main drag I'd point out this and that as we passed. She took it all in as only a child could. I was seeing things through different eyes too, sharing them with her and watching her reactions through the rearview mirror. Flashbacks of those family vacations I took with my parents ebbed and flowed like waves on the beach. Mama and daddy would point things out to me and made sure I had the opportunities to experience what life had to offer.

Pigeon Forge is the Myrtle Beach of the mountains. The landscape is dotted with souvenir stores, amusements, miniature golf and restaurants galore. These sites and sounds are lost in a sea of ants, tourist scurrying about to collect memories and leave hard earned cash in their wake. It is a vacation Mecca. You don't come here to do nothing. Cheap thrills at expensive costs are just part of the experience. I had been here more times that I could count but yet returning was always something I looked forward to doing.

Watching as a tiny child experienced it for the very first time made it even more special. I was glad we had decided to come and had been able to bring her along. I had rounded yet another fostering curve and was feeling a new appreciation for taking the time to be a temporary parent. We did it for the boys and now we were doing it for this precious little girl. Life without purpose is no life at all. I'm not sure who might have said that but it struck me as so as I watched that little red headed not so much a stranger any longer, now glancing back at me in the mirror.

As I watched her watching me, she veered her attention to the side window and pointed, "Helicopter, Tommy... helicopter, Tommy." The emotions that flooded me that very second cannot be described in a manner to give them justice. This was the first time she had ever spoken my name. I think at that very moment I understood how a real parent feels with their child says daddy or mama for the very first time. She pointed again and repeated those two words, "helicopter, Tommy," her face beaming with delight; mine tearing up. My heart had melted one more time. Childless for all these years and now I was feeling almost daddy like; too much so. I was treading into dangerous waters; I was just too blinded by the moment to see where this was heading. Right then, nothing else mattered. I had

had a moment, one of those incidences that no one can take away from you. All these years later, the feelings remained the same, stronger than ever and forever etched in my soul.

Over the next couple of days of our little family vacation I never grew tired of hearing, "helicopter, Tommy," as it became her defining statement and the key to my heart. All these years later, I can vividly see that expression on her face as I speak those words for only me to hear again, *helicopter, Tommy*. I was feeling just a bit too comfortably and fatherly during that mountain retreat. I must confess it was feeling quite fine too. Upon returning, my brain had shifted gears in the foster care world. I began thinking adoption, if given the opportunity. For once I was hoping there would be no reunion with her mother. I shouldn't be thinking that way but why lie about it. If things didn't work out, that as slim as it is, was supposed to be a potential option if all others were taken off the table. One can daydream. Danger Will Robinson, sometimes caring too much can be oh so harmful. I continued to play out my daddy fantasy, Brittany and I becoming almost inseparable. It just felt as if it was meant to be.

Crying Uncle

Brittany and I had fallen back into our daily routine. She was my car buddy on the trek to work Mondays through Fridays. I'd drop her off at the nursery and look forward to the reunion on the return trip. Talk of helicopters had ceased. There were none buzzing the skyways of our little town, a far cry from the mountain paradise tourist trap. She was still putting words to abbreviated sentences but her expressions were what got me. That blazing red hair perfectly framed those blue eyes and deep dimples when she smiled. She smiled a plenty too. Hardly had I ever witnessed her in a bad mood. She wasn't the type to throw any temper tantrums. Occasional fronds would indicate all was not well but with some probing we'd get to the bottom of her woes. Most were nothing.

Parents often brag on their children for one reason or another, saying his or hers is a perfect child. In my eyes Brittany won the perfect award hands down. I'm not just stating this just because I'm bias. She had the perfect demeanor, the best disposition and an astounding outlook on life; given that she was a three year old having been plucked from her maternal mother and placed with strangers. Transitioning from day one with us until now had been a mere eye blink. We and she fit like a puzzle piece. This is one of those times you're supposed to say it was just meant to be. Could this be why I had never had any children? The plan all along had been for this to happen in my life when I needed it the most. Destiny or something close to it had chosen this path at just the right time.

I do tend to beat the dead horse about not being a parent, and I have spurts where I do dwell on it. I'm an only child but what further complicates my precarious only child status is the fact that I could be the last link to carry on the family name. That is a huge responsibility. I think about this fact more often that I have ever admitted to anyone. Male cousins with the same last name are almost nonexistent. Do you understand what pressure that places on my wide shoulders? I do. I've royally failed in carrying the torch and passing it on to the next male in the family. Fact, if I had children there is no guarantee that I would be blessed with a son, but right now I am batting zero in life's World Series. In my current marital situation there is no opportunity for producing any offspring. I accept it as is, not to be, I suppose. I really have no other choice given the current hand dealt. Destiny deals the hand.

It's amazing how taken I have been by the red haired little girl landing on our doorstep. I've allowed my emotions to control my common sense by falling in love with her. She has certainly touched something in my heart that I never knew existed. Funny, I've thought about how I would be open to adoption, but doesn't that sort of contradict my thoughts and worries of carrying on the family name. A daughter couldn't cure my current woes in that department. Still, I don't believe I would hesitate if given the opportunity to make her my daughter.

Why am allowing this to consume me? I am but a foster parent, not a real one. We're mere rental property; governmental housing so to speak. No. we're more. I'm more. This just feels too right; not like the others, children just passing through until their screwed up lives were repaired. Am I just fooling myself? No, this can happen. I have purpose. This was real and was meant to be if ever anything was.

Keeping the reins on me when kids are involved is a full time job. I love buying toys for them and take pride and joy in watching them play with their new possessions. Now given, doll buying was above my pay grade so we allowed her to pick. She clung to her new best friend. Every child deserves a playmate, that security blanket that grounds them. She had found hers in that little doll. While I over did it with toys, my wife ensured Brittany was dressed like a red haired angel. Everything was just falling in place. Brittany had become family; almost as if she had always been part of ours forever. I think I had been bewitched, spellbound by her, and her being completely satisfied with her existence with us. I embraced the daddy feel to it. I realized for the first time that I could actually do this and wasn't half bad at it.

Our social services contact had called and had scheduled a visit for the afternoon. The braggart side of me could hardly wait to show her how well adjusted Brittany had become. I was also eager to hear any updates about her situation and if there might be any opportunities in the near future for contemplating adoption. I had kept these feelings close to the vest for now, even though I had casually mentioned it in conversation with my wife; more as a general statement, not sharing with her the quest I actually had in my heart. Brittany had only been in our care for about six weeks so it was really just a tad too early for me to start tossing out my pipe dreams. Six weeks, it had certainly seemed much longer for good reasons.

I watched her playing with her doll, occasionally looking over at me, holding her up and smiling. I melted as I always did when she gave me that look. I wondered if she thought of me as her dad. I hoped she did. This had been the closest time ever for me to feel like one. Taboo, I know, I'm coloring outside the foster care lines by allowing myself to become too attached to a child, but sometimes your heart overrules your head. With the four boys, they were family. The Amazon twelve year old came with too much baggage that just sort of overwhelmed me. The three little ones had been more than a handful. Now, with Brittany, it had just fallen in place. I was Goldie Locks living the three bear's saga, porridge too hot, too cold and then just right.

The social worker arrived punctually as always and we gathered in the den to exchange information. Her job was to interview us and determine how we rated in the foster care world and assess how the children in our care were fairing. I had no doubt that we would pass with flying colors. We always did. After a few preliminary exchanges, the conversation took on more serious tones. She informed us that they would be returning Brittany to the care of her pregnant mother. DSS had decided the mother had cleaned up her act prompting the return of her child. If I had been standing I would have fallen ungracefully to my chair or the floor. This was the worst possible news; at least from my selfish perspective. Normally I should have been happy for the reunion but not this time. I asked was she sure this was the right thing to do? I had never asked that question before so she met my eyes, sensing my apprehension.

She continued, saying DSS's first priority remained reuniting the children with their parents, once it had been determined to be the best possible scenario. I don't think she had just made that statement just to reinforce the rules. She had directed it specifically at me, or so it felt. She could tell I had crossed the line, even though she never directly called me out on it. My insides were an emotional train wreck, but I tried to maintain stoned faced and unaffected. I'm sure she saw through that too. I wanted to fire off a series of questions to gain a foothold on the decision, but even I knew barking up this tree was futile. They had made their decision, end of the story. I had no say so. I did muster up one, asking what would happen if it didn't work out this time; would she be placed back in our custody. She sort of fronded and then said probably not. I wanted to ask why not, but I could read between the lines; she had me pegged.

Before departing she informed us that she would pick up Brittany Saturday, and for us to have her possessions ready then. That was less than two days from now. I didn't know how I was going to get through this. She and I would have one final road trip to share in the morning. I couldn't fathom saying goodbye. My helicopter had crashed and burned. I should have known better, not to have gotten so involved, and actually I had. Still, I had done it anyway. There really had been little chance of her ever staying with us permanently. Deep down, I had known that too. So why had I allowed it to have gone so far down a hopeless trail. The unexpected bond with the red headed stranger had happened, that's what. Six weeks and now I couldn't imagine life without her. The stress of losing her was consuming me. It hurt to breath. She was going back to her mother, a woman we didn't know, and I would never see her again.

I sat there and watched her playing with her doll, Brittany oblivious to what was about to come. Somehow I was going to have to man up and hide my emotions. It would only harm her if this ended in a tearful blubbering send off. My chest was about to explode just thinking about it. In the past six weeks I had finally understood the significance of fostering and now I hated that I had ever decided to become one. Toss training out the window. No amount had prepared me for this. Never get attached to the children. Never say never. Number nine had been my undoing, my curse, and now I questioned whether I had what it took to continue. Crying uncle seemed the logical solution. Being a foster parent was strictly a volunteer venture. I envisioned my run being over. I didn't want to this anymore. I had had enough.

Fairy tales usually have a happy ending and teach wonderful lessons. Don't hold your breath for either. Okay, so Brittany being returned to her mother should be the happy ending, right? And, we having provided her with a temporary wonderful life should have been a powerful lesson learned. Sorry, I'm not feeling it. This is more the nightmare than the feel good ending. Sure, I'm approaching this selfishly but that little girl had kidnapped my soul; what can I say?

Her departure on that Saturday is a blur. I suppose the mind blocks out what it doesn't really want to remember. It was without tears and I didn't actually say goodbye. The social worker did her job and took her away. I averted staring into those blue eyes and did not want to observe any confusion on her face. It was simply over. I was left with nothing but a big old black hole in my heart. I no longer had any aspirations of being a foster parent. Personally I didn't feel I could do the next child or children justice. I would never be able to give them what they needed, fearful of this happening again. It would not be fair to them or me. I could not be an affective foster parent if I pushed back. I had already made that mistake with the twelve year old Amazon; pulling away when I had discovered the sexual abuse and her attraction to men.

After less than two years, we hung up our foster parenting hats. I had once thought I had found my purpose. I hadn't. There were far better people suited for doing this than me. I would miss the children, one in particular, but I could no longer do this and feel good about it. I had to survive somewhat of a grieving process, mopping about, lost and without answers. I know this sounds a bit melodramatic but getting beyond it did take considerable healing. All I had were a few photos taken during Brittany's stay. After a short period I had to put them away. Viewing them wasn't helping, knowing I would most likely never see her again.

DSS did tell us a few months later that she and her baby sister had been removed from the household. The mother's transformation had been short lived. Brittany and her sister had been placed whereabouts unknown; such was the way of foster care. I had no dog in the hunt anyway. We had dropped out. I still thought about adoption, but refused to venture down that path, fearful it would only lead to more doomed failures. I wasn't ready or willing to open old wounds just to find out. I only hoped she was being loved and taken care of; not that anyone could love her more than I had.

'Helicopter, Tommy...helicopter, Brittany'…

'Don't cry because it's over, smile because it happened.'
- Dr. Seuss
'If ever there is tomorrow when we're not together, there is something you must always remember. You are braver than you believe, stronger than you seem, and smarter than you think, but the most important thing is, even if we're apart, I'll always be with you.' - Winnie the Pooh

'A hundred years from now it will not matter what my bank account was, the sort of house I lived in, or the kind of car I drove . . . But the world may be different because I was important in the life of a child.' - Forest E. Witcraft

Remember, Even Superman had Foster Parents.

T. Allen Winn

As an only child and a 'born and raised' southerner, the byproduct of the good ole Palmetto State and historical Abbeville, South Carolina, the kid developed a vivid imagination, improvising to entertain oneself, family and friends; still do, not a bad attribute for the writing arena. As an adult with no children, not by choice, just luck of the draw, the grownup version has been happily married pert near twenty years, piling up the years like freshly stacked cordwood. Sarcasm, wit, with a smidgen of southern swagger has been ones mantra, obviously influencing the writing style.

To overcome boredom in 2003, age 50, during business travel, too many nights in hotel rooms, the greenhorn took a stab at writing a novel. The plot originated from childhood memories, a simple cartoon series drawn to entertain friends, titled the *Bugsters*. Four months and 650 pages later, the 'end of the world as we know it' saga, renamed *The Lord's Last Acres*, was a done deal. The monstrosity is a prime candidate for trilogy surgery. Boredom conquered, writing became a new pastime, almost replacing golf. In a span of eleven months, losing one's entire bloodline, mother to pancreatic cancer, father to Parkinson and Alzheimer's, and a 94 year old grandmother, an only child fought off stints of self diagnosed depression by penning the memoir, *The Caregiver's Son, Outside the Window Looking In*, a means to cope with grief and for his eyes only at the time.

Fast forward to 2011, Abbeville in the rearview mirror, now living in Pawley's Island, S.C., a gentleman knocked on the door one afternoon. The new neighbor, holding his recently published novel, realized he wasn't being greeted by the previous homeowner, that neighbor also aspiring to write a book. After admitting to dabbling in writing, the gentleman asked if his new acquaintance had a manuscript. Smiling and responding ten, he then announced he had started a publishing company. You can't make this stuff up or ignore the obvious signs. *Road Rage*, the first Detective Trudy Wagner novel, was submitted, a plot developed while the small town transplant dealt with the hazards of driving in a tourist community. Friends and family suspect the author could be the novel's depicted serial killer, purely circumstantial of course.

Life rebooted at age 57 ½, clutching that first published novel. Currently there are sixteen completed and unpublished novels on the old laptop waiting their turn to see the light of day, with at least ten more in various stages of completion. Even with a forty hour work week, this writer often juggles three or more novels. Asked how it is possible to keep these straight; keep what straight is the reply. Additionally, approximately one hundred short stories of humorous golf misadventures and southern nostalgia have been compiled. A close friend stated now that T. Allen Winn books are in print, when he's gone, his life will be more than mere scribbling on a tombstone. Above dirt, the journey continues.

www.ingramcontent.com/pod-product-compliance
Lightning Source LLC
Chambersburg PA
CBHW021139080526
44588CB00008B/130